C0-CDO-130

Beyond Acting White

Beyond Acting White

Reframing the Debate on Black Student Achievement

Edited by
Erin McNamara Horvat and
Carla O'Connor

ROWMAN & LITTLEFIELD PUBLISHERS, INC.
Lanham • Boulder • New York • Toronto • Oxford

ROWMAN & LITTLEFIELD PUBLISHERS, INC.

Published in the United States of America
by Rowman & Littlefield Publishers, Inc.
A wholly owned subsidiary of The Rowman & Littlefield Publishing Group, Inc.
4501 Forbes Boulevard, Suite 200, Lanham, Maryland 20706
www.rowmanlittlefield.com

PO Box 317
Oxford
OX2 9RU, UK

Copyright © 2006 by Rowman & Littlefield Publishers, Inc.

All rights reserved. No part of this publication may be reproduced,
stored in a retrieval system, or transmitted in any form or by any
means, electronic, mechanical, photocopying, recording, or otherwise,
without the prior permission of the publisher.

British Library Cataloguing in Publication Information Available

Library of Congress Cataloging-in-Publication Data

Beyond acting white : reframing the debate on black student achievement /
edited by Erin McNamara Horvat and Carla O'Connor.
    p. cm.
  Includes bibliographical references and index.
  ISBN-13 978-0-7425-4272-3 (cloth : alk. paper)
  ISBN-10 0-7425-4272-6 (cloth : alk. paper)
  ISBN-13 978-0-7425-4273-0 (pbk. : alk. paper)
  ISBN-10 0-7425-4273-4 (pbk. : alk. paper)
  1. African American students. 2. School integration—United States. 3. African
Americans—Education—Social aspects. 4. Academic achievement—United States.
5. Educational equalization—United States. 6. Minorities—Education—United
States. I. Horvat, Erin McNamara, 1964– II. O'Connor, Carla, 1966–
  LC2717.B48 2006
  373.1829'96073—dc22   2005025927

Printed in the United States of America

♾™ The paper used in this publication meets the minimum requirements of
American National Standard for Information Sciences—Permanence of Paper for
Printed Library Materials, ANSI/NISO Z39.48-1992.

Contents

Acknowledgments

We owe a debt of gratitude to the many people who contributed to the publication of this volume. First and foremost, we would like to thank the Ford Foundation for its generous support of this work. The foundation supported a conference held in February 2004 at Temple University in Philadelphia that brought together the contributors to this book as well as a wide array of individuals from the foundation, policy, and scholarly worlds. The foundation also offered critical support during the editorial process. The convening of the conference informed the content and organization of this book and the development of individual chapters. Loren Harris, a program officer at Ford, was a partner with us in shaping our vision of a conference that would assist the authors in crafting chapters that could cross the traditional boundaries that often separate the policy, practice, and scholarly communities. His commitment to finding ways to support the development of more equitable schools and strong, sustainable communities was critical to our work.

Additionally, we are grateful to those who participated in this conference. The insight and critique that was freely shared at that meeting was invaluable to the authors of individual chapters and to us as editors in crafting this volume. We especially thank Margaret Beale Spencer, Camille Charles, and Robert Sellers for their careful reading of chapters and useful feedback to the authors and us.

We must acknowledge the significant contribution made by John Ogbu and Signithia Fordham to our work. While they neither participated in the conference nor read the chapters that appear here, their work was critical in providing the groundwork for the conversations about race and achievement that shape this book. Both of them also supported our work at a very early stage by participating in a panel session at the Annual Meeting of the American Sociological Association in 2003 that provided the impetus for this book.

We must especially thank the contributors to this volume. Typically, edited collections are plagued by long delays and, at times, acrimonious discussions between authors and editors. We experienced none of this. The contributors hit the deadlines we gave them with astonishing accuracy. They also responded to our suggestions with grace and good humor. We thank them for their patience and for struggling through the ideas of the book with one another.

Kathy Mooney expertly edited each manuscript. Her work greatly enhanced the accessibility of the volume. Additionally, Cynthia Overton and Janeen Waller-Evelyn, graduate students at the University of Michigan, provided much-needed administrative support in our efforts to stay true to our timeline.

Finally, we would like to thank our families. Carla's two boys, Kai and Al III, inspire her each day. In contemplating what they have already experienced and have yet to experience as black children growing up in this society, she finds reason to pursue the questions and dilemmas that are featured here. Her husband, Al Jr., keeps her sane when her work life is crazy (Thank you, Al, for letting me wake you at 2:00 and 3:00 in the morning so that I can work through my ideas. Your calming spirit and intellectual challenge contributed significantly to the development of this project). Like Carla, Erin's husband, Paul, and her two girls, Katherine and Margaret, provide both inspiration and support. Kate is a city kid who contends with issues of race, class, gender, and equity on a daily basis in Philadelphia's public schools. Her critical questions and real-life experiences enhance Erin's work every day. In addition, the steadfast support and probing questions of nonacademic family and friends have augmented this work a great deal. They help Erin remain grounded in the here and now while theorizing about how we got where we are as a society and how we might work toward a more equitable and just future.

Foreword

Beyond Acting White: Reframing the Debate on Black Student Achievement accomplishes two very important ends. First, it highlights the persistent problem of academic underachievement among black students and its social consequences (e.g., enduring poverty, health vulnerabilities, incarceration, job loss, family destabilization, etc.). Shining a penetrating light on how black children, and adolescents in particular, suffer in U.S. schools is especially necessary in this era of political conservatism, with its emphasis on blaming the victim and its insistence that everyone is equally capable of pulling themselves up by their bootstraps—even those who have no boots. There is abundant evidence that fifty years after *Brown vs. Board of Education*, U.S. schools remain largely separate and very much unequal. Significant differences persist in access to per-pupil funding, teacher quality and level of certification, safety and comfort of physical facilities, rigor of the curriculum, breadth and depth of curricular resources, extent of technological infrastructure, and integration of technology into classroom instruction.

Second, this book helps reframe explanations for the persistence of the achievement gap, in particular by wrestling with John Ogbu and Signithia Fordham's popular "acting-white" explanation. As O'Connor, Horvat, and Lewis note in the introductory chapter, this hypothesis has taken on a life of its own. It is rare for "scientific" arguments that emerge from the academy to be taken up by the popular press and sustained for nearly two decades. It is also unusual, in principle, for so many in the academy to climb on the bandwagon in support of a hypothesis that is generally presumed to have broad explanatory power, but whose empirical base consists of small samples that were neither randomly selected nor strategically representative. I argue here that the acting-white hypothesis does not have broad explanatory power for at least two reasons. First, it is an ahistorical argument. Second, it reifies folk theories about black inferiority, and, in so doing, invites discussion about what is fundamentally an absurd question.

AN AHISTORICAL ARGUMENT

James Anderson (1988) and many other historians of U.S. education have documented that after the Civil War, Blacks, on their own, with no assistance from the government, founded an unprecedented number of schools, including over 1,500 Sabbath-day schools. The rate of literacy achievement among Blacks from the end of the nineteenth century to the first decade of the twentieth century, documented extensively by W. E. B. DuBois (DuBois and Dill 1911), is an astounding achievement. The more than decade-long work to prepare the legal foundation for arguing the *Brown vs. Board of Education* case before the U.S. Supreme Court is further evidence of a community that places a high premium on education. As Toni Morrison documents in her children's book *Remember: The Journey to School Integration*, the young children, teenagers, and young adults who were the first to integrate the schools of the South did not see consciously carrying themselves in ways to dispute assumed racial stereotypes as a burden, but rather as an opportunity. Many African American parents, especially in the South, told their children that in order to be prepared to take advantage of opportunities for economic and educational upward mobility, they had to be better than Whites (meaning they had to work harder, meet higher standards, take the moral high ground, and persist). Whatever Ogbu and Fordham may have observed in the three *neighborhoods* in California, Washington, DC, and Ohio since the late 1980s is not consistent with the historical response to education within the African American community.

A REIFICATION OF FOLK THEORIES ABOUT BLACK INFERIORITY

A folk theory asserts that black inferiority has been a part of the fabric of U.S. society since the earliest days of the Republic. Thomas Jefferson, for example, articulated a theory about the inherent inferiority of black people in *Notes on Virginia*. I believe the acting-white hypothesis—that black students fail in school because they assume an oppositional stance toward academic achievement, viewing such achievement as acting white—has been sustained because it fundamentally reifies and affirms this folk theory. This is ironic because Ogbu also offers an ecological model that does consider historical and political factors beyond the individual. In this sense, his hypothesis is a step above explanations that impute inferiority as inherent, tracing it to sources ranging from cultural deprivation to genetic composition.

Like a magnet, the acting-white hypothesis continues to pull us into the mire of either defending the idea that black people are not intellectually inferior or in one way or another affirming that such inferiority exists (e.g., as a result of family socialization, neighborhood socialization, or peer network socialization). One example of this dilemma is Christopher Jencks and Meredith Phillips's (1998b) classic volume, *The Black-White Test Score Gap*. The authors clearly believe themselves to be taking a progressive position against explanations based on assumptions of black inferiority, such as those advanced in *The Bell Curve: Intelligence and Class Structure in American Life* (Herrnstein and Murray 1994). Ironically (and unintentionally), Jencks and Phillips assert that the notion of black inferiority must be countered empirically. For instance, they review studies conducted to prove that black people are not inherently intellectually inferior. This literature, done in part as a response to Arthur Jensen's (1969) *Harvard Educational Review* article, includes studies that examined I.Q. scores for black twins who had been raised separately, one in a white home and one in a black home.

Why are investigations of this sort considered necessary—or even valid? To my knowledge, there are no comparable studies examining the potential genetic basis for the differences in test score achievement between white and Asian and white and Asian American students. If test score data can serve as an adequate and reliable basis for evaluating potential genetic differences in populations, then perhaps we should undertake empirical studies to determine whether there is a genetic basis for why Asian and Asian American students typically outperform their white counterparts, particularly in mathematics and science.

The very question is absurd, however; and no scholar, to my knowledge, takes it as a topic worthy of empirical investigation. Thus, it might be useful to reframe how we think about the question of the black-white achievement gap. From a moral perspective, the persistence of this gap is a stain against us as a nation and an affront to our moral integrity. That is the reason to continue to press forward in making public the nature of the discrepancies in opportunity to learn based on race/ethnicity, income, and gender, and for organizing political action to address the problem.

RECONCEPTUALIZING THE NATURE OF THE PROBLEM

At the same time, good scientific explanations for the causes of the problem are a necessary foundation for the formulation of constructive public policy. Reframing what is often cast as a "colored people's" problem as instead a question of understanding the ecological nature of human development might provide us some leverage. What we are confronted with is a classic instance of trying to understand dynamic relations among

- individual agency, traits, and genetic endowments (as opposed to genetic endowments of groups of people);
- the possibilities for and constraints to participation in different contextual levels (e.g., the family; community-based structures such as schools, churches, arts organizations, etc.; peer social networks; work); and
- the networks of activity through which macro-level social, political, economic, educational, and health care–related policies are enacted.

This is the problem that Urie Brofenbrenner (1979) raises in his ecological systems theory, that Glen Elder (1985) raises in his analysis of generational cohort effects, and that Margaret Beale Spencer (1995) raises in her Phenomenological Variant of Ecological Systems theory. It is a systems analysis problem, not simply a poor colored people's problem. This perspective shifts the goal to one of understanding how systems of bias and oppression are operationalized and how forms of socialization at different contextual levels can provide resources for resisting these oppressive structural forces.

A better understanding of the social and cultural ecology of human development would potentially benefit all people; it also would provide a more informed basis for articulating public policies; and, most importantly, it would help free us from the web of constrictions that descend when characteristics other than political significance are attributed to the construct of race. We need to stay focused on explaining how racism is structurally operationalized and avoid becoming entangled either with defending or arguing against ideas that are inherently absurd—such as that one so-called race is either inferior or superior to another. This means recognizing that the system of white supremacy as it is operationalized in the academy (Lee, Spencer, & Harpalani 2003)—and let us be clear that it is there—holds the purse strings, literally and figuratively, to sustain the idea that black intellectual inferiority requires empirical explanations in one direction or the other.

The chapters in this volume offer a welcome alternative. They provide rich explanations of the complexity and nuanced stances that highlight the heterogeneity within the black community. They offer important insights into how class, gender, immigrant status, age, and the material conditions of neighborhoods influence academic effort and achievement. They document how racism is operationalized in the day-to-day life of schools, as well as through broader economic and political forces. They demonstrate the crucial role of nurturing relationships with adults in mediating how children and adolescents interpret the immediate threats in their neighborhoods and schools. This is a comprehensive attempt to broaden how researchers, educators, public policymakers, and the media understand the achievement gap. Without question, this book will become a classic point of reference for future considerations of how best to address the moral stain of the persistent achievement gap.

Carol D. Lee

Introduction: Framing the Field: Past and Future Research on the Historic Underachievement of Black Students

Carla O'Connor, Erin McNamara Horvat, and Amanda E. Lewis

Why are black students underperforming in school? Researchers continue to pursue this question with vigor not only because Blacks currently lag behind Whites on a wide variety of educational indices (e.g., test scores, grade point averages, high school graduation rates, college attrition, and completion), but because the closing of the black-white achievement gap has slowed and by some measures reversed during the last quarter of the twentieth century (Grissmer, Flannagan, & Williamson 1998; Hedges & Nowell 1998; Nettles & Perna 1997a, 1997b). The persistent "gap" in educational outcomes between Blacks and Whites has substantial social implications. Black people's experience with poor school achievement and equally poor access to postsecondary education reduces their access to important social and economic rewards (e.g., all the familial and economic benefits of high wage jobs). However, the underperformance of a large number of black students stands in stark contrast to abundant evidence that black youth articulate high aspirations for their own educational and social mobility—aspirations that actually exceed those articulated by their white counterparts (Cheng & Starks 2002; Kao & Tienda 1998; MacLeod 1995; Qian & Blair 1999). Why, then, do Blacks lag behind Whites in school?

Satisfactory explanations remain elusive, despite extensive research. Ironically, the lack of a definitive answer is in part because the conversation about black students' performance is commonly cast in terms of a "black-white" achievement gap. This framing implicitly situates Whites as the normative referent for interpreting how black students perform in school. Academic and public attention is thus directed toward what it may be about Blacks or blackness that produces underachievement. The contributions of other factors, such as the culture and structure of schools and society, and

1

the attitudes and perspectives of Whites (including schooling agents) go un-examined. Moreover, the social construction of a "black-white" achievement gap inadvertently homogenizes the experiences of both groups. As a result, white poor and working-class students' academic (under)performance is understudied; and both researchers and the public lose sight of the variation in school achievement among Blacks (e.g., the fact that some black students succeed in school and perform comparably to Whites goes unnoted).

Even with these embedded limitations, however, the notion of a black-white achievement gap can be productive. Focusing on "the gap" provides a reference for marking and subsequently exploring racial inequities. We can use these demarcations to advance policies and reforms aimed at producing equity, so long as we also challenge, complicate, and extend the oversimpli-fied conceptualizations of those phenomena that are said to lie at the heart of the gap. Toward this end, this volume uses as a point of departure an espe-cially popular explanation of the gap—the notion that black students disen-gage from academic learning and reject schooling because they believe it is a "white" thing. Although this theory, heretofore referred to as the "acting white hypothesis" originated in empirical research (Fordham & Ogbu 1986), over time it has taken on a life of its own. The findings and discussion presented in this volume aim to extend our thinking about and beyond the acting white hypothesis. Moreover, the chapters that follow provide starting points that ac-ademic and policy communities can use to foster conversations and stimulate investigations that will enrich our understanding of black people's ability to succeed within and progress through the educational pipeline.

We begin, in this chapter, with an overview and critique of research in the field to date and suggest new directions in which the research community might move. We document the general parameters of the black-white achievement gap and analyze existing explanations for this difference. We discuss why the acting-white hypothesis that grew out of Ogbu's cultural ecological theory (CET) has assumed center stage, and why CET and its at-tendant focus on the cultural opposition to acting white provide only limited insight into the underachievement of Blacks. We then outline productive av-enues for new research that complicates and moves beyond the notion of acting white. Lastly, we give an overview of the organization of this volume, highlighting the significant themes addressed by each of the chapters.

DOCUMENTING AND EXPLAINING "THE GAP"

Empirical Evidence

The persistent gap in education between Blacks and Whites has been documented in several areas, most notably in standardized testing, high

school completion rates, secondary school achievement and track placement, and postsecondary school attendance and completion. A detailed discussion of the nature and extent of the achievement gap exists elsewhere
(e.g., Hallinan 2001; Jencks & Phillips 1998a); here, we outline some of the
central parameters.

Historically, Blacks have underperformed on standardized tests relative to
their white peers (Jencks & Phillips 1998b). However, discussion of an
"achievement gap" did not enter public discourse until the years following
Brown v. Board of Education, when measurable strides were made in giving black students more adequate educational opportunities. In fact, the gap
in standardized test performance between Blacks and Whites narrowed sub-
stantially during the first decades after the Brown decision (between 1965
and 1992) (Cook & Evans 2000; Hedges & Nowell 1998). Researchers attributed this narrowing to the rapid closing of group differences at the bottom
of the distribution of test scores (Hedges & Nowell 1998). Blacks continued
to be underrepresented in the upper tails of the distribution of achievement
test performance.

In the post-*Brown* years, Blacks also made substantial progress in high
school completion rates. High school graduation rates for all racial and ethnic groups have increased steadily since the 1960s. In 2000, Asians and
Whites had the highest rates (around 85 percent) (NCES 2001); Blacks, with
graduation rates close to 79 percent, seemed to be approaching parity (NCES
2001). This progress was not echoed in college attendance or completion
rates, however. By the mid-1980s, Blacks were enrolling in college at a lower
rate than they had been in the mid-1970s, and their rate of college completion had slowed (Marks 1985; Nettles & Perna 1997a; NCES 2001). Relative to
Whites, Blacks were only 65 percent as likely to have attained a Bachelor's
degree and only 58 percent as likely to have achieved an advanced degree
(NCES 2001). Further, the overall rise in educational attainment that had
been documented since the 1960s largely reflected gains being made by
black women and not black men. Researchers have attributed these (now-
slowed) gains to the higher rates at which black women—and not black
men—were attending and completing college (Nettles & Perna 1997a). In
addition to these important gender dynamics, there are social class dynamics to the achievement "gap." It is not only working-class and poor black students who are underperforming. Some local measures show Whites of lower
socioeconomic status (SES) outperforming Blacks of higher SES (e.g., Ann
Arbor Public Schools 1998; Rioux 1997). Consistent with this finding, the
achievement gap between Blacks and Whites widens as one moves up the
social-class hierarchy (The College Board 1999).

Blacks also continue to be overrepresented in lower ability and special
education classrooms, while they are underrepresented in higher-ability
classrooms and gifted classrooms (Hallinan 2001; Kovach & Gordon 1997;

National Academy of Sciences 2002; Oakes 1985). They are three times as likely as white students to be labeled as retarded or behaviorally disturbed (Akom 2001; National Academy of Sciences 2002; Skiba 2001), and they are disproportionately represented among the discipline, suspension, and expulsion rolls of America's schools (Ferguson 2000; Noguera 2003).

Clearly, despite a narrowing in some areas, the achievement gap has remained a persistent problem, and one that has affected many points along the educational pipeline. The resulting constrained opportunity for black students takes on special meaning in our current postindustrial economy, where academic credentials are a requirement for entry into living-wage occupations (Bowen & Bok 1998). We cannot effectively address either the gap in educational outcomes or its many ripple effects until we first understand its root causes.

Theoretical Explanations

Researchers have advanced numerous theories to account for the continued underperformance of black students relative to their white peers. They have linked the gap to levels of innate intelligence, cultural deficiencies or differences, cultural and social reproduction, and capital investment and distribution. The roles of within-school (e.g., tracking and ability grouping) and across-school inequities (inequitable resource distribution) also have been examined repeatedly (Cook & Evans 2000; Hallinan 2001; Oakes 1995). Despite their number and variety, these efforts have had significantly less impact than Ogbu's cultural ecological theory. Over the last twenty years, CET has assumed a prominent place in both academic and popular discourse regarding the underachievement of black students.

Despite CET's prominence, the model is rarely taken up in its entirety. This is due in part to its complexity and comprehensiveness (discussed in detail below). Methodological, funding, and time constraints have prevented researchers from designing and implementing empirical studies that account simultaneously for each facet of the model. Instead, researchers have selected particular aspects of CET for further exploration. Of special concern has been how an oppositional cultural frame of reference, an accordant oppositional identity, and the presumed "fear of acting white" are implicated (or not) in the poor school performance of black youth.[1] In fact, this last aspect of the theory has been popular outside as well as inside academia. Articles in major newspapers, news magazines, and journals regularly attribute Blacks' underachievement to black students defining their identities in opposition to Whites and to their fear of (being accused of) acting white if they do well in school.

In the following section, we outline CET's several interrelated tenets and discuss how and why the notion of an oppositional identity and the acting-white hypothesis seem to have gripped the imagination of academics and the general public. We also situate the emergence of CET in its disciplinary, historical, and political contexts.

CULTURAL ECOLOGICAL THEORY IN CONTEXT

According to CET, Blacks in the United States interpret their oppression as systematic and enduring due to the historical and contemporary experiences with institutionalized discrimination (e.g., slavery, job discrimination, structural disadvantages, and racial discrimination in schools) they have experienced. Consequently, they generate theories of "making it" that contradict dominant notions of status attainment and produce disillusionment about the instrumental value of school. They also develop substantial distrust of school and of its agents. Both their disillusionment and distrust suppress their commitment to school norms. Additionally, according to the theory, Blacks identify schooling as a white domain that requires Blacks to "think" and "act" white in exchange for academic success. Not wanting to compromise their own racial identity or risk losing their affiliation with the black community, black youths limit their efforts in school because they find it difficult to withstand the psychological strains involved in crossing cultural borders. This last element of Ogbu's cultural ecological theory raised the specter of a potential conflict between "being" (i.e., "acting" and "thinking") black and doing well in school. The 1986 article Ogbu coauthored with Signithia Fordham subsequently imprinted the acting-white hypothesis on the imagination of the American public. That article also explicitly proposed the idea that black students continue to underperform in school as a result of their cultural opposition to acting white.

CET and the accompanying acting-white hypothesis have important historical antecedents. The history of research dedicated to understanding racial differences is long and varied. Much of this research has been conducted in an effort to understand social mobility in the United States and can be linked to the dominant narrative of status attainment which "promis[es] that all Americans have a reasonable chance to achieve success as they define it— material or otherwise—through their own efforts" (Hochschild 1995, p. xvii; for additional discussions, see Hallinan 2001; McQuillan 1998). This American "dream" forwards the myth of a meritocracy and provides a powerful backdrop for educational research and discourse in this country— particularly with regard to interpreting educational opportunity.

Education is the most-often cited way in which Americans can pursue economic success and social mobility. Educational opportunity is, according to the dominant narrative of status attainment, a taken-for-granted right that can be pursued by all with equal vigor. Some groups' inability to "pull themselves up by their own bootstraps" and access this allegedly free and available resource is often blamed on a lack of individual initiative (Shaw & London 2001).

This "bootstrap ideology" has shaped more than folk theories of educational opportunity. It has affected, as well, how researchers frame and investigate questions of differential outcomes. The expectation that schools will provide an opportunity for upward social mobility is deeply ingrained in our national consciousness, despite evidence that, in fact, over time, schools often have served as the mechanism by which society has managed, controlled, and limited not only aspirations toward but some social groups' experience with upward social mobility (Bowles & Gintis 2002; Brint & Karabel 1989; Clark 1960; Hochschild 1995; McQuillan 1998). Much research, including that which can be captured under the titles of social or cultural reproduction theories (e.g., Bourdieu 1977; Bourdieu & Passeron 1977; Bowles & Gintis 1976, 2002; Bernstein 1977; Willis 1977), has been directed toward understanding why, if all individuals have equal access to educational opportunity, some groups do not have the same outcomes from schooling as others.

The tension between the implicit notion that education ought to serve as a pathway to opportunity and the lived reality that the opportunity structure in our nation and our schools has not functioned as such for many, including many black students, lies at the heart of discussions of the achievement gap and the many attempts to explain its causes. That is, do schools provide a universal opportunity for success (in which case black students would be to blame for not taking advantage of this opportunity) or do schools exacerbate already unequal opportunity structures (in which case black students' underperformance would be understood as a result of constrained opportunity)? Individual investigators and whole fields of research have struggled with this quandary by differentially focusing on structure and agency in investigations of the achievement "gap."

In these investigations, structure refers to social structures, such as economic forces, labor market forces, social class inequalities, and racism, while agency refers to an individual's capacity to take action. Various interpretations of the relative roles and influence of agency and structure play out across these studies. Some researchers have taken a structural approach. They have carefully examined structural forces, evaluating the ways in which they limit, constrain, and shape individual action. Others have been more concerned with examining how individuals make choices or take up their educational opportunities, in the midst of structural constraints. Over time, research, particularly Ogbu's, but also the work of many authors in this volume, can be thought of as having taken a both/and approach. That is, these studies have acknowledged the importance of structure and context in shaping individuals' choices, but they also explore how individuals engage with structural constraints to sometimes reshape the very structure itself. Many of the chapters presented in this volume aim to bridge this agency/structure divide by providing insight into how the gap is produced by structure and agency and by their dialectical interaction.

Also at the center of discussions of the achievement gap are different understandings of what race means. With the passage of the Civil Rights Act of 1964 and the implementation of national programs aimed at desegregation, social scientists began investigations aimed at understanding the achievement gap between Blacks and Whites. In the 1970s, these focused on biological, cultural, and familial differences between Blacks and Whites. Genetic or biological understandings of race (and thus of the causes of black school performance) that were reinvigorated by Jensen in 1969 (Flynn 1980; Jensen 1969) have been almost entirely debunked. But, as evidenced by Herrnstein and Murray's *The Bell Curve*, published in 1994, this sort of controversial and attention-grabbing research has a lingering appeal (Fischer et al. 1996; Jacoby & Glauberman 1995).

Another strand of the early research into differential educational achievement focused on the role of the family in passing on educational and social advantage and disadvantage. Daniel Patrick Moynihan et al. (1965) had initially focused national attention on the alleged "breakdown of the black family" and can be seen as initiating broad interest in culture of poverty explanations for differential educational achievement (Hallinan 2001). The following year, the Coleman report (Coleman et al. 1966), commissioned by the federal government to examine differences in educational opportunities among Blacks and Whites, concluded that the role of schools in the transmission of educational advantage or disadvantage was relatively small compared to the critical role of the family. Although many culture of poverty theories (including the Moynihan report) or research that substantiated the logic of these theories (including the Coleman report) suggested that the origins of the supposed "ills" of black families and communities were structural oppression and economic inequalities, these structural origins quickly faded into the background as causal significance was assigned to Blacks' lack of the "cultural right stuff" (Darity 2002, p. 1). The perhaps unintended legacy of this work stemming from the culture of poverty argument (e.g., Deutsch 1967; Lewis 1966), suggests that certain families and communities have deficient familial forms that do not support educational achievement. Such cultural theories of racial disparities, including those currently on offer as explanations for the achievement gap (e.g., Thernstrom & Thernstrom 2003), ignore or distort the interaction between individual and structural forces that shape lived experience, action, and outcomes.

Ogbu's cultural ecological theory represented an effort to link the structural conditions of life in this country to just such lived experiences on the part of minority students in U.S. public schools. CET is rooted in Ogbu's

initial examination of how historical experiences with and perceptions of a
limited opportunity structure (or "job ceiling") informed the poor performance of black and Mexican American youths relative to Whites (Ogbu 1974,
1978). In these early publications, Ogbu also began to draw distinctions between immigrant minorities and involuntary minorities (initially referred to
as castelike minorities); these differences, in turn, provided the basis for his
account of why some minority groups experience more success in school
than do others.

Ogbu defined immigrant minorities as nonwhite people who came to the
United States voluntarily; this category includes immigrants, refugees, bina-
tionals, and migrant workers (Ogbu 2003).[2] In contrast, involuntary minori-
ties are nonwhite people who are in the United States because they were initially colonized, conquered, or enslaved by white Americans (Ogbu 2003).
Ostensibly in this country against their will, these minorities include "Native
Americans, Alaskan Natives, black Americans, Puerto Ricans, original
Mexican Americans in the Southwest, and Native Hawaiians (Ogbu 2003,
pp. 50–51). Over the next two decades, as he made adjustments to CET,
Ogbu continued to elaborate on and refine the formative distinctions between these two types of minorities. He traced the more successful academic
experiences of immigrant minorities compared to involuntary minorities to
two sources: differences in the incorporation, subordination, and exploitation of the two types of minorities; and differences in the nature of these minorities' responses to their history and treatment (Ogbu 1987, 2003).

According to Ogbu, immigrant minorities, having been incorporated into
the United States voluntarily and in the pursuit of greater educational, social,
economic, or political opportunity, use compatriots in their "homeland" as
their frame of reference. This reference enables them to develop a favorable
disposition toward the American opportunity structure and to acquiesce to
discrimination. When they encounter differential rewards and opportunities,
they focus on being better off than those who remain in their country of
birth. Immigrant minorities can rationalize the discrimination they experience in light of being "guests in a foreign land," who have no choice but to
tolerate such treatment. Additionally, they know they have the option of returning "home" if things become intolerable in the United States. When voluntary minorities encounter social obstacles (including the cultural barriers
and differences they face in schools), they perceive them as merely temporary
—they are "barriers to be overcome" in their pursuit of the American dream.
Consequently, they do not interpret learning school norms "as threatening to
their own culture, language, and identity" (Ogbu 1987, p. 328). In sum, voluntary minorities' frame of reference makes it possible for them to craft folk
theories of "making it" that are consistent with the dominant narrative of status attainment. In turn, they develop a pragmatic trust of white people and
the institutions they control and willingly adapt to the norms and expecta-

tions of American schools. All of these factors are said to contribute to their more competitive performance in school.

In contrast, involuntary minorities situate Whites as their frame of reference and "often conclude that they are far worse off than they ought to be because of white treatment" (Ogbu 1987, p. 331). Furthermore, "they know from generations of experiences that the barriers facing them in the opportunity structure are not temporary" but systemic and enduring (Ogbu 1987, p. 325). They are aware not only of how historical and contemporary expressions of subjugation and exploitation limit their access to social and economic rewards upon their completion of school, but also of how schools' structural inequities (e.g., "biased testing, misclassification, tracking, biased textbooks, biased counseling") already circumscribe their potential to be viable competitors in the contest for social rewards (Ogbu 1990a, p. 127).

It is involuntary minorities' knowledge of and experience with structural barriers to upward mobility that cause them to question the instrumental value of school and to develop a deep distrust of whites and the institutions they control (notably, schools). Consequently, they come to privilege their collective identity and favor collective struggle in the effort to cope with their oppression (Ogbu 1989). Collective identity buffers involuntary minorities psychologically and enables them to "maintain their sense of self worth and integrity" despite their subjugation (Ogbu 1990a, p. 62). Their engagement with collective struggle provides an instrumental means for reducing or eliminating barriers to mobility (Ogbu 1983, 1990a). Although involuntary minorities' collective orientation may help them maintain their mental health, and may improve their likelihood of experiencing greater social justice, it also produces maladaptive educational consequences. Unlike immigrant minorities, involuntary minorities perceive the cultural differences they encounter in school as "markers of identity to be maintained" not "barriers to be overcome" and develop an oppositional stance and identity vis-à-vis white Americans and what they see as indices of white culture. (Ogbu 1987, p. 327). They consequently "equate following the standard practices and related activities of the school that enhance academic success with 'acting white'" (Ogbu 1987, p. 330). With little evidence that they will be appropriately rewarded for their efforts in school and the accordant notion that schooling is the province of white Americans and threatens their own cultural identity, involuntary minorities have little reason to work hard in school and consequently experience poor or underachievement.

CET was a welcome advance over other theories on offer in education. In contrast to genetic models of academic underperformance (e.g., Herrnstein & Murray 1994; Jensen 1969), CET seemed to explain why the relationship between ability (however imperfectly measured by standardized test scores) and academic achievement was weak in the case of black Americans (Ogbu 1989). Unlike models of cultural deprivation (Bloom, Davis, & Hess 1965;

Deutsch 1967; Gottlieb & Ramsey 1967) and cultural difference (Hale 1982; Kochman 1981; Shade 1982; Tharp 1989), it seemed to explain why some minority groups (read immigrant minority groups) did better in school than Blacks even when their culture was "more different from the dominant group in culture and language" (Ogbu 1989). Unlike social and cultural reproduction theories (e.g., Bernstein 1977; Bourdieu & Passeron 1977; Bowles & Gintis 1976; Willis 1977) that emphasized how social class positioning was implicated in the achievement process, CET seemed to explain why middle-class Blacks sometimes fared less well in school than lower-income whites (Jencks & Phillips 1998b; Steele 1992, 1997).

CET's prominence advanced dramatically when Fordham and Ogbu used the theory's logic to explain why black students at a high school in Washington, DC, distanced themselves from what they perceived to be white modalities of success in school. Echoing McCardle and Young (1970), who found that black students in Madison, Wisconsin, feared the loss of their collective black identity during the period of desegregation, Fordham and Ogbu (1986) reported in an *Urban Review* article that the students in the study (which had been conducted by Fordham) felt that they would compromise their racial identity if they sought academic success.[3] These same findings became the subject of public discourse given the popular press coverage of the phenomena in print media.

Since the publication of the 1986 *Urban Review* article, as many as 158 popular press articles (including editorials) have made reference to the acting-white hypothesis.[4] Moreover, since the first popular press mention of the premise in 1987, the number of print media references to acting white has grown aggressively. In the five-year span from 1987 (when the first such article was published) to 1991, twenty-five articles made reference to the phenomenon; during the next five years (1992–1996), forty-two articles did so; and in the next five-year span (1997–2001), forty-five articles. In 2002 alone, partly in anticipation of the publication of a major new work by Ogbu (2003), twenty-two articles referred to the acting-white hypothesis. Between January 2002 and April 2004, partly in response to Ogbu's death in August 2003, but also in response to the Supreme Court decision to uphold the right of universities to consider race in admissions procedures, the number jumped to forty-two articles. Coverage has not been limited to local and national outlets (e.g., *Omaha World Herald*, *St. Petersburg Times*, *Washington Post*, *New York Times*), but has included international media such as the *London Times*, *Toronto Star*, *Sydney Morning Herald*, and (Montreal) *Gazette*.

This popular press interest in the acting-white hypothesis, while useful in focusing national attention on the achievement gap, has distorted some key features of CET and has obscured some critical factors that contribute to the gap. Arguably, the overall effect of this media coverage has been to divert attention from the enduring structural constraints that shape black people's ability to succeed in school and in society more broadly and to focus national concern instead on alleged "problems" within black students, families, and communities. Below, we offer a brief review of the efforts of the popular press to make sense of the gap, as well as a more detailed analysis of its effects.

TREATMENT IN THE POPULAR PRESS

During the first year of popular coverage, most references to the fear of acting white or being accused of acting white in relation to black school performance were closely aligned with how Fordham's and/or Ogbu had rooted this phenomenon (Fordham & Ogbu 1986; Ogbu 1987). In accordance with their conceptualizations, the articles conveyed that this fear developed in response to black people's historical and contemporary experience with racial oppression and with U.S. society's differential reward and opportunity structure. For example, citing an interview with Fordham, one publication explained, "While this response—fear of acting white—is clearly visible in the students' behavior at school, its development and persistence are attributable to the oppressive conditions confronting Black people in America" (C. Stafford 1987). Another noted, "Fordham's study traces the anti-studying peer pressure to the inferior schools and low-level jobs that many Blacks have faced over several generations" (Fisher 1987).

As early as 1988, however, the notion of "the fear of acting white" began to take on a life of its own in the popular press. In general, the hypothesis was stripped of any reference to the structural antecedents Fordham and/or Ogbu had invoked. Additionally, prior to 2002 and the anticipated release of another major work by Ogbu, few articles specifically attributed the theory to either Fordham or Ogbu. In fact, most references to the relationship between the fear of acting white and black underachievement presented the phenomenon not as an academic hypothesis but rather as a foregone conclusion, a taken-for-granted reality. Before 2002, only seven articles challenged the validity of the hypothesis, refuted its impact, or tried to convey the point that—as Diane Ravitch cautioned—"way too much has been made of the purported unwillingness of black students to study for fear of 'acting white'" (as cited by Charen 1997).

The subject of the fear of the acting-white phenomenon has been taken up by a wide cast of characters: teachers incorporate it into articles and editorials about their experiences in predominantly white and predominantly black high schools; parents mention it in letters they write to newspaper editors about their own experiences, or those of their children, or their friends' children; columnists refer to it when reporting on special programs that were designed to combat its occurrence (e.g., Carl Rowan, advocating for his Project Excellence in Washington, DC) (Rowan 1988). Even the leadership of the NAACP and the National Urban League has commented on the belief that black students have a fear of acting white. For example, in his keynote address before about 3,000 people at the 87th National Conference of the National Urban League, then-president Hugh Price urged that efforts to improve educational opportunities for black youth should begin "by putting a stop to the anti-achievement peer culture in our own community. . . . The word among all too many of our youngsters on the street . . . is that doing well academically means acting white. Our children must understand that 'dissing' education is tantamount to signing a death warrant for their dreams" (Mooar 1997). Even members of the entertainment industry have found reason to invoke the acting-white hypothesis. After the release of *Malcolm X*, an interviewer asked film director Spike Lee, "Why is the life of Malcolm, Spike Lee's Malcolm, needed right now?" Lee responded:

> It's needed for the same reason that Malcolm was needed when he was alive, and even more so today. One of the things that Malcolm stressed was education. Well, we're just not doing it. It's such a sad situation now, where male black kids will fail so they can be "down" with everyone else, and if you get A's and speak correct English, you're regarded as being "white." Peer pressure has turned around our whole value system. [*New York Times* 1992, p. 13]

Book reviews and other references to D'Nish D'Souza's (1995) *End of Racism*, John McWhorter's (2000) *Losing the Race*, and Debra J. Dickerson's (2004) *The End of Blackness* also have provided occasions for rearticulating and reinvigorating the acting white hypothesis (Brown 1995, p. 4; Brown 2000, p. 4; Stern 1995, C6; Sewell 2004). Both D'Souza and McWhorter have, in addition, contributed op-ed pieces and/or have spoken out in other venues, invoking the phenomenon in their arguments against affirmative action and other policy interventions aimed at restructuring educational and social opportunities for minorities (Gaines 1996, p. 35; McWhorter 2002, B4). Columnists and academics—sometimes, as in the case of Thomas Sowell and William Raspberry, one and the same—have referenced the theory to substantiate their charge that black people should assume personal responsibility for their failures and stop assuming the role of the victim (e.g., Raspberry 1989, A19; Sowell 1997a, 3G; Sowell 1997b, p. 25). Henry Louis Gates, in a 2002 article in the *London Guardian*, associated the fear of acting white with one of the many ways Blacks themselves have "'reforged the manacles' of the slave era" (Jaggi 2002, p. 20).

Over time, the acting-white hypothesis increasingly has been invoked to suggest that black culture rather than racism or other structured inequities (e.g., low teacher expectations, poor curriculum, inadequate school funding) is responsible for (or, at the very least, more responsible for) the low achievement of black youth. Before 1995, three of the fifty-one (approximately 6 percent) articles that referenced the acting white hypothesis conveyed this perspective. Spurred by the publication of D'Souza's (1995) *End of Racism*, three such articles (representing about 33 percent of the articles referencing the fear of acting white) were published in 1995 alone. Between 1995 and April 2004, twenty-four of 107 articles (a little over 22 percent) called for black responsibility in light of the acting-white hypothesis.

In anticipation of the release of what became Ogbu's (2003) last work, a study examining the underachievement of middle-class Blacks in Shaker Heights, Ohio, the popular press refocused some attention on Ogbu's conceptualization of the structural causes that gave birth to the fear of acting white. For example, an article in the *Plain Dealer* (Santana 2003b, A1) directed readers "to the legacy of slavery, racism and deprivation that combined to feed hostility toward the white majority." A *New York Times* article (Lee 2002, p. 9) indicated that a "long history of discrimination helped foster what is known in sociological lingo as an oppositional peer culture." These same articles also drew attention to other presumed cultural adaptations that could be attributed to Ogbu's cultural ecological theory (CET itself is not mentioned, however). The articles indicated that the fear of acting-white phenomenon was one among other cultural orientations (e.g., black students identifying rappers rather than parents as role models; black parents failing to supervise their children's homework completion and track their progress through school) that reflected "a long history of adapting to oppression and stymied opportunities" (Lee 2002, p. 9).

Other articles echoed (albeit imprecisely) Ogbu's 2003 heightened emphasis on community forces (or the way members of a minority group perceive, interpret, and respond to education as a result of their unique history and adaptations to their minority status in the United States). In his book, Ogbu (2003) argues that these "community forces" do not offer a complete explanation for the differences in school performance among minorities. He notes in his preface that "there is no presumption that community forces are the only cause of, or play the most important role in the academic gap [between Blacks and whites]" (Ogbu 2003, p. viii). He adds, however, that "community forces can and should be studied in their own right, just as societal and school factors are studied in their own right" (Ogbu 2003, p. viii). Nevertheless, articles in the popular press, such as one written by William Raspberry, concluded that "Ogbu sees culture as the *overriding determinant* [of the black-white achievement gap in Shaker Heights] (though he would acknowledge the effect of racism)" (Raspberry 2002, A23; emphasis added).

Most other references to the acting-white hypothesis were disconnected from CET and Ogbu's last work. Still, they concluded, as Raspberry did, that black culture was a powerful—if not the most powerful—factor explaining the achievement performance of Blacks, relative to other variables.[5] Importantly, many of the articles that marginalized or were inattentive to structural factors and made passing or decontextualized references to the acting-white hypothesis were written in response to the Supreme Court decision to uphold affirmative action in university admissions. In these instances, most references to the acting-white hypothesis were offered in the effort to report on the perspectives of those who criticized the Court's decision (Young 2003, A13; Healy 2003, Al; Brown 2003b, 6; Richey 2003, p. 1). One such article quoted one member of the Center for Equal Opportunity who claimed:

> The question underlying the University of Michigan cases is why are so few African-American 17 and 18 year olds academically competitive with white and Asian 17 and 18 year olds. . . . The answer to that question is not discrimination. . . . The answer is extremely high illegitimacy rates, poor public school, and a culture that too often views studying hard as "acting white." [Richey 2003, p. 1]

As early as 2002, Fordham was reported as "fear[ing] that the acting-white idea had been distorted into blaming the victim" (Lee 2002, p. 9).

The cumulative result of the print media's simplification of the acting-white hypothesis and its near-total silence regarding the structural factors CET identifies is that the public has become firmly focused on the culture of black Americans as the source of the achievement gap. This, in turn, makes it easier for conservative activists to orient public sentiment toward policies and practices that would further circumscribe the already inadequate gains that have been made since the civil rights movement. CET and the acting-white hypothesis are vulnerable to more than political exploitation, however. These conceptualizations also are flawed by inherent theoretical and conceptual weaknesses, problems we outline below and that the contributors to this volume take up, as well.

THE NEED FOR FURTHER INVESTIGATION

A growing body of literature highlights problematic aspects of Fordham's and Ogbu's work. These limitations rest with how CET in general and the acting-white hypothesis in particular fail to contend substantively with (1) the theoretical unpacking of race as a social phenomenon; (2) the heterogeneity of the African American experience; and (3) the specifics of social context (particularly how these specifics are articulated by the culture and organization of individual schools and communities).

Unpacking Race Theoretically

Research on the educational achievement, outcomes, and experiences of black youth must necessarily attend to race.[6] But undertheorized, oversimplified, or inaccurate conceptualizations of race work against robust inter-pretations of how race impacts the educational realities of black students. Consequently, in conducting educational research we must pursue more ac-curate and precise ways of capturing race as a social phenomenon.

The imprecise specification of race in survey research aimed at docu-menting and explaining "the gap" derives from the desire to uncover signif-icant statistical relationships. But treating race as a variable makes it almost impossible to unpack its phenomenological, operational, and performative dynamics. Like other qualitative research that examines the relationship be-tween black identity and achievement, both Fordham's and Ogbu's ethno-graphic work (including the work they discuss in their coauthored "Coping with the Burden of Acting White" article) takes up race in these more com-plex ways. At the same time, however, their work often suffers from what Walter Benn Michaels (1992) has referred to as the "anticipation of culture by race" (p. 677). Michaels argues that such anticipation occurs when we pre-sume that to be a member of a particular race, you have to do certain things, but these certain things are not considered authentic to the race in question unless the person doing them is recognized as a member of that race. He stated the case in terms of members of the Navajo nation, but the logic of the argument applies to other races and ethnicities as well. In his words, the an-ticipation of culture by race occurs when "To be Navajo you have to do Navajo things, but you can't really count as doing Navajo things unless you already are Navajo" (Michaels 1992, p. 677).

When we anticipate culture by race, we not only reify race as a stable, ob-jective, and measurable category, but also link it deterministically to culture. When race is operationalized in this way, we lose sight of black heterogene-ity, including the diverse ways by which individuals make sense of what it means to be black. We underconceptualize how "blackness" intersects with class, gender, and ethnic identities. Further, we limit our analyses to how "blackness" is reflected in the meanings students bring with them to school and other institutions and simultaneously silence the meanings that are im-posed on black students by institutional structures (including schools) and their agents. And the near-unilateral focus on making sense of "blackness" in this literature also stops short of examining how the social construction of "whiteness" is simultaneously implicated in the achievement performance of black students.

The anticipation of culture by race also prevents us from considering whether the behaviors and attitudes that are documented among Blacks are indeed "black" attitudes and behaviors, or whether, instead, these attitudes and behaviors are hallmarks of another social category of which black (as well as white and other) youths are a part (e.g., adolescence) (Cook & Lud-wig 1998). If we are to address these limitations as they are articulated in the empirical research that undergirds the acting-white hypothesis, we must

improve the theoretical precision with which we document and conceptual-
ize race. In so doing, we need also to more closely examine the ways in
which black heterogeneity, class, and gender intersect and more carefully
evaluate the impact of institutionalized constructions of race (including but
not limited to whiteness) that are articulated via inequities and struggles that
occur in schools and other institutions.

EXPLORING THE HETEROGENEITY OF THE
AFRICAN AMERICAN EXPERIENCE

Critics of CET and the acting-white hypothesis regularly point out that Blacks
are not simply raced. They are also positioned by gender and social class.
Additionally, black families not only vary in structure, norms, expectations,
and value orientations (Allen & James 1998), but also in terms of how they
racially socialize their children (Spencer 1983, 1990; Stevenson 1994; Swanson, Spencer, & Peterson 1998). Black youths' peer groups, moreover, are
differentially constituted and exhibit different norms and beliefs. Finally, the
experience of being black shifts across historical time as a consequence of
how opportunities and constraints are differentially reflected from one era to
another.

In light of known heterogeneity in the black experience, we have already
developed evidence that gender (Carter 1999; Fordham 1996a, 1996b; Kao &
Tienda 1998); social class (Hochschild 1995; Foley 1991); peer group norms
(Cook & Ludwig 1998; Ferguson 1998; Hemmings 1996; Horvat & Lewis
2003); family history, resources and interactions (Clark 1983; MacLeod 1995;
Mickelson 1990; O'Connor 1999); and historical time (MacLeod 1995;
O'Connor 2002) all moderate the meaning and expression of racial identity.
And despite the preoccupation with how black students perform relative to
their white peers, we also already have evidence of substantive variation in
how Blacks perform in school (e.g., Attaway & Bry 2004; Bryk, Lee, & Holland 1993; Cross & Slater 2000; Dachter-Loury 1989; Grissmer, Flanagan, &
Williamson 1998; Nettles & Perna 1997a, 1997b; Wang & Gordon 1994). The
evident variation in the black experience and in black achievement performance, therefore, compels us to establish more precise empirical and
conceptual connections between these two indices of variability.

The acting-white hypothesis, as it was first introduced in 1986 and further
elaborated in Fordham's solo publications (Fordham 1988, 1996a, 1996b),
recognized high achievement on the part of some black students. Additionally, Ogbu (e.g., 1981, 1989) acknowledged variability in the achievement
performance of black Americans, despite his evident focus on a comparative
examination of Blacks as a whole vis-à-vis other minority groups and Whites.
Both Fordham and Ogbu, however, treat these expressions of high achieve-

ment as exceptions, and marginalize the significance of substantive within-group variations in black achievement that are not simply the province of individual distinction. Social class not only differentiates the performance of Blacks, but at least one measure of social class—namely wealth—eradicates the gap between Blacks and Whites on some educational measures (Conley 1999). Additionally, black women academically outperform black men at dramatic rates. These considerable distinctions in black achievement cannot be reduced to individual variation. They require greater empirical and theoretical attention.

EXPLORING THE CULTURE AND ORGANIZATION
OF SCHOOLS AND COMMUNITIES

In homogenizing African American experiences, the acting-white hypothesis also overlooks the possibility that the specifics of any given context might moderate the meaning and performance of racial identity, thus disrupting its relationship to academic achievement in ways unaccounted for by the model. Unfortunately, the failure to attend to how the contexts and demands of particular environments affect the development and adjustment of minority youth is not uncommon. As Spencer, Swanson, and Cunningham (1991) point out, with few exceptions (e.g., Bell-Scott & Taylor 1989; Holliday 1985; Taylor 1976), "studies that explore contextual effects are seldom conducted on minority youth" (p. 368). Similarly, both Ainsworth-Darnell and Downey (1998) and Cook and Ludwig (1998) emphasize the importance of context. They urge attending to the specific complexities of daily school experiences in different school settings in order to gain a more complete understanding of black students' persistent lack of achievement.

In accordance with this charge, we must further explore how the culture and organization of local schools reify race and impose specific meanings of blackness. Race is more than a product of how African Americans make sense of themselves as racial subjects and then enact this sense-making in relation to school. It is also a consequence of how schools and their agents racialize black subjects. For example, Ann Ferguson (2000) found that both black and white boys are apt to perform their masculinity (or their position as males) by transgressing school rules. She stresses that black boys more often find themselves "in trouble" because of how their performances are interpreted, rather than what actions they perform. More specifically, Ferguson found that when white boys transgress, school officials presume that "boys will be boys," attribute "innocence to their wrong doing," and believe that "they must be socialized to fully understand the meaning of their acts" (p. 80). In contrast, when black boys transgress, their acts are "adultified." That is, "their transgressions are made to take on a sinister, intentional, fully conscious tone that is stripped of any element of naivete" (p. 83). Having framed the young black transgressors as "not children," the interpreters (most of whom are white and constitute authority, and therefore power, in the school setting) are necessarily directed toward treatment "that punishes through example and exclusion rather than through persuasion and edification, as is practiced with the young white males in the school" (p. 90). Too often we have treated race and even racial subjectivities as something that students bring with them to school rather than understanding them as coproduced in relation to educational practices and processes.

Schools are not, however, the only institutions that racialize black bodies and frame black actions. The culture and organization of communities (physical and affective) and neighborhoods also can operate in ways that reify race and make sense of and shape blackness in ways that inform black achievement. Thus, the study of the institutionalization of blackness both within and outside of schools is warranted.

BOOK OVERVIEW

The chapters that follow address the limitations outlined above. Taken in total, the chapters not only explore the heterogeneity in black identity, experience, and response but how the demographics and organization of schools, public discourses, racialization processes, and material conditions impact how black people experience school. We have divided this volume into three sections that highlight the different ways in which these issues can be taken up in relation to making better sense of the black-white achievement gap. Further, these chapters signal promising avenues for future research. Below, we provide a detailed overview of the chapters and the contributions that they make to our understanding of where future research efforts aimed at understanding and ameliorating the gap ought to be directed.

The Organization of Schools and Student Agency

The chapters that we have selected to begin this volume amplify the importance of examining the intersection of school structures, race, and individual processes. Given the research presented here, it is clear that efforts aimed at ameliorating the gap need to be directed at what happens inside schools and classrooms. While social class differences among families, parenting practices, and a host of other factors certainly impact students' ability to engage in school, educators have little control over what happens inside students' homes. Moreover, as the chapters below argue, school structures are deeply implicated in maintaining racial inequality in access to opportunity in schools. Both Mickelson and Velasco and Tyson make strong cases for the need in the research community to systematically examine the ways in which our school structures reinforce and reify existing racial disparities in achievement. Highlighting the relevance of tracking and ability grouping, both chapters argue that early and persistent notions among students about who is smart and who is not are implied and reinforced by the historical and present-day structures of schools, including the hierarchal organization of instruction and ability grouping. These chapters are especially important because they both connect these structural arguments with the lived experiences and responses of students in schools and their interpretations of their own and their peers' ability and life chances. These authors make apparent how structure and agency work in concert in schools to perpetuate the black-white achievement gap.

In their chapter, Mickelson and Velasco focus on black high achievers in the Charlotte-Mecklenburg, North Carolina, school district. Unlike much other research that has examined the gap and the notion of acting white, Mickelson and Velasco acknowledge both the structural factors impacting black students' lives and illustrate how these structural factors (primarily tracking) influences their lived experiences, the choices they make about classes, the ways that they are viewed by peers, and how they respond to these peer assessments of them.

We would like to highlight two critical contributions made by Mickelson and Velasco in their examination of these students' experiences as high achievers and our often failed or incomplete efforts to understand the lived meaning of the notion of acting white. By examining the intersection of race, school structure, and individual difference, these authors endeavor to move the debate away from a dichotomous conversation about either the presence or absence of acting white in schools. They complicate our understanding of how and when the acting-white label is used and what it signifies for students. Their work highlights the complexity of not only the participants' lives within schools but also the complexity of the ways in which race and achievement are institutionalized in these sites. Their work hints at the heterogeneity of the black experience, taken up in more detail later in the book, and draws attention to the significant and enduring role of school and classroom structure in perpetuating the achievement gap.

Tyson also takes up the issue of tracking/ability grouping, and her findings are consistent with those of Mickelson and Velasco in her emphasis on the role of school structures in perpetuating the achievement gap and reifying raced notions of ability in school settings. However, Tyson layers on top of this structural analysis of school settings a much-needed focus on life stage development. Tyson's body of work presented here makes clear the need for researchers to examine the achievement gap in light of the developmental stages students move through. Her findings indicate that younger black students have a very strong desire to excel academically and that the notion of oppositional culture or the importance of what it means to act white does not emerge until adolescence. Yet, by the time they reach adolescence, students have certainly begun to have been sorted and labeled as "smart" or not.

It is clear that a promising avenue for future research on the gap ought to be aimed at identifying the processes that explain these developmental and academic shifts. More work on student's early school careers is also warranted. Such work must examine how individual differences are interpreted in school settings. Additionally, this work must explore how race (that of the students as well as that of the educators) influences educators' interpretations of ability as well as their proclivity and capacity to maximize the learning opportunities of all students, especially students of color who are underrepresented in the upper echelons of our tracking system.

The Heterogeneity of Black Identity, Experience, and Response

The authors contributing to this section of the book take up more directly the ways in which students' lived experiences are far more complex and differentiated than other explanations for black underachievement would suggest. All three contributors to this section highlight the variation found in black students' experiences and how students actively create their identities and respond to the structures of school and society. These three chapters also draw attention to the value of examining the achievement gap from an ethnographic perspective, allowing researchers to gain insight into the complexity and multifaceted nature of students' lives. These authors reveal the ways in which race, class, gender, and ethnicity interact to shape how students are situated within and react to school. By extension, the research presented here draws attention to the fact that solutions aimed at narrowing the achievement gap must take into account the multidimensional nature of students' social realities.

The chapter by Annette Hemmings provides an anthropological perspective on black student achievement and the ways in which individual and publicly available discourses regarding the identity and potential of black people (or blackness) are played out in school settings and interplay with black achievement. Focusing on the micro-level cultural realities of two students' lived experiences as they come of age in specific high school communities, this chapter sheds light on how students' narratives and dispositions toward achievement change over time as they progress through high school and move into adulthood. This chapter reminds us of the important role of individual agency and how social structures frame but do not wholly determine how students articulate their identities and navigate their social world. It also reveals how students differentially make sense of and respond to publicly available discourses on blackness in the process of doing their own identity work. This work highlights the dynamic nature of identity formation and development for young people and illustrates the ways in which students will articulate different identities as they struggle to find the formula and representations that suit their lived realities.

Prudence Carter's examination of the influence of gender on academic achievement among black and Latino youth further takes up this theme of identity construction and the complexity of factors that impact the ways that students engage with school. Exploring the nexus of race/ethnicity and gender, Carter's work brings into focus the ways in which racialized gender construction affect students' orientations toward schooling norms and expectations. More specifically, she shows how black and Latino youths' constructions of femininity and masculinity are aligned or not with conceptions of what it means to act white; and how these constructions subsequently impact the inclination with which males versus females are more likely to embrace those styles, codes, and behaviors that increase the probability for academic success. This research not only highlights the extent to which gender has been woefully under-studied in relation to black achievement performance. Moreover, it demonstrates that research efforts aimed at understanding the variation with which Blacks perform in school must be theoretically and empirically attentive to how the intersections of "particular" identities are framed and articulated in relation to schooling.

This theme of broadening our conceptual lenses such that the race of students is not treated in isolation of other social positions is also taken up in the next chapter by Sherri-Ann Butterfield. Butterfield's work examines how ethnic identity is implicated in black students' dispositions toward and activity in school and further complicates our understanding of how intersecting identities affect students' educational orientations. Her analysis centers on black West Indians who do not fit neatly into the logic of Ogbu's cultural ecological theory. Focused on second-generation immigrants, Butterfield finds that her research participants report that their parents imagine the American opportunity structure in ways that are consistent with how CET captures the orientations of voluntary minorities. Yet these same young people also report being confronted with the racial challenges common to involuntary minorities. In their effort to make sense of and negotiate the narratives of opportunity that are transmitted in their households and their own experience with racial discrimination, which they read as systemic and enduring, they engage in school in ways that would not be predicted by Ogbu's model. Importantly, the nature of their engagement is not only framed by their distinct experiences as second (as opposed to first generation immigrants) but by the demographics of the schools they attended. Butterfield's work conveys that researchers need to be quite careful and deliberate in conceptualizing immigrant status and how this status is uniquely articulated and experienced in specific settings to impact achievement orientations and performance. Taken together, these three chapters provide evidence that future research and the theoretical models and adaptations that emerge from the research need to take into account the ways in which the multiple identities of students intersect with social space to influence experiences in and outcomes from schooling.

The Structuring of Race and Material Inequities

The final section of the volume reinvigorates our attention to the structural realities that frame the achievement gap. In the final two chapters, the authors take up the question of how the structural conditions of American society influence the complex ways that students experience school.

Ainsworth and Wiggan force us to pull back our lens again to a wide-angle vision that focuses on the structural impediments to equal opportunities for achievement in schooling between Blacks and Whites. While not discounting the individual level decisions made by families and students that affect their ability to achieve in school, the work of these authors points to the important role of "material conditions" in shaping opportunities to achieve and enact social mobility through educational institutions. While in this chapter they present a detailed analysis of research that points to the importance of neighborhood context in shaping opportunities for achievement, these authors call for research that focuses on the ways in which the structural conditions of our society—such as housing discrimination, racial inequality in schools, and uneven opportunities for employment based on social location—influence efforts to close the achievement gap. In their examination of neighborhoods, Ainsworth and Wiggan direct us to a multidimensional approach that would reveal how neighborhood context influences individual outcomes.

We conclude the substantive chapters of the volume with a piece by Amanda Lewis. In the work presented here, Lewis argues that research efforts need to be focused on the ways in which the racialized structural realities of school and society must be taken into account before we can look to individual attitudes and behaviors as a way to make sense of the achievement gap. She argues that our lack of attention to the structural impediments to school success has limited our ability to develop effective social policy aimed at ameliorating the gap. Lewis further demonstrates how culture operates as structure—how durable patterns of meaning-making and human interaction systemically accord some and not others educational privilege and reify power differentials between racial/ethnic groups in ways that impact educational opportunities and outcomes and inform achievement gaps.

Lewis uses a detailed ethnographic study of the everyday lives of students in three schools to illustrate how the racialized structure of American society permeate daily interactions in schools. Her work again reminds us that despite CET's attendant focus on both the structural and cultural forces that shape black achievement, in recent years the structural aspect of the theory has received far less attention than the cultural aspect that draws attention to the attitudes and values of black students and their families. In contrast to this problematic turn, Lewis's work focuses squarely on the structural conditions that shape black achievement, including the ways that structured inequalities are articulated in the micro-dynamics of U.S. schools. If we are to better understand the origins of the achievement gap we must attend, as Lewis does, to the ways in which white cultural and economic hegemony continue to structure the daily lived reality for students in schools.

As a whole, this volume calls for research that fundamentally acknowledges and explores the ways in which the raced and classed realities of American society impact the lives of students in schools. This research needs to be aimed at all levels of the problem. We need to understand how schools perpetuate systemic inequality, how students' identities are complicated by their own social location, and how the structural aspects of our lives bound the daily decisions, actions, and choices made by students and their families in relation to school. It is through such multilevel analyses that we might better understand how and why educational opportunities are maximized for some and limited for others such that achievement gaps, including the black-white divide, persist.

NOTES

1. In an article published after his death, Ogbu (2004) criticizes how CET has been captured in academic discourse. Among other things, he takes issue with the ways CET has been reduced to "oppositional culture" and has become indistinguishable from the acting-white hypothesis. In this article, he stresses that "although black collective identity and cultural frame of reference are oppositional, only one of five categories of Blacks among both adults and students is explicitly opposed to adopting White attitudes, behaviors, speech" (Ogbu 2004, p. 28). He explains, moreover, that in his own study he has "generally found that there are relatively few students who reject good grades because it is White [and] on the contrary they want to make good grades and many report that they are well received by their close friends when they get good grades" (Ogbu 2004, p. 28). Having offered this clarification, he notes, however, that "what [black] students reject that hurt their academic performance are "White" attitudes and behaviors conducive to making good grades" (i.e., and depending on the school context: "speaking standard English, enrollment in Honors and AP classes, being smart during lessons, having too many White friends," "studying a lot or doing homework everyday," "acting like a nerd," "taking mathematics and science classes," "spending a lot of time in the library," "reading a lot") and "experience peer pressures from other Black students to discourage them from adopting such White attitudes and behaviors" (Ogbu 2004, pp. 28–29). In directing our attention to black

students' opposition to "'white' attitudes and behaviors conducive to making good grades" Ogbu (2004, p. 28), nevertheless, forwards essentialized conceptions of whiteness (and by implication blackness) and continues to convey that black underperformance in school derives, in part, from black students' opposition to whiteness (with the analytical emphasis being on how Blacks conflate whiteness not with competitive educational outcomes [i.e., "good grades"] but with "behaviors" and "attitudes" that produce these competitive outcomes).

2. Ogbu does not consider the political contexts that shape the less-than-voluntary migration of some refugees, nor how these conditions might affect their perceptions and experiences once in their new surroundings.

3. CET has since been substantiated by research on other minority groups (e.g., Matute-Bianchi 1986; Gibson & Ogbu 1991). And the notion of an identity-achievement strain among African Americans, which would be consistent with the "acting white hypothesis," has been supported by the work of Ford and her colleagues (Ford, Harris, & Schueger 1993) as well as by Steele (Steele 1992; Steele & Aronson 1995). Moreover, Fordham's (1988, 1991, 1996a) sole-authored publications have reinforced the notion of a relationship between acting white and Blacks' academic achievement.

4. These articles were identified through a LexisNexis bibliographic search. We searched for all articles published between 1984 and 2004 in "major newspapers" and "magazines and journals" that featured "acting white," "race," or "black" anywhere in the text. We incorporated the additional qualifiers of "black" and "race" because an initial search using just "acting white" retrieved references to a large stream of articles that referred to acting White House representative and the like. Our qualified search produced 210 articles. Of these, fifty-two referred to acting white in relation to areas other than Blacks' academic or educational achievement (e.g., speech, dress, social relations, representation of black families in sitcoms). Two of these fifty-two articles did, however, associate acting white with the generic notion of "excellence." The remaining 158 articles referenced the notion of acting white in relation to educational achievement or attainment.

5. Notable exceptions to this trend were three articles that referred to the work of Ronald Ferguson (and the Minority Achievement Network), or referenced the perspectives of Pedro Noguera (Santana 2003a, A1; Pappano 2003, B9; Winerip 2003, B8).

6. This discussion of unpacking race is taken largely from a chapter written by O'Connor, Lewis, and Mueller for a forthcoming edited volume.

I

THE ORGANIZATION OF SCHOOLS AND STUDENT AGENCY

1

Bring it On! Diverse Responses to "Acting White" among Academically Able Black Adolescents

Roslyn Arlin Mickelson and Anne E. Velasco

Even as Americans celebrate the fiftieth anniversary of the epochal *Brown v. Board of Education* (1954) decision, race-related gaps in academic achievement remain intractable and perplexing problems. On the national level, the achievement gap has been narrowing since the 1970s, although in the last decade the rate of closure has slowed (Campbell, Hombo, & Mazzeo 2000). The processes that generate the racial disparity in achievement are the subjects of ongoing investigation. Among the most provocative, controversial, and widely debated explanation is John Ogbu's (Ogbu 2003; Ogbu & Simons 1998) cultural ecological model (CEM) of minority achievement, one component of which is the concept of oppositional cultural frameworks (OCFs). "Acting white," Signithia Fordham and Ogbu's (1986) notion that African American students forego academic achievement because they fear their peers will label them as traitors to their race, is a related concept that too often becomes confused with the larger, more complex theory of oppositional cultural frameworks.

Much of the scholarship in the area of the gap focuses on low-achieving students and the role OCF ostensibly plays in their outcomes. In contrast, this chapter focuses on high achievers. Our goal is to examine high achievers who have found ways to be academically successful in the same educational environments in which so many African American students have not. Our study examines how the structure of schools and classrooms intersect with students' peer cultures—which may include an OCF—to shape their reactions to race issues, including their responses to acting white.

OCFs have several aspects. They include (1) disdain for public and/or private behaviors that lead to visible displays of academic competence or that lead to good grades (such as volunteering answers in class, doing homework during lunch, using Standard English in conversation, and studying for tests); (2) values and behaviors that resist the official educational agenda (which calls for complying with school behavior codes and mastering the curriculum); and (3) rejection of popular culture norms (meaning those defined by dominant middle-class, white dress styles and taste in music, TV, and other media). Someone who is labeled acting white accepts and exhibits many of the mainstream, white values, norms, and behaviors described above. Acting white is considered evidence of weak social identity as a black person and lack of race solidarity.

Several researchers have investigated the effects of OCFs on achievement, sometimes mistakenly fusing the acting-white hypothesis with the OCF model as they explore the roots of the race gap. Some find support for the model (Farkas 1996; Farkas, Lleras, & Maczuga 2002; Lovaglia et al. 1998; Mickelson 2002; Portes & Rumbaut 1996; Solomon 1992; Steinberg, Dornbusch, & Brown 1992; Waters 1999), but many researchers who investigate oppositional culture are less convinced. Some report that it does not exist (Ainsworth-Darnell & Downey 1998; Cook & Ludwig 1998; Downey & Ainsworth-Darnell 2002; R. Ferguson 2001), or that what is labeled oppositional culture is actually something else, or that oppositional culture operates differently from the way Ogbu describes it (Carter 2003; Cousins 2006; Horvat 2001; O'Connor 1997, 1999, 2001). Other researchers do not question the existence of the acting-white label as something to be avoided; rather, they question whether it is related to achievement, or whether black students' primary response to the actual or threatened labeling is always academic withdrawal. We fall into this last category in that our findings illustrate that the responses to being labeled acting white vary, and, in some cases, the label seemed to spur students to even higher achievement.

Using data from a series of interviews of academically successful black high school students in Charlotte, North Carolina, we find that an OCF exists among many, but certainly not all, black students. The acting-white label is certainly associated with the behaviors other researchers have documented, such as the use of Standard English, certain taste in clothing, demeanor, etc. But, we also find that the acting-white label is associated with academic achievement.

Additionally, we found a range of responses to the acting-white label among the academically talented and accomplished black students we interviewed: (1) Some students acknowledged being the recipient of the insult but promptly dismissed it. (2) Some students were greatly disturbed by it—some even admit to crying about it—but, with the help of parents and others, managed to work through that distress. (3) Others rejected the label as being "anti-Black" but were challenged by it. In some way, it motivated them to actively "represent their race" and assume a "Bring it on!" attitude.

We also found that structural or organizational features of schools are one set of contributing factors to the academic race gap and to OCFs. Scholars frequently note the ways that the organization and structure of schooling shape, channel, and trigger students' behavior. Supporters (including Ogbu) and critics of the OCF model readily acknowledge that racism in American culture, along with discriminatory school policies, practices, and organizational structures, contribute to the racial disparity in achievement. Tracking is a good example of this point. Tracking—which segregates students in racially correlated ability groups and thus also imposes racially correlated opportunities to learn—is a notorious structural contributor to the achievement gap. The voluminous literature on tracking indicates,[1] among other things, that a key component of the race gap in achievement is the relative absence of black students in higher-level tracks and their disproportionate enrollment in lower-level ones (Jencks & Phillips 1998b; Mickelson 2001; Oakes, Muir, & Joseph 2000). Research on the black-white race gap on standardized tests shows that although both groups may take similarly *named* courses (e.g., English 12), Blacks are more likely to be in lower tracks where the instructional level is less rigorous than in the higher tracks dominated by white students (Mickelson 2001, 2002, 2003b). As Hallinan and Sorensen (1977) observe, no matter how motivated and capable students are, they cannot learn what they are not taught. Thus, those in lower tracks learn less, and because Blacks are in lower-level courses, they do not perform as well as Whites on standardized tests.

The race gap in achievement is also shaped by another important set of factors—individual student characteristics (e.g., prior achievement and parental involvement) and students' course enrollment decisions. Students can learn higher-level social studies, English, math, and science only if their school offers such courses *and* they enroll in them. Thus, it is the intersection of individual factors (including students' response to peer pressure) with school structures, policies, and practices that generates racially correlated track placements for comparably able students.

In our recent research, we have been interviewing students to understand why there are so few African American students in upper-track high school courses. This chapter reports our findings from a set of twenty-two in-depth interviews with high-achieving African American adolescents who were enrolled in at least two high school Advanced Placement (AP) (or International Baccalaureate [IB]) courses during the previous five years. We explore how they arrived at the top of the academic pyramid and why they were joined by so few of their comparably able black peers. Our interests include the influence of youth culture;[2] the organizational structure of the school (racial composition of the school and of academic tracks); and the role of parents, peers, and educators in Black adolescents' educational careers. We seek to answer the following questions: (1) Does acting white exist as part of

CEM/OCF, and is there a shared definition of acting white that operates among black high school students? (2) Does acting white affect achievement and/or the type of courses students take? (3) Do students who encounter the acting-white slur respond similarly? (4) Is acting white related to the race gap in achievement, consistent with OCF as hypothesized by Ogbu? and (5) How does the organization and structure of a school interact with youth culture to generate student responses such as the decision to enroll in a particular class, to study, or to be motivated to excel academically? Specifically, how might school structure and youth culture interact in influencing whether students enroll in high-level classes *and* how might these interactions influence the labeling of high-performing students as acting white?

Our findings suggest that the Charlotte-Mecklenburg Schools (CMS's) organization of instruction into racially correlated tracks, combined with the presence of an oppositional youth culture—specifically, students' efforts to avoid behaviors that may result in their being labeled as acting white—contributes to the decision of some, but not all, black students to not fully engage academically. At the same time, our findings also refine how an OCF operates differently among black adolescents. We show that while some students may avoid academic achievement and difficult classes due to their fear of being labeled, as Ogbu predicted, others find the cultural stereotypes of Blacks as less intelligent and the acting-white epithet motivating. They interpret these aspersions as a personal challenge, goading them to excel in school and to embrace academic success as a way of "acting black." Both responses support the argument that the acting-white label *is* about academic success and academic disengagement, as well as about the use of Standard English, a particular style of dress, and a specific demeanor as signals of racial group solidarity. In short, this chapter supports Ogbu's claims that oppositional culture exists, and it is about achievement as well as language, fashion, music, etc., and it may result in the avoidance of academic achievement for some. At the same time, our findings support critics who argue that Ogbu's model is too static and deterministic to account for the range of motivations and academic behaviors exhibited by black youth.

STUDY BACKGROUND AND CONTEXT

The findings we report in this chapter are drawn from our ongoing investigation of school reform in Charlotte, North Carolina. Charlotte is the site of the landmark *Swann v. Charlotte-Mecklenburg Schools* (1971) decision, in which the Supreme Court first upheld the use of within-district mandatory busing as a remedy for segregated schooling. The current phase of the research was not conducted solely to investigate the questions addressed herein. However, the wealth of data collected over the course of seventeen years of research in CMS permits us to investigate the questions animating this chapter.

From roughly 1974 to 1992, CMS employed a mandatory busing plan to achieve racial balance among its schools. As a result of the busing, by 1997 the majority of CMS students attended a desegregated school during some portion of their academic careers in Charlotte.[3] Although schools were by and large desegregated at the school level, by the early 1980s, students learned in classrooms resegregated by tracking. This longstanding practice of curricular and programmatic differentiation that creates racially correlated tracking dates back to the early 1970s when busing was at its peak (Mickelson 2001). Then, as now, top academic tracks had only a sprinkling of black students (Mickelson & Smith 1999). Currently, CMS differentiates its high school academic curricula into five tracks. From least to most rigorous they are (1) special education, (2) regular, (3) advanced, (4) academically gifted (also called honors), and (5) AP and/or in some schools, the IB program. Special education is almost exclusively black, while in most schools, AP and IB courses are almost exclusively white.

In the early 1990s, much of the mandatory busing plan was replaced by other desegregation strategies, most notably a program of controlled choice among magnet schools. This policy shift occurred largely because of pressure from two sources: business elites, who complained that the desegregation plan's reputation hindered economic development, and newly relocating middle-class white parents, who were dissatisfied with the race and class integration of the schools they found when they moved to CMS (Mickelson & Ray 1994; Mickelson & Smith 1999).

In 1997, white parents sued the district, seeking a declaration of unitary status[4] and an end to the use of race-conscious policies of any kind (*Capacchione et al.* 1997), and several black plaintiffs (*Belk et al.* 1999) reactivated the original lawsuit, claiming that CMS never fully complied with the original *Swann* ruling. A federal judge declared the district unitary in 1999. After three years of litigation and appeals, in spring 2002 the U.S. Supreme Court upheld the lower courts' unitary decisions. In fall 2002, CMS returned to a neighborhood-school-based student assignment plan, and the district rapidly began to resegregate by race and social class (Mickelson 2003a, 2003b).

CMS's history of struggles over race and education form a part of every student's lived reality. Because of the desegregation plan, ongoing public discussion of desegregation, and the reopened litigation, race and racism are widely acknowledged by adults and children as part of the process of schooling in the Charlotte-Mecklenburg schools (Hubbard and Mickelson 2004). And even though most of the individuals we interviewed had attended desegregated schools during most of their CMS careers, at the secondary school level many learned in racially isolated white upper-track courses. Their classrooms invariably were resegregated such that many of our interviewees were the only or one of a handful of Blacks in that class-room. As a result, throughout the CMS system, all students—Blacks as well as Whites—came to associate track levels with race and academic ability. The racial composition of a particular classroom signaled both its level of rigor and who among the students were its "legitimate" members. Courses with mainly white students conveyed to everyone that the course was diffi-cult, while courses with mainly black students were widely considered easy. In these ways, the public struggle over desegregation of the schools and the racially correlated tracking system provide the context for CMS students' de-velopment of trust/distrust in schools and in educators, their social and racial identities, and their attitudes toward education and their future.

METHODS AND DATA

The findings reported in this chapter derive from a multi-method, multiyear investigation of school reform and educational equity that can be separated into three phases. Each phase grew out of the findings and unanswered questions raised in the previous phase. Table 1.1 summarizes the phases of Mickelson's school reform study.

In 1987, Mickelson began a qualitative study of corporate leaders and school reform (see Mickelson & Ray 1994; Ray & Mickelson 1990, 1993). She found that corporate leaders wanted public schools to improve entry-level employees' work readiness, their attitudes, and their skills. They also wanted the schools to "do something" about desegregation. The findings from the first phase (1987–1994) led to the study's second phase (1995–1999). The second phase included a 1997 survey of CMS eighth- and twelfth-grade stu-dents' attitudes, experiences, and achievement outcomes. The survey was designed to ascertain, among other things, whether previous reforms re-sulted in students' perceptions of greater work readiness, but this phase of the research also revealed data about school-related factors that affect achievement. One specific finding showed that segregation, both at the school level and by track within schools, had a negative effect on student outcomes. And a troubling pattern appeared: academically able black stu-dents typically *were not* found in the top tracks, while Whites with less aca-demic promise *were* enrolled in such classes, along with academically able Whites and a few Blacks (Mickelson 2001).

Specifically, Mickelson compared the twelfth-grade track placement of black and white students who, as sixth graders, scored in the same decile range on the California Achievement Test (CAT). She found that among those who scored in the top decile (90–99 percentile), 52 percent of Whites but only 20 percent of Blacks enrolled in AP or IB English. At the same time, 35 percent of Whites with scores below the 70 percentile were taking AP or

Table 1.1.   Three Phases of Mickelson's Case Study of School Reform in the Charlotte-Mecklenburg School District, 1987–2003

	Dates	Type of Data	Focal Point/Participants
Phase I	*1987–1994*	The Business Agenda and Educational Restructuring	
		Observations	task force; school board meetings; community forums
		Interviews	150 local, state, & national education, civic, business leaders, & local parents
Phase II	*1995–1999*	Business Leaders and School Reform: The Case Study of CMS	
		Surveys	
		Middle School Students	2,400 8th graders
		High School Students	1,800 12th graders
Phase III	*2000–2003*	Academic Pathways and Race Equity	
		Interviews	
		Students	89
		Black Females	27
		Black Males	27
		White Females	15
		White Males	12
		Other	8
		Parents	29
		Black Parents	19
		White Parents	10
		Educators	22

IB English. Only 9 percent of Blacks with weaker academic records enrolled in the most rigorous courses (Mickelson 2001, p. 237).

This finding prompted us to investigate CMS's course selection and placement practices, including its approach to tracking, as well as the roles of parents and students themselves in the choice of courses. Thus, the third phase (2001–2003) of the CMS reform study produced 140 interviews, including fifty-four with academically able black students about their educational experiences. The twenty-two top performers are the subjects of this chapter. The results of the third phase interviews also inform the debate about the black-white race gap by demonstrating how structure and agency, separately and in combination, shape student achievement. Findings from this component of the research (reported in this chapter) are directly relevant to the debate over OCFs and acting white.

Research Design of Phase III

Consistent with our goal of understanding whether acting white exists as part of CEM/OCF and, if so, how it affects student academic behavior, we decided to talk with black students who had achieved academic success.

Given that the OCF is one explanation of black academic failure, by inter-viewing academic successes, we sought to gain some clarification of—at a minimum—how these young people navigated these treacherous social waters. We expected that their experiences would shed light on the OCF process among other students.

Sample

From 2000 to 2003, we conducted a series of approximately 140 in-depth interviews in order to understand why certain students enroll in rigorous college-preparatory courses while other comparably able youth do not. In particular, we wanted to understand, given the paucity of black students in AP and IB courses, why some African American students took such classes in light of the visible association of AP and IB courses with Whites. Were these African American students subjected to OCF pressures? If so, how did they handle the situation? Could their experiences shed light on the choices made by black students who do not excel academically and who eschew AP courses? In exploring this set of questions we expected to learn about students' encounters with OCF.

Beginning in 2000, we obtained a snowball sample of academically able adolescents (both black and white students in grades ten–twelve and recent high school graduates), their parents, teachers, administrators, and coun-selors. We began with children of UNCC (University of North Carolina, Char-lotte) colleagues and younger friends and relatives of UNCC faculty and graduate students. We asked CMS administrators, teachers, and counselors whom we interviewed to recommend additional interviewees. The students we interviewed attended eight of CMS's thirteen high schools. We inter-viewed eighty-nine students split roughly into black and white (and "other"), male and female subsamples. In this chapter, we focus on the high achiev-ing—the most academically gifted and accomplished—African Americans in our sample, eleven young women and eleven young men, ranging in age from sixteen to twenty-one.

We defined high achieving as taking (or having taken) at least two AP or IB classes during high school, with the remaining classes rated no lower than the "advanced" level, which in CMS is considered college preparatory. (A class with the label "advanced" is considered one academic step above a "regular" class, the lowest level—nonspecial education—of difficulty and typically not taken by those who plan to attend college.) At the time of the interviews, some of our interviewees were still attending high school, some had recently graduated, and some were attending college. Our questions fo-cused on their experiences in the high school course selection process.

Interviews

We conducted and recorded interviews based on protocols specifically designed for this study. The protocols were status and, in the cases of our parent and student interviewees, race specific; that is, we developed interviews for students, parents, counselors, teachers, and administrators and had unique versions for black and white students and parents. Two members of the research team conducted each interview.[5] We attempted to match the race and gender of the interviewee with at least one of the researchers (i.e., a black female student was interviewed by a black student researcher and one of the white female authors). Research team members transcribed and analyzed the interviews using conventional qualitative methods of analysis.

FINDINGS

Why More Blacks Are Not in AP Courses

The young people we focus on in this chapter took mainly AP and/or IB courses, the highest-level courses available to high school students. They also tackled multiple extracurricular activities (e.g., sports, music, and service organizations) and exuded great confidence in their abilities and in the academic choices they had made. We hoped they could shed some light on why other academically able black students might make different choices—course selections below their ability levels. Doing so seemed to be evidence that these black youth were avoiding high-level academics.[6]

As our interviewees tried to articulate why black students are so underrepresented in high-level classes, responses tended to fall into three categories: (1) Students want to avoid hard work, and their parents, teachers, and counselors are not pushing them hard enough; (2) Responses to the track structures of the school: Since, overall in CMS, there are fewer black students in upper-level classes, choosing these classes carries a risk of social isolation (see R. Ferguson 2001). Some of our students reported feeling uncomfortable if there were few students in the class who looked like them. (3) Though they would not use this as *their* reason for not taking a high-level class, *other* students might be discouraged by the fear of being labeled acting white.

A common response among our entire student sample—black and white—(regardless of ability level) was that *most* students do not want to be challenged and do not want to work hard. Several of our interviewees even referred to themselves and others as "lazy." In response to this question: "Why do you think there are so few black students who take upper-level courses?" one young woman reported:

> some of my friends do take the easy way and have art four periods of the day, and you know, they don't challenge themselves. [Karen H., seventeen years old]

Other students included the corollary that some of these students do not have parents and teachers encouraging them to challenge themselves. Another student answered the question in this way:

> One, because they aren't pushing themselves, and two, well, two, because they don't have nobody to push 'em. [Kinston J., seventeen years old]

As Tyson (2002) and others have pointed out, most students, regardless of race, seek less challenging classes. High school students are pragmatic when considering the commitment required in high-level courses. Our interviewees said that AP and IB classes are seen as difficult and beyond the intellectual reach of most students, black and white. Because they are concerned about college entrance standards, many students do not want to jeopardize their grade-point average by moving into a more challenging course level where their grades may suffer. They know how labor intensive these courses are, and they want to have time for sports and extracurricular and social activities.

Our respondents indicated that they and others were reluctant to take AP and IB classes because they did not want to be the only or one of few African Americans in a classroom. They saw this possibility as a significant obstacle:

> I guess one of the things that I saw that deterred me from AP classes was not seeing enough of me in AP classes. [Marilyn J., eighteen years old, who overcame her initial discomfort to take numerous AP classes]

> I knew of, yeah, I knew a few people that would . . . based on, like, the number of black students in class . . . that would be the factor whether they took the class or not . . . they just say, like, . . . "There aren't any black people in there; I'm not gonna take that course." . . . I mean, like from the people that I knew . . . like, they would find it way, way easier to make friends with another black person than with a person from another race. . . . Just getting used to that [being one of few Blacks in a class] would probably take a lot of effort before even starting to concentrate on the actual work . . . of the class. [Clarence M., twenty years old]

Since all students seem very aware of the racial composition of the classes available to them, some researchers have speculated that African American students choose not to be in upper-level classes because those classes are seen as a "white domain" (Mickelson 2001; Oakes 1990; Wheelock 1992; Yonazawa 1997). Enrolling and doing well in advanced courses would be interpreted as acting white. But, the desire for more Blacks in a class is not necessarily avoidance of acting white.

What Acting White Means

Many critics of Ogbu's OCF hypothesis do not deny that black students sometimes accuse one another of acting white. What they challenge is Ogbu's interpretation of this charge. Critics agree that acting white is used to sanction those black adolescents who are seen to have rejected their racial identity as African Americans, as signaled by their language, dress, and certain cultural tastes. It is not, critics contend, about sanctioning those who embrace achievement per se. We disagree in that our data suggest that acting white also *can be* invoked to sanction those who embrace achievement. We asked our interviewees to respond to the following question:

> Some people believe that black students do not do as well in school as white students because black students are afraid that if they do well in school their friends will accuse them of acting white. Do you know of students like this, or have you ever experienced anything like that?

Students' answers show that they vary in how they interpret the meaning of acting white. The quotes below offer a nuanced picture of acting white. In fact, we found that a striking characteristic of the label is its fluidity. Students often vacillated—sometimes from one sentence to the next—about what acting white meant to them. The following exchange demonstrates how difficult it could be to elicit a firm definition of acting white. Earlier in the conversation, Kris had indicated that he had been accused of acting white during middle school.

> SM [a white female graduate student]: So, did it [acting white] have to do more with academics, or with, like, social things? It sounds like you're saying academics.
>
> KW: I think, immediately, it was academics, but when you break it down, of course, it's social. Just because, I mean, most people think that black people aren't as smart as white, so. Especially at that age, so.
>
> SM: So, it wasn't, like the way you dressed, the way you . . .
>
> KW: No.
>
> SM: . . . the people you hung out with . . . ?

KW: Like I said, I've always looked like the rest of my friends. I just happened to be smarter. [Kristopher W., eighteen years old]

Despite this sometimes slippery nature of the meaning of acting white, most of our interviewees agreed, contrary to some of Ogbu's critics, that academic achievement *is* a component. Senior Edward L. observed that students who do well are targets of ridicule for a variety of reasons, including their academic achievement.

It's mostly people who are getting good grades and choosing their studying instead of going out, you know, it's like—at lunch, just sit and talk, and they're, like, studying and doing homework or reading a book or doing whatever. . . . And sometimes, it's just—the term "acting white" isn't like even based on things like that; it's based on the way they dress, they way they talk. [Edward L., seventeen years old]

In another exchange, Darryl B., an IB student, began by saying that acting white was not about academics, but he ended by describing how the students in "regular" classes talk about the black students in high-level academic classes. His answer illustrates the division between students as both black IB and regular students seem to interpret it.

AG [a black male graduate student]: Have you ever been accused of acting white?

DB: No, not really. I'm just fine now, you know. Nobody ever calls me a white boy or anything like that. I guess it's really just the company you keep. Uh, you're associated with them. And then, I mean, it's what you do, I guess. What music you listen to, where you . . . what you do on the weekends . . .

AG: So, you're saying that acting white for—at least, as far as being a black student or a black person—is more of a social thing than an academic thing or . . .

DB: Yeah.

AG: Do they go hand in hand?

DB: Nah. Nobody's gonna knock you for doing well. It's not like getting good grades is acting white. That's just doing what you're supposed to do. I wouldn't knock anybody. I don't know, some people might. Like some of the Regular kids, they'll, um, you know, talk about the IB [International Baccalaureate] kids, you know what I'm saying? Okay, there's a wall that we stand in on the [school's] mall, and the IB black kids stand up here, and the Regular black kids stand down here. And they call us the—I think we're the north side or something like that. So, you know, I'll walk down here to talk to some people. They're like, "What you doing down here on the south side?" And I'll just be like, "Man, I'm just here to talk, you know?" [Darryl B., eighteen years old]

Darryl attended Freedom High, which was known for having a high concentration (at least 50 percent at that time of his interview) of black students in its academically rigorous IB program. (And this working- and middle-class school was well integrated at the building level, as well.) Given Freedom High's IB program's racial composition, being black and in IB is normative; IB students accusing a black person of acting white because of his or her academic successes would have been nonsensical. But, outside of that classroom, Darryl's reputation as a high-level student causes him to be seen as "different." Darryl did not belong on the south side of the mall because the regular students there knew he was an IB student. Was he in the "wrong" place because of the way he talked, walked, or dressed, or was it because he was a good student? We can know only Darryl's assessment. Darryl did not see himself as different from the regular students in terms of dress, diction, or cultural style; what he acknowledged is that the IB students stood on the north end of the wall and the regular kids stood on the south. Somehow, the students on the south side saw his crossing from the "north side" to the "south side" as a transgression —Darryl was not one of them.

High school senior Itisha A. described her experiences as an honor roll student. She expressed her disgust for those who labeled her acting white for doing well in school. She deconstructed the implication of the slur by extending its logic.

I was always on the honor roll, or you know, something like that—you know, you get called white, which I think is ridiculous 'cause that's meaning that if you're intelligent, you're white, if you're dumb, then you're black. And you know, and that's a bad, you know, a stipulation to put on yourself as a person or as a race, that this is the only way you can be. That is the stereotype that we've put on ourselves as a society, that black students aren't intelligent, they don't work hard, they don't try. So, when you do, you're trying to be a white student who does work hard and who does try and who has parents that are involved in their education. [Itisha A., seventeen years old]

In the following quote, Richard T. tried to give a definition of acting white in terms of course-level enrollment. He juxtaposed taking higher-level/college prep classes "so you can be like them" [Whites] with doing what the majority of black students do, namely avoiding advanced classes.

In general, I guess a lot of people would say acting white is because you tryin' to kiss up and suck up to people and you tryin' to take all these advanced classes or whatever so you can—so you can be like them [white students], or do whatever, and you should just do what black people do in the majority. [Richard T., twenty years old]

Clifton W.'s analysis traced responsibility for the epithet linking achievement with Whites to disgruntled low-performing students:

I would probably say that that's just a way that they [low performers] can blame or make the people who aren't performing as well feel that they don't have to do well because if they . . . if they don't do well, it's ok, because they're not acting white. I mean, just a way of putting people who are successful down. [Clifton W., seventeen years old]

Barbara T. understands that her academic accomplishments are emblematic of what some black students label as acting white. The personal discomfort engendered in Barbara T. by the label was evident as she struggled to articulate the complex intragroup dynamics that underlie the slur.

I hate to say it, but any, I mean . . . [sighs] It's such a . . . it's such a complicated . . . it's so complicated to answer that question just because . . . I . . . I'm probably the epitome of what it means to act quote, unquote "white." It's when you're, for the most part, you're competent, you know, you believe in education, and, and you, that's a practice for you. You're articulate, and, and—that bothers me that people would define such positive qualities as, have a negative connotation—like as if you haven't maintained truth to your background or something. [Barbara T., twenty-one years old]

Thus, the students indicate that although acting white is about racial solidarity, race identity, social skills, language, etc., for them, and for those wielding the insults, the concept is inextricably linked to academic achievement as well.

INDIVIDUAL RESPONSES TO BEING ACCUSED OF ACTING WHITE

Most of the students who had had the unsettling experience of being accused of acting white noted that the labeling had occurred in middle school (though students said they experienced it, at various times, from elementary through high school). This is not surprising, since middle school is a time when young adolescents are working, often in dramatic ways, to discover who they are. O'Connor (2001) explains that students construct their identities by reflecting and refracting the world made up of their family histories, school sites, and peer group culture. The meanings black students construct about their social positioning and agency are shaped by that world. Adolescents routinely categorize people, relying first on the most visually obvious groupings of gender, race, and language. Because middle school also is the time when ability grouping for academic classes becomes more marked, it follows that students would add this distinction to their repertoire of categories, labeling those in higher classes smart and those in lower classes dumb. What they see—that more white students are in higher-level courses and more Blacks are in lower-level ones—makes it very easy for youngsters to naively confuse correlation with causality. Thus, a structural characteristic of schools provides a ready basis for associating race with academic performance.[7] And because young adolescents often are critical of anyone they see as different, those who deviate from what is accepted as normative behavior are likely to be ridiculed. If students attend schools in which few black students take challenging classes, those who do so could be seen as deviating from normative black behavior or as acting white.

Some students cannot withstand this criticism; they give up completely on academics when their racial identities are challenged. Edward, the high school senior quoted earlier, commented on this reaction.

I've seen this happen to a couple of people, like, to fit in, they'll just change their whole, you know, their whole attitude, you know. And they'll change the way they dress, the way they think, they'll stop doing work, you know. They won't do any type of work, homework. [Edward L., seventeen years old]

Most of the students we interviewed described themselves as able to cope with criticism and peer pressure, even when it caused them pain and confusion.

And that's just when I distance myself from people, 'cause I don't care. I mean, you can, you can say whatever you want to. I know what I'm doing, I know what I'm . . . I know I'm trying to get my grades right, and I know I'm trying to get off to a good school. So, while I'm, supposedly, acting white in school, then what are they acting like when I'm off at school, and they're sitting around the house still, in they parents' house, working at Burger King or whatever? So, I mean, I don't care; they can say whatever they want to. [Kristopher W., eighteen years old]

The young women in our sample reported reacting more emotionally to being labeled as acting white than did the young men.[8] They eloquently described their anguish over having their core identity challenged. As Marilyn reported, she "went home crying" when someone accused her of acting white. Anita H. responded by turning the tables.

> That's happened to me before, but [laughs] I always get 'em because I say something smart like, you know, "Well, um, so you're saying that acting black is to be dumb, you know, to be ignorant?" You know? And then it . . . [the response was] "No, no, I didn't say that!" But in essence, that's what they were saying. [Anita H., sixteen years old]

Anita, Kristopher, Itisha, and many other respondents possessed the analytical skills to deconstruct the insult and then dispose of it. Another strategy was to deliberately embrace the challenge, in order to destroy the myth of black intellectual inferiority while demonstrating black intellectual prowess. There were obstacles to overcome and challenges to meet when a student adopted this course of action.

The Challenges and Opportunities of "Representing the Race"

Even at this relatively early stage in life, these students had encountered racism. They were aware of lowered expectations for black students held by teachers, counselors, school administrators, and sometimes even from their own relatives. They considered the acting-white label to be part of the insidious legacy that impugned black people's intelligence. Some of our interviewees said they deliberately embraced the challenge to do well, to work hard, and to succeed to prove the doubters wrong. They knew they were intelligent, they knew they could handle high-level classes, and they consciously wanted to disprove any notion that black students were not as intellectually competent as white students. And they wanted to reclaim academic achievement as entirely consistent with acting black.

Because the slur acting white often is leveled by lower-achieving students, our high-performing students perceived the label as a reaction to their academic success. But it also implies that they are not really black. They, therefore, sought to assert their "Blackness" by reaffirming academic achievement as acting black. They sought not to change themselves but to change those who accuse and try to marginalize them.

Initially hurt and confused when labeled as acting white, they eventually found the slur motivating. They were incensed by the label's implications: if doing well is equivalent to acting white, then failing is equivalent to acting black. Some saw themselves as being on a mission to "represent the race" by challenging myths and stereotypes about black academic underperformance.

Yeah, it's like some people, not really me, [laughing] but it's like they kinda get a kick out of, you know, just being the only black person in a class. You know, it's like, "I'm, you know, here to kinda be that thorn in your side and show you that, yes, we can do this, too." [Jonathan R., eighteen years old]

I like it 'cause I want to prove that I'm just as good as you, you know. I'm in that class, and I got the highest grade in there, and all of you all are struggling. It doesn't matter that I'm black, you know. So like, um, because I was the first black male in our class, like class rank wise . . . I'm trying to represent my people. Give me the spotlight! [Darryl B., eighteen years old]

Like Darryl and Jonathan, Brian relished the idea of being in the spotlight.[9] He found being on center stage motivating, although he was ambivalent about the pressure this put on him:

that's mainly where I felt that I had to sort of represent the black race, and so, I saw it as something good. I didn't really see it as a pressure. But it did, it does feel kind of strange, though, when you are around people of a different race, and you're, like, the only one there. And, I don't know, it seems . . . at first, you're kind of scared that they might look down on you or something. [Brian N., eighteen years old]

Kinston had a similar perspective on being the only Black in a class and representing the race.

It's, it's pressure. I mean it's a lot. I guess it's a motivator because it keeps me in the books, but at the same time, it's hard knowing that if you fail they are going to try to say everybody that's black [is] going to fail. That's what's hard. It's a lot of pressure, but I like pressure and I like being in the spotlight. I think I do better because of that pressure and stuff like that. [Kinston J., seventeen years old][10]

Unlike Jonathan's and Darryl's obvious relish in grabbing "the spotlight," Brian and Kinston, though seeming to be motivated by the pressure of representing their race, alluded to some of the negative aspects involved in this path.

The few black adolescents in high-level classes inevitably find themselves "invited" by teachers and (white) classmates to "represent their entire race." While at times amused by this idea, our students realized its absurdity and its marginalizing implications for black people. It was just another example of some of the casual racism that they endured from some of their white peers and teachers.

Unlike the young men mentioned earlier, most of the students we interviewed longed to avoid adding the burden of having to represent their entire race to their already challenging academic agendas. Most, nevertheless, had been forced to play the role of "the token black person" in the classroom because there were no others. For instance, when the topic of slavery or of civil rights was discussed, the white students or teacher often turned to the black students for the definitive black opinion. One interviewee described her negative physical reaction to this psychological burden.

> Yeah, it's—it's—it's more like I—all eyes—yeah, all eyes are on me. I—like, I can feel my—like, I can—like I—like I'm embarrassed. Like, I feel like I'm standing up in front of the class and they're all staring at me or something, and I can feel myself getting, like, hot or something. [Madison B., sixteen years old]

THE COSTS OF ACHIEVEMENT

Although the twenty-two students we interviewed were high achievers, intent on tackling and overcoming academic challenges, their success came at a price. African American adolescents must deal with the stresses that all adolescents face and, at the same time, they must struggle with the racialized world in which they live. The issues they deal with are different from and arguably more complex than those of white students. We have mentioned the burden of representing one's race, although some students view this as a challenge and motivator. We will now discuss other costs that our high-achieving African American students incurred.

Living between Worlds

Our high-track, academically successful black students were keenly aware of their separation—which sometimes was physical as well as psychological —from most other black students in their schools. As O'Connor shows, advanced classes often are located on a different side of a school from the less rigorous ones that most black students take. Some of our students made great efforts to spend time with black students who were in the regular classes, and for some isolated high-achieving black students, this was the only way they could have contact with other black students. Still, on a day-to-day basis, high-achieving Blacks spent much more time with white students than they did with black students, and often felt uncomfortable in that white-dominated world.

> It's like you feel like you don't fit in because you don't really fit in with, um, white or other, or just say white people who are in that class because you're not the same as them, and those are the people who are mainly taking the upper classes. And, so you don't really feel like you

fit in with them. You feel like they might look down on you, really, even though they seem to be caring about you. And, plus, you don't really fit in with the, um, African American people who are not taking the higher classes because you're not really thinking about what they're thinking. You're not really doing the same things that they're doing. So, you feel like you don't really fit in with them. [Brian N., eighteen years old]

This passage recall's Darryl's earlier comment about the wall that literally and figuratively seemed to divide groups of black students: "So, you know, I'll walk down here to talk to some people. They're like, "What you doing down here on the south side?"

Internalizing Stereotypes

An unintentional but consequential outcome of having few Blacks in upper-level classes is that some people, black and white, consciously or unconsciously may perceive this absence as evidence of Blacks' intellectual inferiority: if black students were capable of doing the work demanded in those classes, then they would certainly be there. Our interviewees were not immune to this commonly offered logic, as the following exchange between the first author and Madison demonstrates. In describing how others associate white with smart, Madison reveals how this insidious stereotype had penetrated her own worldview:

MB: I find myself having my own stereotypes. Like if I, I mean, 'cause I know my friends, I know they're smart, black, white, or whatever, but um, I guess if, like I'm a [teaching] assistant for this class, and it's a majority black students, and most of them have Fs in the class, and like, the few white students, not all of them, a couple of them have bad, lower grades, but none of them, of course, are as bad as the black students'. So, I guess that's . . .

RM: What do you mean "of course?"

MB: I don't know, I don't know why. . . . [laughs nervously] I heard myself do it. Oh! I don't know why I said, "of course." Um. See I have my own stereotypes. . . . I don't know why that is, 'cause that makes me as bad as a white person saying the same thing. I don't know, and I don't know why I think that.

Later in the interview, Madison was clear about the ways stereotypes about race and intelligence interact with the racially correlated organization of schooling (i.e., on-site segregation and tracking that produces racially identifiable classes) to contribute to perceptions that doing well in school is acting white.

I don't know—I [sigh]—I don't know. I prob—I know—it probably has a lot to do with who you're around. Like, I—I—I guess I would be more around white people if I was, like, coming out of a—a class where I—it would be majority, um, white students. And I'd be around them, and they'd be like, "Oh, well, she—I guess she thinks she's—she's not—she's better than us or she's not as—like, we're not as good as her because"—I don't know, um [sigh]. 'Cause I—I think—I think people associate white with smart, and black with not. So if they see a black person with white people, "Oh, they're smart. They're—they're better, or they think they are." [Madison B., sixteen years old]

Davey G., who was a college student when we interviewed him, had achieved some perspective on his high school experiences and was aware of the insidious ways that racist stereotypes had infiltrated them. As a student at a historically black college (HBC), he realized what he had absorbed by being one of few black students in the mostly white upper-level courses he had taken during high school.

[In high school] . . . there weren't enough [black] students in high [track] classes, and what effect, yeah, I mean the effect that it did have on me was when I saw a class full of black students, which was every class [at his HBCU], I always initially, before I thought about it [snaps his fingers], I came to the conclusion . . . that this class must be . . . That must be the slow class. [Davey G., twenty years old]

STRUCTURES OF SUCCESS

Mickelson's (2001) high school survey data (see table 1.1) revealed that many bright black students do not enroll in AP or IB courses. Given the cumulative effects of racism in schools, and the presence of an African American adolescent peer culture that contains elements of OCFs, we wondered what enabled the students who did enroll in AP or IB classes to make that choice and to succeed in the classes. Why had these twenty-two students enrolled in AP or IB courses? In particular, we wondered whether our interviewees, by definition successful students, had significant support systems that helped them sustain their academic pursuits and navigate the school and adolescent peer culture.

Our interviewees revealed common experiences that launched and supported their success. Relationships with their significant others—friends, parents, and teachers—were important for sustaining the students' emotional and intellectual well-being, especially in the face of toxic epithets like acting white. We found, as well, that the organizational context of learning contributed mightily to academic success. For example, many of the twenty-two students we interviewed had been certified as academically gifted during their elementary school years. This early certification put them on a path for academic success and supported their achievement with stimulating curricula, additional resources, and all-important labels that signaled to school agents that these children were "smart."

Systems of Support: Help from Friends and Parents

In order to persevere in challenging academic classes, students need support. Our research indicates that having friends who are taking the same classes is ideal, but a network of friends who are doing coursework that is at least similar is helpful, too. As Clifton and Brian explained, these friends provide touchstones—people with whom to compare notes, literally and figuratively.

And just, like, in my biology class, um, my friend's in another period, although the same biology class, but we talk about the class a lot, like if I need some information about a homework assignment or anything like that . . . what they did in class that day, I'll call her up and find out what happened in class that day. [Clifton W., seventeen years old]

I think one of the things that also helped me stay in it, like I said, my three best [friends] that go to my school and they stayed in IB, so I stayed in IB. [Brian N., eighteen years old]

Anita described her strategy for maintaining support this way:

So you just have to keep the people around you who are supportive and will help you out in what you want to do, you know, and not um, you know, not listen to that kind of stuff [accusations of acting white] because, you know, where are you gonna be in ten years and where are they gonna be, ya know? So you just have to be strong within yourself to do classes like that, you know, and know that what you're doing is right and will help you. [Anita H., sixteen years old]

Supportive parents can help students manage stressful times by being available, by listening, and by encouraging their children to plan for the future. Marilyn recalled that when she came home devastated because she had been accused of acting white, her parents comforted her.

When I came home crying, they would say, "Baby, don't." I'm sure that's what every parent says to their kids, but, um, it helps to have parents you can come home to and cry, you know. They're still supportive, and they still tell you, "Well, they'll be flipping burgers at McDonald's while you're . . . ," . . . you know. [Marilyn J., eighteen years old]

Davey's mother often comforted and encouraged him.

My mother and I had a lot of these conversations . . . but the pressure you're referring to [dealing with accusations from other black students about acting white], I learned to live with it. You know. And, she would always tell me, "You know, one day, Davey, you'll be doing this and that, and this and that, and you'll forget all about it." So, I don't know. I put it behind me at that moment. [Snaps his fingers.] [Davey G., twenty years old]

Systems of Support: Help from Teachers and Counselors

Students particularly value their teachers' assessments. The right words from a teacher or counselor can motivate a student to challenge him or herself—conversely, an educator's words can undermine a student's self-confidence.

My English teacher told me to go ahead and take AP, he felt, like, he—he could see that's what I thought [that teachers felt that black students weren't as smart as Whites] and tried to reassure me that that wasn't true. [Marilyn]

Counselors, mentors, advisors, people that I'm close to and not close to always say, "Are you sure you want to do that? It will be hard." Some say [snaps fingers], "I know you can do it. Tackle it, handle it, finish it, do it, complete it. Congrats, you're almost done." They give encouraging words while others may give . . . they may tell me that there will be many obstacles in my future: "Are you sure you wanna do that?" [Davey]

Systems of Support: School Opportunity Structures as a Context for Acting White

Support from significant others makes it possible to succeed in top classes, but the structure of opportunity in a school is even more important. If students do not enroll in top tracks, they cannot succeed in them. We observed a notable trend among IB students from two CMS high schools. The first, Menlo Park, is approximately one-third minority. It is located in a very affluent part of Charlotte and has a reputation as a rigorous school. Very few Blacks enroll in Menlo Park's IB program. Freedom High, located in a mixed working- and middle-class bucolic suburb on the suburban fringe of the county, is about one-half minority, in large part because a sizable number of black students opted to enroll in Freedom High's IB program to avoid their neighborhood schools. The Freedom High transfer students' poorly regarded home school, Gardner High, does not offer an IB program. An unintended consequence of this set of circumstances is that the IB program at Freedom is approximately 50 percent black.

In a diverse school in which critical numbers of minority students take upper-level classes, acting white was not an issue. IB student Karen H. compared her prior experiences in an integrated Florida high school's IB program with IB experiences at her current CMS school, North County High, a racially isolated white suburban school.

> [Acting white for Blacks] . . . really that wasn't a problem until I got here because, um, the classes in Florida, the IB program was so diverse, it had students from everywhere, so it really wasn't an issue there with the students. But, here, it's like, if you get an A on something, other black students, typically female, you know, look at you, and [say] "Oh, she acts so white," and, you know, it's really discouraging [laughs] . . . it seems like they don't want you to succeed. [Karen H., seventeen years old]

We found that black IB students at Freedom were much less likely than their counterparts at Menlo Park to face peer criticism for their academic endeavors. We found Freedom High's black IB students were less often harassed by the epithet because participation in the IB program was more normative than at Menlo Park. The following quotation from Freedom High IB student Darryl highlights the power of school opportunity structure norms to influence students' track level enrollment decisions by normalizing IB courses as a place where Blacks belong.

> Ok, um, in the IB program, there were, I think there were fifty-three IB seniors, and, uh, I think almost, like, thirty of 'em were black. Most of 'em were black. And, uh, in my classes, it'd be a good mix of everything, Blacks, Whites, Asians. That's what IB really was, so. . . . [Darryl B., eighteen years old]

Support systems provided by family members, peers, and educators, in conjunction with a school social organization that normalized Blacks' participation in the top academic tracks, made the difficult road that bright black students must travel a little easier.

CONCLUSION

The starting point of the research reported in this chapter is the paucity of Blacks in upper-level tracks and, by extension, how that imbalance contributes to the race gap in academic achievement. Our findings help answer the question that follows from this starting point, namely, why aren't there more Blacks in the most academically rigorous classes? Our findings also address the debates concerning CEM/OCF. The organizational dynamics of schools, such as race differences in opportunities to learn and to prepare for these classes, discriminatory practices by educators in making placement recommendations, and structural features of schools' daily operations are part of the answer. Our data suggest, however, that we cannot fully understand the reasons for black underenrollment in rigorous college-prep courses without examining the choices made by the students themselves. Personal beliefs, peer culture, parental expectations, and the structure of opportunity at specific schools all influence the decisions that academically able students make as they select courses and allocate time and energy for studying. Our findings point to one additional aspect of this process; that is, some students' desire to avoid being labeled by peers as acting white.

John Ogbu's compelling and controversial theory that black youths' oppositional cultural frameworks lead them to discredit and avoid behaviors contributing to academic success provides one explanation for the educational choices of some black students. Following Ogbu, one could argue that one reason so few of Charlotte-Mecklenburg schools' academically able Blacks enroll in top-level classes is because taking such courses could result in their being labeled as acting white. Since this is a damaging epithet that connotes a lack of social solidarity with other Blacks, identity-conscious adolescents would likely seek to avoid the risk. Two groups of critics challenge Ogbu: those whose work casts doubt on the existence of OCFs, and those who believe that such frameworks exist but question the way Ogbu describes their function, their etiology, their distribution among minority youth, and their relative importance for explaining the race gap. We fall into the second group.

We found all twenty-two students we interviewed were aware that the most rigorous classes were considered white territory—by Whites and Blacks alike. Our respondents refused to comply with those expectations. For some, an awareness that many Whites think Blacks do not belong in top-track classes and cannot perform at a sufficiently high level was motivating. This goaded them into proving that black students are as academically competitive as white students, and that valuing and pursuing academics is part of what it means to be black. But they had to prove this to other black students, as well as to white students and teachers.

Our investigation was a response to earlier survey findings that showed CMS's pervasive use of academic tracks had a powerful effect on academic outcomes (Mickelson 2001). Due to within-school segregation by tracking, and to the growth of resegregation at the school level during the 1990s, many Blacks and Whites are now learning in racially separate environments. This pattern of second-generation segregation blunted the full potential for equality of educational opportunity that came with desegregation. Another important consequence of the second-generation segregation, as our data show, is that, throughout the Charlotte-Mecklenburg schools, many students came to associate track levels with race and academic ability. The students in our sample confirmed that the racial composition of a particular classroom signaled its level of rigor and ostensibly who belonged in it. Courses with mainly white students were understood to be the difficult ones, reserved for smart people; classes with mainly black students were widely understood to be the easy ones. To the extent that the demography and structure of the school created or reinforced the association of "smart" with "white," we saw the intersection of school structure and peer culture shaping the individual student's behavior.

Our findings contribute to the ongoing debate on OCFs and the race gap in achievement in several ways. While our findings are consistent with Ogbu's theory that an OCF shapes the achievement behavior of black students, they also lend support to those who find his OCF model inadequately narrow in its focus, overly deterministic, and failing to account for observed variations in black students' responses to social and academic pressures. Like the youth whom Tyson describes (chapter 2 in this volume), our respondents reacted to the acting-white slur in various ways. Some got angry, a few felt that their identities were challenged, and others powerfully reaffirmed academic achievement as integral to Blackness. By definition, though, our respondents did not succumb to the pressure to underperform lest they be labeled as acting white. Another striking similarity between our findings and Tyson's is the powerful role that school social organization and structure play in generating and exacerbating the association between student race and academic achievement. Specifically, our respondents reported that the racial composition of their schools and their academic tracks were clearly factors in how students in their schools understood the relationship between race and achievement.

On the other hand, our findings also indicate that Ogbu is correct both about the influence of OCFs on some students' school behaviors and about the acting-white label as a part of such frameworks. In contrast to Tyson's findings, the students we interviewed maintained that acting white is, at least partially, about academic achievement and about engaging in behaviors that typically lead to achievement (e.g., enrolling in AP courses, participating in class, doing homework, studying for tests, and performing well on them). Acting white also includes using Standard English, participating in mainstream white cultural forms instead of mainstream black cultural forms, associating primarily with white friends, and displaying other signifiers of weak social identity as a black adolescent.

The twenty-two high-performing students we discuss in this chapter are a subset of the fifty-four black students we interviewed during Phase III of the larger study (see table 1.1). Most of the fifty-four black students acknowledged that high-achieving Blacks faced accusations of acting white at some point in their academic careers. And our twenty-two high-performing interviewees, while noting the label's social dimensions, invariably identified an academic aspect as well. Typically, our respondents recounted being accused of acting white when they were in middle school. By the time they reached high school, being labeled white for their achievement was not commonly an overt problem; there is ample evidence, however, that the slur, which contributes to pervasive stereotypes of black academic inferiority, along with school structures that segregated black and white students at the classroom level, affected them at a subconscious level. Recall Madison and Davey's disturbing comments:

> the few white students, not all of them, a couple of them have bad, lower grades, but none of them, of course, are as bad as the black students'. [Madison]

> when I saw a class full of black students, which was every class [at his HBC], I always initially, before I thought about it [snaps his fingers], I came to the conclusion . . . that this class must be . . . that must be the slow class. [Davey]

These comments provide evidence that black students are affected by the processes and structures within schools that contribute to the labeling of academic achievement as acting white. Schools reflect—in fact, magnify—the larger culture in which cultural stereotypes regarding race and intelligence abound, and the social organization of school by tracks reinforces a notion that white equates with smart and black equates with dumb. When particularly strong group norms in middle school and high school governing solidarity within race are added to this mixture, we begin to understand how this label attaches to high achievers.

Fortunately, all of these stellar students worked through the pain, shame, and aggravation of being accused of betraying their race, but their responses to being labeled acting white varied. Some ignored it; some consciously sought to reaffirm that acting black included academic excellence; others embraced the challenge to disprove the underlying assumptions of the acting-white epithet. We found that our students managed to cope with the accusation and even thrive because of certain factors:

- They were guided into high-level classes and supported in them by parents, peers, and educators.
- The demographic and social organization of particular schools was such that the concept of acting white was nullified. There was a critical

mass of black students participating in upper-level classes at these schools, which made the slur ridiculous (see the earlier discussion of Menlo Park vs. Freedom High).

- Many of these students were "certified" as academically gifted students early in their school careers. This helped inoculate them against the "slings and arrows" of racism that they would encounter on their school journeys by providing them with an early imprimatur of their academic competence and self-worth.

Obviously, our high achievers are not typical of all students, black or white. Nor are their reactions necessarily typical of all academically able black students—our purposive snowball sample was self-selected. We have no idea how many academically able students accommodate the threat of being labeled as a race traitor by withdrawing from academic pursuits. Members of our sample implied that although they had not let this threat inhibit their academic performance or dissuade them from enrolling in top-level tracks, they had many peers for whom the opposite was true. Our respondents were aware of academically able Blacks who, in order to avoid being accused of acting white, deliberately chose not to enroll in higher-track classes and not to maximize their academic achievement.

The interviews we conducted with older adolescents do not permit us to investigate the developmental aspects of OCF, as does Tyson. It is noteworthy, though, that many of our interviewees recall that their own experiences with acting-white slurs initially occurred during their middle school years. Based on the data provided in our interviews, we concur with Tyson's notion of the importance of children's developmental trajectory for understanding if, when, and how OCF affect students' achievement attitudes and behaviors.

Our findings suggest that both sides of the argument over the causes of the racial disparity in achievement are partially correct. We demonstrate that an OCF exists, and that it is about academics as well as the use of Standard English, and the choice of clothing, hairstyle, demeanor, and other markers of racial identity. In some cases, we believe that the OCF contributes to the race gap in academic outcomes, as Ogbu proposed. Because of the power of acting white to shame them as traitors to the race, some portion of black adolescents do decline to behave in ways that lead to academic success. They choose not to do homework, not to study for exams, not to participate in class, and not to take rigorous college-level courses.

At the same time, our findings suggest two elaborations or corrections to the OCF model that are consistent with the arguments of Ogbu's critics. Just because the acting-white epithet is leveled at a black adolescent, it does not mean he or she will respond by withdrawing from academics. Our interviewees reacted in an entirely different manner—they were stirred to excel academically precisely to counter the insidious claim that being black some-how means you are not smart—or at least not as smart as Whites. With their academic success, high-achieving black students prove that the blanket no-tion that being black means you cannot/should not do well in school is in-sulting, demeaning, racist, acontextual, ahistorical, and empirically false.

The second elaboration to Ogbu that our findings suggest is that school or-ganizational features—such as racially correlated academic tracks—create, sustain, and reproduce racial differences in educational outcomes and in stu-dents' worldviews regarding race, ability, and achievement. To be fair, we must acknowledge that Ogbu (2003) does identify tracking as a source of black underachievement. Our findings suggest *how* tracking intersects with black peer culture, and with larger racial stereotypes, to inform students' de-cisions about whether or not they will be comfortable and successful in a higher track class. To the extent that black students associate white with smart and black with dumb, we must assume that growing up in a school system constantly waging battles over desegregation and consistently reseg-regating students into racially correlated tracks contributes to the core beliefs upon which OCFs are built.

Ogbu never claimed that all Blacks eschew achievement; nor did he ig-nore the racism that is part of what we accept as the fabric of American so-ciety and public education. His critics do not deny that the acting-white epithet exists in black youth culture. Rather, they challenge Ogbu's interpre-tation of OCFs as centered on achievement behaviors, his relative inattention to variation in black performance, and to issues of context, gender, and so-cial class. Our findings suggest that one way those with differing perspec-tives might talk with instead of past one another is to acknowledge the va-lidity and the incompleteness of both sets of arguments. The resulting conversation would go far toward resolving the controversy over acting white and would bring greater clarity to the larger issue of Black-White gaps in higher-level course enrollments and achievement.

NOTES

The research reported in this chapter is supported by grants to the first author from the Ford Foundation (985-1336 and 1000-1430). In addition to the authors, Anthony Greene, Shannon Maples, Sean Langley, Aminah Muhammad, and Stephanie South-worth conducted many, and participated in some of the analyses, of the interviews we quote in this chapter. We wish to acknowledge their contributions.

1. For reviews of the relationship between tracking and achievement, see Loveless (1999), Lucas (1999), Mickelson (2003a, 2003b), Oakes (1985, 1990, 1994), Welner (2001), Welner and Oakes (1996), Wheelock (1992), and Yonazawa (1997).

2. A given youth culture is tied to the economic context and historical moment in which the students live. It is also linked to adolescent development and the degree to which adolescents are socially constructed as neither adults nor children. A given youth culture will have multiple subcultures. Subcultures are raced, gendered, and incorporate elements of social class and sexual orientation specificity.

Norms, values, and artifacts (material aspects) of a youth culture are signifiers of membership in it, and that members are neither adults nor children. Signifiers include distinctive music, clothing, language, behaviors such as risk taking, sullenness alternating with exuberance, subjectivity to peer pressure, moodiness, distancing from parents, argumentativeness with peers and adults, optimism, and idealism. We loosely adapted this definition of youth culture from Nancy Lesko (2001). From a youth culture perspective, an OCF reflects norms and attitudes of involuntary minority youth.

3. Although most CMS schools were desegregated during our respondents' educational careers, most of the students were resegregated by track once they reached secondary school, often a school that was officially considered desegregated. During elementary school, white students were much more likely than black students to be placed in gifted education programs, and Blacks were more likely than Whites to be identified for special education (Mickelson 2001).

4. Unitary is a legal term that describes a school system that has formally transitioned from a "racially dual" (i.e., segregated by race) system to a "unitary" (i.e., a single, desegregated) system. The status is assigned officially, by a court, typically the one that originally found the district to be a dual one.

5. The research team consisted of the authors (middle-aged, white female sociologists) and nine graduate and undergraduate research assistants (RAs). The RAs, drawn from sociology, political science, criminal justice, and social work, included three black males, two white males, two black females, and two white females. The diversity among team members permits our data collection and analysis to cross the generational, race, and gender barriers that often constrain or limit qualitative research.

6. We use our sample of high achievers as informants not only because they are articulate about this issue, but also because our subsample of the population of academically able Blacks who do *not* enroll in higher-level tracks is woefully small. Of all of the black students interviewed, even those not selected for the subsample in this chapter (the high achievers) were taking some "Advanced" classes. We interviewed very few students who would be considered "Regular" students (i.e., no college-prep classes). Also, we found it interesting, but not surprising, that the lower-level students in our black sample did not report as many accusations of acting white. We speculate that because they did not participate in such high-level classes, they apparently did not trigger this label.

7. We are keenly aware that racial stereotypes about intelligence are an integral part of American culture. Such stereotypes reinforce the associations of achievement with race that follow from the visibly disproportionate representation of Blacks in lower-track classes and Whites in more rigorous ones. Stereotypes held by counselors and teachers, for example, also are likely contributors to reinforcing the disproportionate representation of black and white students within these tracks. To illustrate, in early fall 2001, hundreds of CMS middle school students, a majority of whom were black, were found to have been enrolled in lower-level mathematics classes even though all had passed or excelled on their previous year's EOG (End of

Grade Test) math standardized tests (they had scores of 3 [proficient] or 4 [above pro-ficient]). Several weeks into the fall semester, in response to this discovery, the su-perintendent ordered the misplaced students to be moved into higher-level, recon-stituted math classes. The superintendent said that a number of decisions led to the misplacement of so many Blacks into lower-level math courses, including racial stereotyping: "I think people need to face that there are issues of bias and prejudice that play into this" (Cenzipur 2001, A7).

8. Horvat and Lewis (2003) report similar findings. They discuss how young women are able to diffuse the anxiety caused by the accusations of acting white through supportive friendships with other peers who value education.

9. Our analysis extends Steele and Aronson's (1998) work on spotlight anxiety. Some of our evidence supports their argument that the spotlight results in academic disengagement because academically able youth, for whom achievement is very salient, fear confirming the stereotype of black intellectual inferiority. They disengage as an alternative to risking these prospective public "failures." In addition, we find student responses to the spotlight issue include those who respond differently. Some, we find, use the spotlight to thrive!

10. Whether, in fact, the spotlight pressure leads to better performance as Kinston claims, or depresses his performance as Steele and Aronson predict, is beyond the scope of this chapter.

2

The Making of a "Burden": Tracing the Development of a "Burden of Acting White" in Schools

Karolyn Tyson

Much of the scholarly and popular discourse on black students' relationship to school and achievement has been shaped by Fordham and Ogbu's (1986) "burden-of-acting-white" hypothesis. The authors trace the achievement gap between black and white students to a peculiar, negative "cultural orientation toward schooling" in the African American community—a consequence of the history of oppression and discrimination suffered at the hands of Whites in America. Ogbu (1987) has theorized, further, that school learning is perceived by African Americans as another way in which whites are attempting to destroy black cultural identity. African American students therefore resist what schools have to offer, in part to maintain their authentic black identity and in part because school learning is not worth the effort—in the end, it does not pay off for Blacks. Consequently, those black students who do strive for academic excellence, Fordham and Ogbu contend, face ridicule and ostracism from their black peers.

Data I have collected in four research projects over the past nine years tell a different story about black students and their relationship to school and achievement. Some black students are indeed accused of "acting white" by their peers, but I find that the notion of a relationship between race and achievement, including the idea that excelling in school constitutes acting white, is manufactured in schools, primarily through highly visible institutional patterns of tracking and achievement. My findings, key aspects of which I discuss in this chapter, highlight three significant limitations of the original conceptualization of the "burden-of-acting-white" thesis: (1) the role of culture is misspecified; (2) the treatment of schooling context (including achievement outcomes and course, program, or track placement patterns by race and social class) is inadequate; and (3) the importance of human developmental processes is insufficiently addressed. Systematic attention to these factors, I argue, would help make sense of the inconsistent findings reported by researchers who have conducted empirical investigations of a burden of acting white or an "oppositional peer culture" among black students. The failure of researchers to come to a consensus regarding the problem of a burden of acting white after more than eighteen years of study is both a testament to its complexity (Kao, Tienda, & Schneider 1996) and a clarion call for a new approach.

In this chapter, I use empirical data drawn from interviews and classroom observations of various cohorts of black students from elementary to high school to highlight the contextual aspects of a burden of acting white with respect to academic achievement. I trace the journey children make through school, assess the impact of early experiences on later attitudes and behaviors, and consider the influence of particular school structures. I begin by discussing the three key limitations to the burden-of-acting-white hypothesis noted above and then suggest an alternative framework for understanding the development of the burden of acting white.

CULTURE, CONTEXT, AND HUMAN DEVELOPMENT IN A BURDEN OF ACTING WHITE

Culture, as others have noted (Gould 1999; Trueba 1988), forms the core of the original burden-of-acting-white thesis. Fordham and Ogbu (1986) posited that Blacks have constructed a set of cultural norms in opposition to those of the dominant culture. A communitywide rejection of the standard norms of academic success creates a burden of acting white for black students who strive for high academic achievement. The authors acknowledged the influence of institutional and structural factors (e.g., economic inequality, a job ceiling, unequal reward structure) in the development of a burden of acting white, but they traced the root problem to the "cultural orientation toward schooling which exists within the minority community" (p.183). According to Fordham and Ogbu, African American students undervalue education because they do not perceive schooling to be as relevant to Blacks as to Whites, and they also believe that, unlike Whites, education does not pay off for them. Thus, black students are less motivated than other students to work hard in school and consequently do not put forth the effort necessary to excel. In short, the authors formulated—intentionally or not—yet another cultural deficit argument (Gould 1999; Harpalani 1999, cited in Spencer et al. 2001; Mahiri 1989). For, in order to effectively address the problem of black students' underachievement, Fordham and Ogbu imply that the norms and values of black culture must change.

The conceptualization of culture in the acting-white thesis is itself problematic, however. Rather than perceiving culture as providing students with "tools" to help them make sense of and act in the particular situations they confront (a perspective Swidler [1986] proposed), Fordham and Ogbu see culture as providing the values by which students determine whether or not school is a worthwhile investment. That judgment, once reached, shapes their behavior. I argue that a conception of culture as a "toolkit" is much more useful theoretically. Findings have been mixed regarding the existence of a burden of acting white, or even of an "oppositional peer culture" among black students. If culture supplies values, then African American values must differ across schools and samples of students. In other words, for the mixed findings to make sense, African Americans would have to value education in some settings and not in others. But why would this be the case? Definitions of culture vary, but most agree that it is shared among a particular group of people. Given this basic premise, the particular "cultural orientation toward schooling" that Fordham and Ogbu posit Blacks have should be relatively stable across school settings and student samples. However, if culture is conceived of as a toolkit, the inconsistent findings make more sense, for they alert us to look for possible variation in the school environment. Students may be confronting different situations in schools that lead to different meaning making, and consequently, to different strategies of action (Swidler 1986).

Another drawback to accepting the model of culture as supplying values is that it leads to a narrow focus on attitudes and behaviors as primary explanatory factors. That focus, in turn, diverts attention from important contextual, school-based factors. These include institutional patterns of segregation based on race and socioeconomic status (SES) in courses, programs, and achievement (e.g., honor roll, junior marshal), which appear to give rise to the idea of a relationship between race and achievement. Much of Fordham's and Ogbu's work, individual and collaborative, has been based on ethnographic studies (e.g., Fordham 1988, 1996a; Ogbu 1985, 1991b). Yet, in developing their theory of a burden of acting white, they appear to have missed an opportunity to attend to specific details of the school context. Students' day-to-day experiences in school certainly influence how they think about education and achievement (Hemmings 1996; Mickelson and Velasco this volume; Steinberg 1996). In their effort to make sense of student narratives in light of racial inequality in the United States, Fordham and Ogbu (1986) overlooked *local* structures of inequality, specifically those within individual schools (e.g., tracking).[1] Paying closer attention to factors within schools and classrooms helps clarify why some studies find evidence of a burden of acting white or an oppositional peer culture among black students (Farkas, Lleras, & Maczuga 2002; Neal-Barnett 2001; Steinberg, Dornbusch, & Brown 1992), while others do not (Ainsworth-Darnell & Downey 1998; Cook & Ludwig 1998; Downey & Ainsworth-Darnell 2002;

Ferguson 2001; Kao, Tienda & Schneider 1996). Equally important, a more local focus can uncover the mechanisms and stages through which such a "burden" might develop.

My final point, which, again, others have made as well (see Spencer et al. 2001), is that most examinations of the burden of acting white have not taken into account the different needs of human beings at various stages of the life course. Few studies have paid attention to a child's need to develop a sense of competence or an adolescent's need to establish a sense of identity and place (in the family, the peer group, the community, etc.). Thus, the consequences of a failure to achieve these developmental goals, as well as the strategies students might employ to compensate for such a failure, also have received little or no systematic study. I maintain that developmental processes are significant factors in academic performance. Frequently, students who lack opportunities for academic success find other ways to achieve a sense of competence and worth in school (Sennett & Cobb 1972; Stinchcombe 1964). I argue that in cases where the lack of academic opportunity afforded to Blacks appears to be systematic, black students are likely to make sense of these patterns in ways that allow them to maintain their personal dignity and worth. Steele and Aronson (1995) have convincingly shown that commonly held stereotypes—such as that Blacks are less intelligent than Whites or that they simply are not capable of high academic achievement—can undermine the test performance of college students. Steele (1992) also has argued persuasively that these and similar stereotypes contribute to "disidentification" with school and academics among younger black students. Indeed, disidentification, according to Steele (1992) and Osborne (1997), is just one strategy black students might employ to deal with the realities of their school settings.

To fully appreciate the role of the developmental process in this context, analyses of black students' achievement orientation must include students of all ages. Paying attention to younger students would contribute to a better understanding of the factors that shape a burden of acting white where it does manifest itself. With few exceptions (e.g., Ford & Harris 1996), research thus far has focused on adolescents. Yet as Elder (1998) reminds us, there is a cumulative effect of experiences, with childhood experiences contributing to the choices adolescents make and the ways they think about the world. Thus, the experiences of younger students might provide clues about the outcomes we observe among adolescents. Given ongoing debate amid contradictory research findings, analyses that provide a clearer understanding of how students make sense of and organize their school lives under particular circumstances and at different stages of schooling are essential. I offer below an alternative framing of the burden of acting white that mitigates some of the most serious limitations of the original thesis.[2]

REFRAMING A BURDEN OF ACTING WHITE

Field research in schools and interviews with more than 250 students in elementary, middle, and high schools reveal a somewhat different and more complicated process than Fordham and Ogbu (1986) and Ogbu (1987) described with respect to black students and their relationship to education, learning, and achievement. I find that, as has been the case historically, black students generally value education and acknowledge an important connection between school performance and later life chances.[3] Moreover, black students in my studies rarely equated whiteness with academic ability and/or high achievement unless patterns of achievement by race (and usually social class) in their own school settings were stark. That is, I found some evidence to support a burden of acting white for black students, but only in particular contexts. The acting-white hypothesis was most relevant to black students in school settings where only Whites (usually wealthy Whites) or disproportionately few Blacks had opportunities to participate in higher-level programs and courses, such as programs for academically and intellectually gifted (AIG) students and honors and advanced placement (AP) courses. Students who had not experienced such explicit linking of race and achievement —those who attended all-black schools or schools that had more racially balanced classrooms—rarely recalled ever being accused of acting white specifically because of their achievement or achievement-related behaviors.

It appears, then, that in schools where higher-level classrooms and programs are disproportionately populated by Whites, and scholastic achievements and honors also appear to be reserved for whites, academic achievement is simply added to the list of behaviors around which students (Blacks and others) draw racial boundaries. It is not until adolescence that these boundaries seem to become significant and are articulated, though; because at this life stage, they have implications for identity development, group membership and allegiances, and position in the ever-important hierarchical social structure of middle and high schools. This correlation with life stage may partially explain why the relationship between accusations of acting white and high academic achievement or academic striving is so often misinterpreted. Among adolescents, academic success and accusations of acting white are often conflated because it is the higher-achieving black students who are most likely to exhibit white styles and preferences and/or to have more contact with Whites.

For instance, in racially mixed schools, high-achieving black students tend to be racially isolated in high-ability classes and programs (see Mickelson and Velasco this volume). Therefore, their chances of forming friendships with and adopting certain preferences and styles of speech, dress, and behavior from white students are greater than those of other black students who have less contact with white students. Although opportunities to form interracial friendships exist outside of the classroom and school, segregated residential patterns continue to limit such opportunities, especially for Blacks (Massey & Denton 1993; Massey et al. 2003; Pattillo-McCoy 1999); and students tend to self-segregate at lunch and in other nonacademic settings (Tatum 1997). In addition, as Fordham (1988) noted, high-achieving black students are more likely than their lower-achieving peers to employ "raceless" strategies. In her study of a predominantly black urban high school, Fordham found that high-achieving black students believed Whites required racelessness in exchange for success. In order to be acceptable to and accepted by white America, the students felt they had to distance themselves from "authentic" African American cultural norms.[4] In sum, it is not always high achievement in and of itself that leads to the accusation of acting white. Rather, sometimes it is particular behaviors, such as a strategy of racelessness or hanging out only with Whites, that mark the high-achieving student for this charge.

In the following sections, I describe my previous research and use key findings from four studies to illustrate (1) that young black students have a positive orientation toward schooling and achievement and consequently find the experience of low achievement punishing; (2) that black students' early attitudes toward school and achievement can and do change over time as a result of particular schooling experiences and developmental needs; and (3) that a conception of culture as supplying tools better explains the documented attitudes, behaviors, and achievement orientation of black students of all ages than does a conception of culture as supplying values.

EMPIRICAL EVIDENCE: OVERVIEW OF FOUR RESEARCH PROJECTS

Table 2.1 presents basic information about four research projects I have been involved in. Each examined, to varying degrees, black students' attitudes toward school and their achievement orientation. All included interviews and, with the exception of one study, classroom observations over an extended period.

Study I

The first study was conducted over an eight-month period in 1996–1997. I used ethnographic methods and interviews with parents, teachers, principals, and students to examine the educational experiences of working- and middle-class black children in two all-black elementary schools, one a Christian independent school (Alternatives) and the other a public school (Madison). Both schools were located in Hopeville, one of the largest metropolitan areas in the southeast.[5] The study's purpose was to examine the

Table 2.1. Selected Characteristics of Studies

Study	Methods of Data Collection	Number of Schools and Classrooms	Students' Race and Median Household Income	Dates, Length of Data Collection	Interview Participants
Study I In Their Own Words I (PI: K. Tyson)	Ethnography, interviews, documentary data	Madison Elementary 1 3rd-grade classroom 1 4th-grade classroom Alternatives 1 3rd-grade classroom 1 4th-grade classroom	Black $60,000–$79,000 Black $40,000–$59,000	1996–1997; 8 months	40 Students 36 Parents 4 Teachers 2 Principals
Study II In Their Own Words II (PI: K. Tyson)	Ethnography, interviews, documentary data	Linwood Elementary 1 3rd-grade classroom 1 4th-grade classroom	Black $6,000–$8,499	2000–2001; 7 months	20 Students 11 Parents 2 Teachers
Study III NCDPI (Co-PIs: W. Darity, D. Castellino, and K. Tyson)	Extant data, surveys, interviews	6 high schools 2 middle schools 3 elementary schools	Black (53), Asian, white (53), Hispanic, Native American (income data not available)	2000–2001; 5 months	125 Students 57 Teachers 18 Counselors 15 Principals
Study IV(A) Effective Schools (Co-PIs: W. Darity, D. Castellino, and K. Tyson)	Participant observation, interviews, surveys, documentary data	19 high schools 65 students	Black $50,001–$70,000	2002–2004; 30 months	65 Students 50 Parents

mechanisms by which school environments shape student outcomes (attitudes, behavior, and achievement).

Study II

A few years later, I conducted a second, similar study in a high-poverty, predominantly black public elementary school (Linwood) in a smaller metropolitan area of another southeastern state. This time, my goal was to assess how low SES factors might affect the school-related attitudes and behaviors of black students. I wondered how the schooling experience at an institution like Linwood differed from the experience at schools like Madison and Alternatives, and how those differences affected student outcomes.

Study III

The third study was a larger project undertaken with a team of researchers on behalf of North Carolina's Department of Public Instruction (NCDPI).[6] Over a five-month period in 2000–2001, we investigated the underrepresentation of minority and low-income students in academically rigorous courses and programs (e.g., "gifted" programs and AP and honors courses) in the state's public schools. Here, too, we assessed achievement orientation, attitudes toward school, and classroom structure, but this time, there was a larger and more diverse group of participants. The team interviewed 125 white, black, Hispanic, Native American, and Asian students in grades one through twelve in eleven North Carolina public schools and conducted surveys of 1,112 schools in the state. This study, and the one described next, also included analyses of extant data from the North Carolina Department of Public Instruction.

Study IV

The fourth study began in 2001 and data collection ended in 2004; it included the same team of researchers as in Study III.[7] This project had two components; one examined six North Carolina schools that had been successful in closing the achievement gap between black and white students (Study IV [A] in table 2.1); the other examined the practices and strategies of high-achieving black students in high schools in three North Carolina school districts (Study IV [B] in table 2.1). Each component was intended to investigate the black-white achievement gap from the vantage point of success. The study's overall rationale is that high-achieving black students can provide us with a view from the inside, helping to uncover the barriers and challenges that may be preventing other students from achieving similar success. We used a variety of research methods in this study, including classroom observations, group and individual interviews, and surveys.

Each of the four studies contributes to an understanding of black children's relationship to school and achievement. As a whole, the studies include a diverse group. There are elementary, middle, and high school students; the students come from poor, working- and middle-class backgrounds; and there are both high and low achievers.

FINDINGS: THE VALUE OF SCHOOL AND THE IMPORTANCE OF ACHIEVEMENT

Analyses of the interview and observational data across the four studies show that both younger and older black students say they value education, express a desire to do well academically, and hope to be acknowledged for their performance by parents, teachers, and peers. Elementary school students, especially, expressed very little ambivalence toward high achievement. In the classroom, at assemblies, and at award ceremonies, they openly celebrated their own achievements and those of their friends. They gave one another high fives, danced, and sometimes sang in celebration of an achievement, big or small. There was no mistaking how these children felt about success, or about failure. When they did not do well, students cried or sulked, became angry, quiet, or even abusive toward their peers. These children understood that academic achievement mattered. It not only brought them immediate positive results (e.g., praise, honors, rewards), it also promised positive outcomes in the future (e.g., enrollment in a good college, employment in a good job, a nice home, a decent quality of life).

From their earliest years in school, students receive messages about the importance of academic achievement. They learn that grades and standardized test scores hold meaning as indicators of ability, competence, and most critically, potential for adult success. These messages are not easily forgotten or dismissed, because evaluations (in the form of achievement test scores, in-class grades, report cards, etc.) are a regular and ongoing part of most students' schooling experience. These assessments determine grade promotion, academic placement, and other critical decisions (Parsons 1959). Most of the students in the four studies described here firmly believed that school evaluations had important consequences for their future. This was especially true among the younger students, as the following quotes demonstrate.

> Sherry: I wanna be a doctor when I grow up. I just wanna be a doctor. So when I grow up, I can't get anywhere with an F. I can't get anywhere with that. I can only get somewhere with a A. [Study I, Alternatives School, fourth grader, March 21, 1997]

Denise: It ["M" on a report card] means mastered, and I want to master everything.

Interviewer: Why?

Denise: 'Cause I don't want to be homeless.

Interviewer: Why would you be homeless?

Denise: If I didn't get good grades, I might not be able to get a house or get a good job. [Study I, Alternatives School, fourth grader, March 26, 1997]

Moreover, grades and test scores are usually the first formal evaluations children receive regarding their ability. Because both students and parents consider the school an authority on such matters, these evaluations are significant (Weinstein et al. 1980). In fact, students reportedly rely more on cues from teachers about their "smartness" than they do on their own performance assessments (Weinstein 1981). Not surprisingly, then, early school evaluations contribute to the perceptions children form of themselves and others (Rist 1970; Tyson 2002), and shape their expectations regarding how they will do in the future (Wittrock 1986).

Early perceptions of ability are significant. They can influence the decisions that students subsequently make with respect to effort expended on schoolwork, course choices, and post–high school plans, as well as how attached they feel to school. Evaluations that students receive from school appear to color their expectations for the future, which suggests an internalization of institutional messages (Entwisle & Hayduk 1978; Leacock 1969; Stinchcombe 1964). As early as third and fourth grade, some participants in the studies had a solid sense of themselves as students: some saw themselves as smart and successful and others saw themselves in an opposite light. These also tended to be students who had had significant and persistent experiences either with success or failure. Even among the younger students, those with the poorest scholastic records (i.e., those who were retained, received remedial services, or got low grades or low test scores) tended to be more pessimistic about their ability to do well in the future (Tyson 2002). Allen and Lynette, both third graders at Madison (Study I), are clear examples. Neither student was looking forward to the next grade; each envisioned academic troubles in the future. Allen feared that the work would "get harder and harder" in fourth grade and that he "might fail and get kept back." So he preferred to avoid school altogether and "just stay home." Students who had skipped a grade, or who had been identified as academically gifted and continued to do well, tended to be more optimistic. Although they were not always certain how they would fare in the future, they were hopeful that they would do well if they continued to "work hard" and "study."

Fortunately for some students, but unfortunately for others, evaluations can and often do change. Such changes can cause a corresponding shift in self-perceptions. Rhonda, for example, a fourth grader at Alternatives, recalled not feeling "intelligent" when she was in daycare, where other students called her "dumb" and "stupid," and later when she was retained in kindergarten. Things turned around for Rhonda at Alternatives. When she transferred there, she was skipped a grade and placed into her age-appropriate grade. With improved grades Rhonda saw herself differently. "It makes me feel intelligent [to earn] As and Bs and sometimes Cs," she confided. At Madison Elementary, another fourth grade student, Brian, had nearly the opposite experience. He said he had always thought of himself as "so smart," until he got to the fourth grade and "started failing." Brian's academic troubles led to his removal from the school's gifted program. He was "shocked" by his low performance and "embarrassed" to let his friends know.

Formal academic evaluations in the form of grades and test scores are not, however, the only sources of information students use as they build perceptions of themselves. They also consider their performance relative to other students. They may compare themselves to their closest friends (information about a friend's performance is usually the most easily accessed) as well as to other students in their class, school, or community. Part of Brian's embarrassment, for example, likely stemmed from the fact that many of his friends were among the highest achievers in his class. Students are very aware of the general achievement patterns in the classroom and school (see Mickelson and Velasco this volume; Tyson 2002). They know who is and who is not numbered among the "smart students." They make such determinations based on how frequently students raise their hands, how often their responses are correct, how well they do on tests, the classes they are enrolled in, and the amount and kinds of awards and honors they receive.

Schools provide many opportunities for students to learn who the smart people are, and by extension, who they are not. Public posting of the honor roll or principal's list, awards ceremonies, and participation in the school's gifted program all are clear, public indicators of achievement. The gifted program is an especially powerful tool in this regard. Many gifted programs, in North Carolina and elsewhere, are structured as "pull-out" programs. Students leave the classroom for specialized instruction with another teacher a few times a week. Leaving the room confers on these students a public acknowledgement of high ability, a distinction that does not escape their classmates. Children who attended elementary and middle schools with gifted programs had little trouble telling us which students such programs were for (e.g., "the academically intelligent people," "only for intelligent persons") or naming the students who participated in these kinds of programs. For example, when I asked Allen, the Madison third grader mentioned earlier, about his classmates, he commented that "most of 'em" were "good and smart." When asked how he knew they were smart, Allen replied, "'Cause most kids are in Quest [the gifted program], and [the] other kids [go] with Miss Grady, like me."[8]

This awareness of achievement takes on particular importance when race, gender, social class, or any other identifiable characteristic seems to separate the smart and/or rewarded from the rest of the class (see also Mickelson and Velasco this volume), a point discussed further below.

FINDINGS: LOW ACHIEVEMENT
AND THE NEED FOR FACE-SAVING STRATEGIES

Across all grade levels, individual black students in all four studies seemed more troubled by their own poor academic performance than they were by concerns that they might be ridiculed by their peers for high academic achievement. I found little evidence that black students in these studies operated under a set of norms or values that are in opposition to the dominant norms that encourage achievement and success in school. Rather, it was because they are guided by these dominant achievement-oriented norms that some black students, like other low-achieving students, faced a burden.

The desire for achievement and recognition was clear among students at the de facto segregated Madison Elementary, for example. There, good scores on the year-end Iowa Test of Basic Skills (ITBS) earned students an invitation to the "lock-in," a Friday night sleepover at the school that included pizza and movies. Those students who met the achievement criteria received invitations in the form of a letter, handed out in the classroom, while the other students looked on. The invited students celebrated their success, jumping up and down and cheering. At first, the other students sat quietly watching; later, as the following field note excerpt documents, they began announcing their own plans for that Friday night.

12:00 P.M.: Mrs. Miller hands out ITBS letters inviting students to the lock-in. The students cheer. Hope, Trey, Tiffany, Angel, Tammy, Brad, Regina, and three other students are invited. Doreen, Rayna, Lynette, Allen, Dion, and Stacey did not get letters.

Allen says he "can spend the night over [at his] friend's house." Rayna says she can "play video games all night long." . . . Lynette says she'll have a lock-in at her house "better than any lock-in [they] could have."

2:22 P.M.: Trey asks a question about the lock-in.

Allen tells me he stays up on Fridays until one o'clock in the morning.

Doreen, who did not receive a letter, mentions to the teacher, Mrs. Miller, that she made the lock-in last year, but otherwise she remains quiet. Shortly after the class is dismissed, Doreen's mother comes into the room to see Mrs. Miller.

She says her "child is in tears because she didn't get a letter." [Study I, Madison Elementary, third grade, June 3, 1997]

The students who did not receive letters attempted to hide their disappointment and embarrassment in front of their peers by "playing it off" (i.e., pretending not to care). Some covered by saying they would be doing something better, or just as good; others said they had been invited in the past. Although as far as I know only Doreen cried, all those who were not invited were upset.

In general, the study findings (especially the observational data) show it was not high achievement that caused black students the most distress but low or poor performance. In the elementary grades, this unhappiness was palpable. For example, when asked how school was going so far, Madison third grader Lynette replied:

Bad . . . I just don't get it. I wish we never had school and our parents just taught us. . . . I try and sit there and try to understand, [but] it doesn't come to my head. [Study I, February 12, 1997]

Older students tried to be less conspicuous about their feelings, particularly in public. Yet younger or older, black students who participated in the studies were not indifferent to the experience of low academic performance or to being perceived as "dumb" or low achieving. Thus, I would not describe any of them as "disidentified" with academics, as Osborne (1997) defines the concept. Some showed signs of alienation and disengagement (either in their behavior or in their narratives), but I could find no student among those interviewed for whom good performance was not rewarding or poor performance not punishing. The extent to which they showed distress or worry about achievement varied—especially among the older students. Still, every student interviewed revealed some sign of concern.

When referring to their own academic performance, the lower-achieving students, including adolescents, almost always presented narratives tinged with melancholy. Consider the words of Terrance, a high school sophomore:

Interviewer: Do you see any sort of divisions in courses people take?

Terrance: Sometimes people tend to make fun of us because we're in regular classes and they think they're a step above us, but I really don't think . . .

Interviewer: What kinds of students make fun of you students in . . .

Terrance: The students in the honors courses.

Interviewer: What do they say?

Terrance: They say, like, we're stupid or something. Or, I'm stupid because I should be in that class and I'm not.

Interviewer: You've heard them say things like this?

Terrance: Uh-hum.

Interviewer: And what do you say in response?

Terrance: I just say—I just walk away. And I say under my breath, "I know I'm not stupid, because if I was, I would've dropped out of school long time ago." [Study III, March 2, 2001, Avery High School]

There was no mistaking the hurt in this young man's voice or words. Being perceived as "stupid" by his peers (both black and white) was not something he took lightly.

For the black students in all four studies, achievement and grades mattered. High achievement (e.g., good grades, academic honors) was perceived as an indication of intelligence, especially among younger students, and was valued.[9] Older students were more cautious about equating grades with intelligence, but they, too, valued earning high grades (though not necessarily working too hard to earn them).[10] They recognized that grades had consequences for adult outcomes, but earning high grades still made most students feel good. Partly, students enjoyed the recognition, but there is also a sense of pride attached to earning high grades. As one junior at Massey (Study IV [B] August 1, 2002) commented emphatically when asked about personal goals for academic achievement: "My goal is to get As every quarter. . . . I want to be on top. I want everybody to know I'm on top." Likewise, a senior at Avery High (Study III) expressed regret over her decision to take honors classes because they "shot down [her] grade point average." She admitted that the only reason she took the advanced courses was to get recognition at graduation for completing the North Carolina Scholars program, but she believed she sacrificed a 4.0 GPA in the process. "If I hadn't gone [into the program], I probably would have had a 4.0" (March 2, 2001). Students were proud of their high achievement because it gave them a sense of accomplishment and was an indication of ability, if not intelligence.

Low achievement, though, was different. There was more variation in how students understood their low grades. Sometimes they attributed low grades to a bad or unfair teacher or a lack of effort on their own part. For instance, when we asked a group of low-achieving black girls at East Side High (Study IV [B], May, 14, 2003) how they felt about their academic performance, all three said that they were disappointed. Yolanda said she knew she could have done better, but she "didn't try." Sugar also claimed she could have done better if she hadn't "slacked off by not going to class." Students were far less likely to attribute low grades to an overall lack of ability. However, they would sometimes say things like, "Math is just not my strong point," and isolate the problem to a specific domain. In general, though, students thought that if they worked harder they would do better.

The reasons students did not work harder are varied and complicated and require more in-depth analysis than can be undertaken here. However, my impression of students like Sugar and Yolanda was that they did not truly believe they could do better. Thus, not trying was a safety net that prevented them from realizing a lack of intellectual ability. So, although there is variation in how students understand low achievement, most students, especially at the elementary level, understand it to have negative implications. As a Madison third grader explained, "If I get Fs—'cause everybody knows that slogan, A's a angel, B beautiful, C crazy, a D, dumb, and F, you a fool—I won't be a popular person. When I get in middle school, all the teachers will say, 'I don't want that boy in my class.'"

Given the association between achievement and how students believe others view them and how they view themselves, it is not surprising to find that low achievers develop strategies to help them maintain positive perceptions of themselves (including pretending they do not care about achievement or rewards) and also to ensure that others will continue to view them positively. In fact, at the elementary school level, being perceived as smart is so important to students that I observed some low-achieving students regularly staging deceitful "ability shows" in an attempt to signal to their classmates that they were doing well academically (Tyson 2002). A typical scenario would involve the low achiever audibly exclaiming "Yes!" and pumping his or her fist in the air when a correct answer was announced. However, from where I sat, I could clearly see that the student did not have that answer or that he or she was erasing one answer and writing in another.

At other times, the student, usually a male, would fervently wave his hand in the air when there was an opportunity for a response, even though he did not know the answer. I learned to detect the underlying deceit by the way the student responded if the teacher did call on him. Caught off guard, the student would back-pedal, saying that he had not meant to raise his hand or that he had forgotten what he was going to say. Sometimes, he would simply stutter until the teacher called on someone else. When another student supplied the correct answer, the poseur would write down the correct answer, then cheer as though he had known that answer all along. This type of ability show was attempted only when other students in the class also were raising their hands, lessening the likelihood that the teacher would actually call on the particular student and expose his ruse. Deceitful shows are significant as "strategies for self-presentation" (Goffman 1959; Hewitt 1984) because they expose the lengths to which young students are willing to go to influence the image others have of them.

Face-Saving Strategies and School Context

Elementary school–aged students are likely to engage in more elaborate deceptions than adolescents, but we found that students of every age tried to avoid negative evaluations of their abilities. Their strategies varied according to their grade, age, school, gender, race, and/or social class. Not all strategies are available to all students, however, and not all strategies are equally effective. Take the case of the three low-achieving black girls from working-class and low-income backgrounds.[11] The girls, students at East Side High School (Study IV [A]), were confronted with a situation in which a teacher publicly humiliated students, calling them "dumb" and "stupid." The girls had been enrolled in the teacher's class at different times, but their responses to the situation were similar: each cut the class regularly. Two of the girls ended up failing the class (the third was still enrolled at the time of the interview). The girls took turns describing their experiences with this teacher.

Stephanie: . . . just criticizing people, "You ain't gon do this, you ain't gon do that." I mean that's all he [the teacher] do half the class period and stuff. I mean you don't wanna hear all that. Just teach me.

Sugar: That's why I failed before, cause I ain't wanna hear all that. I didn't go to class. I didn't wanna hear it.

Stephanie: He's always saying, "You ain't gon make it in your life." . . .

Sugar: Basically, like she says, he just criticizes you.

Stephanie: I mean, I don't know where he be getting that stuff from: "You dumb, well you gon be stupid, you gon be working at McDonald's."

Yolanda: Yup. . . .

Sugar: He will call you by your name. He'll be like, "Sugar, you made the lowest grade in the classroom."

Stephanie: He crazy. . . .

Yolanda: He had called me stupid in front, I think it was a student's mother who was there, and he was like, "You stupid for failing this test. It was the easiest test in the whole wide world." Which it wasn't. And then I had went out the room and then called my mother.

How are these students to understand their teacher's behavior? That his estimations of his students are correct is certainly not an explanation the girls would willingly accept. If they thought themselves to be as stupid as the teacher suggested, they might as well give up and drop out of school—as Terrance, quoted earlier, noted. Perhaps if the teacher had been white, the girls would have relied on their knowledge of race relations and racism (especially in the South) to dismiss his comments; or perhaps they would have been motivated to file a formal complaint against the teacher. Either strategy might have allowed them to avoid doubts about their intellectual ability. But the teacher was black. Thus, it seemed the only way the students could make sense of the teacher's comments and simultaneously deny their validity was to conclude that he was crazy. Of greater consequence, however, is the strategy of action the girls employed. They described the problem with this crazy teacher as one of long standing. They did not believe the school would do anything to change his behavior, so in their view, cutting his class was the only option.

It is in this kind of situation, where students are trying to make sense of and deal with the circumstances they confront in their day-to-day school lives, that culture exerts its influence. Had the girls been white and/or middle class instead of black and working class and low income, they might have perceived other options as available to them for resolving the problem with the teacher, and therefore might have acted differently (see Lareau & Horvat 1999). That two of the girls did not involve their parents suggests they did not see their parents as likely to prevail in a confrontation with institutional agents. Furthermore, given that the problem was not resolved even after one girl did call her mother, that assessment may have been correct.

Nonetheless, the anger and frustration conveyed in these students' words, behavior (avoiding class), and tone should not be overlooked. If the girls were adhering to the norms of a peer culture that disparages academic achievement, we might have expected them to respond by dismissing the teacher's comments altogether or by accepting them as some sort of badge of honor. Yet the students were clearly hurt and embarrassed by their teacher's comments, especially since they had been made in public. The girls' decision to cut class had more to do with their desire to avoid the embarrassment of their teacher's negative evaluations than to avoid achieving school success—which they admitted they desired.

SCHOOL STRUCTURE AND ACHIEVEMENT OPPORTUNITIES

For black students at some predominantly black high schools such as East Side (a historically black high school and 68 percent black at the time of our study), or for students at an all-black elementary school such as Madison, where Blacks comprise all or the majority of the population in higher-level programs and courses, race does not appear to figure into ability distinctions (see Mickelson and Velasco this volume).[12] In many other schools, though, even some that are predominantly black, black students are significantly less likely than white students to have opportunities to participate in higher-level courses and programs, including gifted programs.[13]

Using data collected in school surveys (Study III), we found that in 1999–2000, white students were overrepresented in gifted programs (relative to their proportion in the overall student body) in 93 percent of the elementary schools reporting in North Carolina. One-third of these schools were majority minority (mostly black). Of the 517 elementary schools for which data on enrollment in the gifted program were available, there were only thirty-eight schools (7 percent) in which minority students were not underrepresented in the program relative to their enrollment in the student body. In fifteen of those thirty-eight schools, minority students made up more than half of the school population; and in nine schools, they comprised more than 90 percent of the student body. Put another way, in many cases, in order for minorities to achieve at least parity in representation in a school's gifted program, the student body had to be almost exclusively minority.

In North Carolina, then, black students generally are confronted with the image of an all-white or majority-white gifted program. For example, at Holt Elementary School, where the student body was 74 percent minority (and 71 percent black), the gifted program was 100 percent white. At Georgetown Elementary, 87 percent of the student body was black, but the gifted program was more than 50 percent white. At Jackson, a middle school, black students made up over 50 percent of the student body but just 9 percent of the gifted program. All three schools were among a sample of eleven sites later selected for more in-depth analysis.[14] We followed up the surveys with interviews with students, teachers, counselors, and principals at the selected schools. The interviews sometimes revealed facts hidden in the aggregate data. We learned from a fifth-grade teacher at Georgetown, for example, that whereas none of the fifteen black or minority students in her class were in the gifted program, all five of the white students in the class were.

Overall, the case study data show a systematic lack of equal opportunities to participate in gifted programs for Blacks and other students of color in North Carolina public schools (see table 2.2.) Our case study investigations found no evidence that these students lacked interest in participating in the programs or that few or none met the criteria. The black elementary school students we interviewed were overwhelmingly positive about the gifted program. Most were aware of the special classes, knew what it meant to be "gifted," and wished to be in their school's gifted program. Many of our interviewees, like Mae, Morgan, and Ria, Holt elementary school students quoted below, were confident that they were "smart enough":

Mae: I heard about the AG class. [Mike] told me about it, and he said it's for the, for the academically intelligent people.

Interviewer: And why do you want to be in it?

Mae: 'Cause I feel like I'm smart enough to be in that class. [Study III, fourth grade, March 9, 2001]

Interviewer: Why would you like to do that [be in AG program]?

Morgan: Because I'm a pretty smart girl. [Study III, fourth grade, March 9, 2001]

Interviewer: Is there any other class or anything else in the school that you would like to be in that you know about?

Ria: AG.

Interviewer: Why?

Ria: Because they, uhm, like, [are] advanced math students who are like, smart, and I feel that I should be in it because I think I'm really smart. [Study III, sixth grade, March 9, 2001]

Students also told us that they believed their test scores and grades met the requirements for the program, although they were not always sure what those criteria were. In general, students thought the gifted program would be fun; they had an idea that students in the program were special and were given opportunities to do things that were interesting and exciting. Some students indicated that they believed they needed the "challenge" the gifted program would offer.

Finally, although all schools had a specific set of criteria by which eligibility for participation in the gifted program was established, we learned that in practice, the screening process was quite flexible. For example, the school surveys ($N = 866$)[15] showed that across the state, more than 100 different instruments were used to screen elementary school students for placement in AIG programs.[16] The most commonly used instrument was the state's standardized End of Grade test, which 89 percent of the schools used. Teachers'

Table 2.2. Black Representation in North Carolina Elementary and Middle School Gifted Programs, 2000–2001*

School	Percent Black in Student Body	Percent Black in Gifted (AIG) Program
Georgetown Elementary	87	44
Holt Elementary	71	0
Ivory Elementary	21	17
Jackson Middle	50	9
Kilborn Middle	10	11

*Data are drawn for Study III.

impressions were important, as well. Some form of teacher recommendation, checklist, or observation form was used in 90 percent of all schools reporting, making this the number one screening instrument statewide. Most schools (66 percent) permitted parents to request that a child be screened for the AIG program, or have him or her tested by a clinician outside of the school. Interestingly, though, as we learned from the case study interviews, this information was not widely publicized. For example, none of the three elementary schools we studied included information about the gifted program in the student handbook. One school, Holt, had a pamphlet that described the program, but none of the black students with whom we spoke seemed aware of it, and many told us their parents had not known about the program until they (the children) mentioned it. Indeed, we learned from counselors and teachers that although Holt has an annual Open House, the gifted program is not on the agenda and the pamphlet is not distributed.

Holt may be a rare case, but the gifted programs typically seemed to be underpublicized, if not actually secret. At the three elementary schools in the case study, we found selectivity in getting information about the program to parents as well as ambiguity in determining "giftedness." This combination, as some teachers and counselors at the schools admitted, left the door open for preferential treatment and discrimination. One black female staff person at Georgetown, for instance, who had been working at the school for more than ten years, was sure racism played a role in the racial composition of the school's program for AIG students.

Ms. B.: As you may have noticed, the majority of our AIG kids are white. [She laughs.]

Interviewer: Now why do you think the majority of kids in AIG are white?

Ms. B.: I think there are two reasons, especially—there're probably more than that. One, that's the way the AIG program, to my knowledge, has always been. Based on racism or any other kind of ism—maybe only those kids are seen as smart, I don't know.

She went on to say that some of the white AIG students also were classified as learning disabled. She found this amusing:

Ms. B.: They're LD but they're also AIG. [She laughs.] They have physical limitations but they're still AIG.

Interviewer: Now you say that kind of suspiciously. What do you think is going on?

Ms. B.: What do I think is going on? Bottom line, I guess there's probably some kind of ism going on. . . . First of all, AIG's set up to serve a certain segment of the kids, and white kids fit into that category. . . . They do what, what schools want them to do in terms of equalizing that to success.

School staff at Holt also believed racism played a role in the racial composition of the school's gifted program, although they were much more cautious about what they said and how they said it. Throughout most of one interview, one informant whispered. With his hand partially covering his mouth, he nervously told us, for instance, that the one black child in AIG was placed in the program only after we called to notify the school that it would be part of our state-commissioned study. His revelation explained why the information on the survey, submitted before our visit, showed no black students in Holt's AIG program.

Interestingly, although these racial patterns at the elementary schools were obvious to adults, the students seemed to pay them little attention. Elementary school–aged students in the studies reported on here rarely mentioned the race of their fellow students or commented on the racial composition of classes. For example, not one of the students we interviewed at either Holt or Georgetown mentioned the race of students in the gifted program, even when asked about those students.[17]

ADOLESCENTS AND THE INCREASING SIGNIFICANCE OF RACE

Although the elementary school students interviewed in the studies reported on here (more than 100 students across six schools) rarely referred to others (e.g., friends, teachers) in terms of their race, middle and high school students frequently did so. Moreover, the older students could reflect back on their earlier years in school and recall when they began to take notice of race and, in some cases, when they first developed a level of racial awareness. It may be that young students unconsciously process images of racial patterns even when race appears to have little or no conscious import for them. In any case, we found that as students matured, race seemed to take on new meaning.

Interviewer: But could you tell the difference there, like how you mentioned you don't see many black students on the honor roll here. Did you notice the same thing in elementary school?

Darren: I didn't really. To be honest with you, that reality really didn't hit me till middle school. When I was younger, I mean, I wasn't really high up on the racial issues. [Study IV (B), Everton High School, Senior, December 20, 2002]

Vanessa: I don't think as a child you ever really notice it [race], and then you start reading books like Frederick Douglass's, and you start reading about all these people more in depth, and that's when like, I mean, in elementary school they don't tell you about all the bad things that happen in this country. You read all this in high school. You get all these books about, and you see movies about how it happened and what happened, and that's when your eyes are opened and you see black people become enraged, and the white kids, the real white kids—the "proud to be white" kids, with Confederate flags and things—they're from like Shady Heights [a small predominantly white rural area of the county] and they went to Shady Heights Elementary. So in high school that's like our first time getting to school with white kids who were supreme, and so that's where the faction comes in, because we never— I see, like, girls, like, that I grew up with, and I never—they always talked to me. They were always friendly with me. Now I see them with Confederate flags and everything, and they're just like out there, like, "White is supreme." But they still talk to me. I don't understand that one, but they still talk to me. But I just see a whole different side than I seen when we were in elementary school. Because they've been introduced to—like, we've been introduced to our black history—they've been introduced to their white history and why they should feel like that. [Study IV (B), Everton High School, Junior, July 2002]

For most of the adolescents we interviewed, race did not become an issue until middle or high school. Consequently, middle and high school students were significantly more likely to talk about race; and black and other students of color were more likely to do so than Whites, particularly when the interviewer was perceived to be black.[18] Older students were also more likely to refer to groups in their narratives (i.e., they made more references to "we," "us," and "they" than did elementary school students). The latter tended to refer more to individuals, and when they did engage in group-centered talk, it was usually gender talk (e.g., "the boys," or "the girls"). Among middle and high school students, group-centered talk expanded to include many more references to race, social class or perceived wealth ("the rich kids," "the ghetto" kids), and achievement ("the smart people," "the hard-working people"), and to other social categories ("Goth kid," "your weird people," "preps," "potheads") that generally do not exist among younger students.[19]

Adolescent students' increased focus on group membership is normal. Identity development—figuring out "who you are"—is one of the most important goals associated with adolescence (Harter 1990; Spencer et al. 2001). Group membership takes on particular salience during this period, because it provides cues, to both insiders and outsiders, about expected roles and behaviors. Not all groups are created equally, however. Membership in some groups is voluntary (e.g., preps, jocks), while in others it is not (e.g., gender, race). And some groups have more clearly defined markers, whether ascribed or achieved, that signal who is in and who is out (the boundaries demarcating groups may vary across time and place, however). Group memberships are also valued differently within and across time and place. For example, "preps" may be at the top of the hierarchical social structure in one school and near the bottom in another.

Data from the studies described in table 2.1 illustrate how pivotal the preadolescent/early adolescent period of middle school is in this regard. In interviews, many high-achieving black high school juniors (Study IV [B]) revealed that pressure to conform to the norms of a particular peer group surfaced for the first time during middle school.

Interviewer: All right, let's go back to freshman and sophomore year. You said then you were trying to fit in and follow your friends and so forth. What were you trying to fit in about? Fit in with whom? And what were you doing?

Tommy: Actually that story goes back to seventh/eighth grade year. Seventh grade year was my first year at Wade Middle School. And I was also trying to fit in. I was trying to fit in with the cool crowd and the cool crowd was the African Americans, the black people who were, like, off in their little own island and . . .

Interviewer: Tell me a little bit about Wade Middle School. This is a mixed school, so it's not a predominantly black school, so how . . .

Tommy: Right, it's actually predominantly white. There's a small group of black students, and I was trying to fit in with them because of the fact that they were cool, and you know, I figured—hey, I'm black—you know, I could fit in.

Interviewer: What made them cool?

Tommy: I have no idea.

Interviewer: Who decided that they were cool?

Tommy: They just—they seemed cool when I was a little twelve-year-old or whatever—however old I was. And, ah, yeah. So, see, I have a high vocabulary, and I'm afraid to use it around other people because, they'll be like, "Wait a minute, slow down. Speak in English." And so, I didn't fit in because of that. And I seemed like the nerd back in, uh, back in middle school, and freshman and sophomore year, too. [Study IV (B), Wade High School, Junior, July 10, 2002]

A junior attending a different high school remembered middle school as traumatic.

> Selina: And when I moved to middle school, I was, you know, I was fine until I moved from [East Wade] in sixth grade to seventh grade in [Massey] Middle. It was such—I don't—I don't understand, because, like in [East Wade], I guess it's maybe because it's our first year in middle school, we're, just, you know, all new. But in seventh grade, I was the new student, but yet I got into like, a fight, every month.
>
> Interviewer: Why?
>
> Selina: I don't know, because—the people—I don't know what it is! And I would talk to the counselors, they were like, "You know what? They, um, they're jealous of you" or "They have something—you have something that they don't have." And I'm like, you know, I'm not trying to cause any trouble here, you know, I don't—So . . .
>
> Interviewer: Who would you—who would fight you every month?
>
> Selina [laughing]: The black girls, to be honest with you, yes. [Study IV (B), Massey High School, Junior July 11, 2002]

There is nothing especially unusual about Selina's or Tommy's experiences in middle school. Trying to fit in and/or being picked on or teased about being different are common experiences during adolescence (Kinney 1993). For all the adolescents in Study III, for example, the pressure to fit in or conform to peer norms involved things like acting "cool," "down to earth," or "regular," or simply being like the other students with whom one identified. For black students, being regular sometimes involved adhering to some notion of an "authentic" black self, or, at least, being more like the "average" black student.

The problem for many black students in North Carolina public schools, however, is that the average black student is usually just that academically—average or sometimes below average. Thus, as described above, the general awareness of patterns of achievement, placement, and tracking by race creates yet another marker adolescents use to construct group boundaries. Whatever its academic benefits, tracking provides adolescent students with visible, ready-made categories for classifying and judging one another, determining insiders and outsiders, winners and losers (see Mickelson and Velasco this volume).

That tracking practices become more pronounced in middle and high school, just as students are entering and moving through adolescence, has significant implications for the development of notions of acting white with respect to academic achievement. In situations where black students are disproportionately underrepresented in upper-level courses and on the honor roll, academic achievement becomes one more factor for adolescents to add to the list of racialized markers—a list that includes style of dress (e.g., FUBU vs. Abercrombie & Fitch), musical tastes (e.g., rap or hip-hop vs. heavy metal) and language (Black English vs. Standard English).[20] The things that become racialized are those that students regularly observe racial groups doing differently. Arguably, these differences are simply perceptions that, like other stereotypes, are passed along from one generation to the next, and have no basis in current reality. However, even stereotypes would lose their currency over time if not for the persistence of patterns in everyday life that seem to validate them. Students continue to notice, for example, that black students tend to dress one way and favor certain brands of clothing while white students dress another way and favor other brands (Neal-Barnett 2001; Perry 2002). The particular styles change over time among groups, and even converge at times, but some differences between the groups remain. Consequently, eighteen years after Fordham and Ogbu (1986) first identified the burden of acting white, it remains a reality with which some black students must contend.

A search through the transcripts of interviews with more than 250 students (participants in the four studies) produced references to acting white *only* among the middle and high school students, and mostly among the latter. Marc, a black seventh grader at Jackson Middle School (see table 2.2), reported that black students were accused of acting white for certain behaviors, although he was careful to exclude academic pursuits.

Interviewer: What about different racial groups in this school? Are there, do most, is it really integrated? Do black and white students hang out all the time together, or are they more separate, how does that work?

Marc: Most of the time [black and white students hang out together]— but a lot of the black people think that they're better than the white people, or vice versa. Or the black people will always pick on the white people about what they do . . . and if you're black and you act like you're white, then they would hold it against you. The black people would not like you as much . . . if you're black and you act like you're— you do stuff that the white people do, then, then, like, skateboarding and stuff like that, then they say that you're white and that you, I don't know how to really say it, they just say that you're really white and that you don't care about everybody else that's black.

Interviewer: What are other things that white people do, that if you do as a black person, the other black kids will make fun of?

Marc: Like, if you surf or if you talk differently, like "dude" or something like that.

Interviewer: Are there other things besides, like skateboarding or surfing, that are labeled as "white"?

Marc: Mm, just about everything that black people don't do. Like if it's not associated with, like—I'm not talking about with the school—but drugs or shooting or something like that, then it's considered black. [Study III, Jackson Middle School, seventh grader, March 16, 2001]

One of the few black students in his school's gifted program, Marc admitted that he was teased by other Blacks for how he talked and for doing other things that Whites do, but he denied that being smart was among them.

In one sense, Marc's narrative is not unique; other students offered similar, though slightly less detailed descriptions of demarcations of racial group boundaries. Nor was Marc the only student to report being teased or accused of acting white. What was unusual to find in these interviews, though, was the charge of acting white with specific reference to academic achievement or achievement behaviors. Where we did find evidence of this, it was *only* among students who were in situations where none or very few other Blacks were in the more rigorous courses and programs. But, and this is an important qualification, not *all* students in such situations were accused of acting white. Even when asked point-blank, some high-achieving students denied being labeled as acting white.

Interviewer: Have you ever been accused of acting white?

Marguerite: Hmm, no.

Interviewer: Never?

Marguerite: Hunh-uh.

Interviewer: Middle school, elementary?

Marguerite: Middle school, actually I would have said "yes" in middle school, but no, no one ever said anything. It was more like, I guess it was more me, because at our middle school, most of the folks were predominantly black. Our middle school was predominantly black, and in our AG class, it was all white, so I guess it was more mentally. [Study IV (B), Vanderbilt High School, Junior, August 2, 2002]

Again, in some cases acting white and achievement are conflated, but in others they are not. In most cases, whether academic achievement and acting white are fused depends on the specific behavior displayed by the high-achieving student and how others perceive it. Marguerite and Marc each regularly hung out with other black students who were not in the upper-level courses, which meant that although each was isolated from other

Blacks in some contexts, they were well integrated in other, important contexts. Moreover, in Marc's case, although he was in the gifted program, his grades were not always good (some Cs and Ds) and he was not in any honors classes (e.g., pre-Algebra). Thus, as a whole, his achievement would not be considered stellar.

Racial isolation, being one of a few or the only black student in a gifted program, was a common experience for the adolescents in this study, especially among the subsample of high-achieving students (Study IV [B]). Many vividly recalled the isolation they had felt in lower grades.

Marguerite: You just kind of feel like, "Why am I one of the few in here?" I guess that it was an identity issue, and I guess that by the time I got in high school, I was used to being in classes with the white people, so it wasn't as much of an issue, and I don't know. . . . Yeah, and I'm taking, I'm, you know, my sixth-grade year, all my classes are with black kids, my English and my math classes. Then in seventh-grade year, I'm put into the class [AG] where it's mostly white people, and one hour, two hours out of the day I sit with white people, and the rest of the four hours with the black people. [Study IV (B), Vanderbilt High School, Junior, August 2, 2002]

Younger black students who witnessed racial isolation at the time of the interview, either as participants in an AIG program or as outside observers, never mentioned the racial composition of the programs. It was the older students, maturing adolescents, who were most likely to reflect on race in this context and to question similar disparities in their past. With access to a more sophisticated lens through which to view their environment, and equipped with new language and cultural understandings, the older students were perhaps reframing how they perceived earlier events. Nonetheless, it is clear that although students may not talk about race early on, the image of segregated classrooms remains etched in their minds.

Adolescents also were aware of being "the only one" in their current advanced classes in high school.

Selina: It would be, like, me and some other person in the class of like, maybe twenty people. So, I mean, not that it's a problem to me, but yet, that's—it's pretty apparent. I went to take an AP History test this past May and, um, I was the only black person in like a whole room of, like, maybe two hundred kids taking the test. [Study IV (B), Massey High School, Junior, July 11, 2002]

Interviewer: Your honors courses—is it the same thing in there—you've got your black students over there and your white students over there? Let's even look at Chemistry, Honors Chemistry. Let's go to that class.

Hakim: OK, I'm going to be honest with you.

Interviewer: Be honest.

Hakim: Um, mostly in honors courses, they're mostly white people. . . .
And, and, you know, there's pretty, you know, it's uneven, really, you
know, mostly white people that takes it, and . . . I think in one course I
was the only black boy. I'm not sure. I think so.

Interviewer: OK. And what, how do you feel about that?

Hakim: That's all! I mean, that's pretty much it. I was the only black boy
and that's just it. I noticed that one day when I was [laughs] at the back.
And I just said, "Hey, I'm the only black boy!" you know. [laughter]
That's all, I mean, you know? [Study III, Clearview High School, Junior,
March 8, 2001]

Although some students, like Hakim and Selina, did not seem too concerned about the racial disparities they observed in their classes, others
found the pattern troubling. A common complaint from high-achieving black
students was that there were few other Blacks in advanced classes. Some
students wanted to see more African Americans have a chance to succeed at
higher levels, especially because they thought their peers were capable of
higher achievement. Other students wanted to change the environment in
advanced classes, in which they sometimes felt isolated and stigmatized.

CONCLUSION

The primary goal of this chapter was to reconsider the burden-of-acting-
white hypothesis in light of specific school contexts and particular life stages.
How and when does academic achievement become a marker of race, a
group boundary signifying what is black and what is white? I have argued
that schools create and sustain structures that conflate race and achievement,
but that this fusion has little salience for students until they reach adolescence. Even then, only students who experience institutionally imposed and
sustained patterns of achievement by race are likely to grapple with the burden of acting white. Moreover, as discussed in this chapter, data drawn from
interviews and classroom observations do not support the notion that an oppositional culture is pervasive among black students. Black students, in general, and young black students in particular, value education and want to do
well academically.

I contend that an inability to realize the goal of high achievement is the
real burden many black students face. Hewitt's (1984) symbolic interactionist perspective suggests that for some low-achieving students, teasing and

ridiculing the high achievers is a way of regaining a sense of dignity and power in the face of their own disappointment and resentment:

> Becoming aware of their imagined negative appearances to others, people may seek to defend themselves in various ways—by rationalizing what they see as their own failures, by attacking others, or perhaps by resolving to excel in the very qualities they feel lacking in themselves but present in others. [p. 119]

Thus, when black students disproportionately experience low achievement in the context of disproportionate white high achievement, some emphasize their black authenticity, seeking dignity in racial solidarity. Like the working-class, low-achieving grade school boys in Sennett and Cobb's (1972) study of the injuries of lower-class status, some low-achieving black students wear racial solidarity as a "badge of dignity."

Researchers have recognized that early academic evaluations are connected in important ways to later outcomes (Kao, Tienda, & Schneider 1996), but some theoretical and/or methodological models assume that student attitudes are static and that these attitudes determine achievement outcomes (Rumberger & Larson 1998). Results from the research I have been involved in, however, suggest that attitudes and achievement have reciprocal effects. Although the data discussed in this chapter are cross-sectional rather than longitudinal, the findings point to important links between early school evaluations and adolescent outcomes. Of most significance is the clear evidence that black students begin school achievement oriented and engaged with the process of learning. For those whose attempts to attain high achievement are successful, school can be a relatively satisfying experience. For those whose attempts are not successful, going to school may seem worthwhile only insofar as it affords an opportunity to socialize with friends and/or to engage in other enjoyable activities, such as sports, theater, art, or music.

Over time, low achievers may come to focus on characteristics that do not depend on the school's valuation. Reorienting their goals (Kao, Tienda, & Schneider 1996) may bolster these students' self-perceptions and help ensure positive evaluations from others (Stinchcombe 1964).[21] Accomplishments that adolescents commonly use to stand in for academic achievement include being cool or tough, being a comedian or class clown, being a good dresser, or being a good athlete. Excelling in one or more of these areas provides an identity that elicits respect, fear, and/or admiration from other students and simultaneously diverts attention from low academic performance. These categories of behavior or personal style also are available to high-achieving students who, as they become older, may wish to downplay their academic performance. This "identity work," which is a normal part of adolescent life both in and out of school, may include behaviors that are labeled as acting white.

The failure to recognize and build on the early achievement orientation of black students relieves school agents of any obligation to address site-specific patterns of racial disparity in academic placement and achievement. As we found in the NCDPI study, teachers and administrators typically explain these gaps by tracing the problem to the students themselves: black students are "averse to success" or "black students don't place a high value on education." Relying on these explanations permits school personnel to ignore their own role in creating and/or maintaining racist structures and to absolve themselves of any institutional responsibility for ongoing racial disparities. If these patterns are the result of choices the students make, and if these decisions in turn are rooted in the students' culture, schools can hardly be expected to change the status quo.

As this chapter has shown, however, black students begin their journeys through school enthusiastically. They do not arrive with notions that academic achievement is for Whites only. Instead, such ideas develop in the process of schooling as maturing students search for tools (language, theories, etc.) to make sense of the stark racial disparities in placement and achievement that characterize some schools. Thus, to truly understand the burden of acting white with respect to academic achievement, we must begin in the schools, for that is where the association between whiteness and achievement originates for many children. As students mature, they increasingly perceive the lack of minority students in rigorous courses and programs as embarrassing and insulting. They then use the cultural tools available to them to understand why such disparities exist and to maintain a positive perception of themselves in the face of this insult. With each succeeding generation, American schools help perpetuate inequality and group animosity.

Students' actions are not based on cultural values, but rather on their ideas about their chances for success and their perceptions regarding what options are available to them under a particular set of circumstances. Recall, for example, the narratives of the high school girls whose abilities had been publicly belittled by their teacher. Students draw on their cultural knowledge to make sense of such circumstances and to guide their response to the situation. Students with an array of resources available to them, such as those supplied by highly educated, well-informed, or well-connected parents, might have pursued a different solution to the problem of a verbally abusive teacher. With multiple options available, the girls might have been less likely to undermine their own desire to succeed by cutting this teacher's class.

I urge researchers and educators interested in understanding how adolescent peer cultures develop and affect achievement outcomes to pay closer attention to students' early school experiences and to how these influence their later attitudes and behaviors; to evaluate students' actions in light of the needs and goals associated with their developmental life stage; and to systematically investigate school and classroom context, including the structural barriers built into the academic programs of most middle and high schools. Setting our research sights at a more local level will help provide answers to the puzzle of why evidence supporting the acting-white hypothesis or supporting the theory of a black peer culture that demeans academic striving more broadly is present in some settings and not others. Even more important than this, though, researchers must pay more attention to how persistent experiences of relative low achievement affect students' achievement orientation over time. Research of this type among Blacks and other minority groups is essential, since it is these students who continue to be systematically denied opportunities to participate in more rigorous academic courses and programs.

NOTES

1. See, for example, studies by Hubbard and Mehan (1999), Lucas (1999), and Oakes (1985).

2. My primary concern in this chapter is with acting white with respect to academic achievement. It is important to remember, however, that African Americans and other students of color may be accused of acting white for any number of reasons, including musical tastes, hairstyle and clothing preferences, speech, friendship networks, and leisure activities. In fact, acting white is most frequently used in these contexts, and not with regard to school performance. See McArdle and Young (1970) for examples of early uses of the term.

3. The belief among American Blacks that education functions as a means to social, economic, and political advancement dates as far back as slavery and the antebellum period (Franklin 1981).

4. The characteristics of "authentic" black culture and identity are highly contested (Favors 1999).

5. This work was supported by a dissertation fellowship from the Spencer Foundation.

6. My co-investigators on this project were William Darity, an economist, and Domini Castellino, a psychologist.

7. This study was supported by a grant from the Spencer Foundation to co-investigators Darity, Castellino, and Tyson.

8. Ms. Grady provided remedial instruction at Madison.

9. Working "too hard" in school, though, generally is *not* valued. Several studies have found that the average high school student, regardless of race, displays a particular disdain for students who work too hard in school (Cookson & Persell 1985; Kinney 1993; Steinberg 1996).

10. These findings may result partly from the institutional context of the schools the students attended and the composition of the student samples. First, the samples included younger students, who tend to be less conscious of race and racial difference (see Spencer 1984), and second, they included many high-achieving students,

who are most likely to reject the notion that doing well in school is acting white (see Mickelson and Velasco this volume).

11. For the purposes of the study, a school counselor identified students as high or low achieving, based on their grades.

12. At East Side, for instance, the honors biology and English courses we observed during 2002–2003 were majority black.

13. Students cannot self-select into gifted programs in the same way they can, theoretically, self-select into AP and honors courses in high school. Participation in AIG programs is based on a variety of factors, typically some combination of any of the following: test scores, teacher recommendations, IQ scores, grades, and work portfolios.

14. These schools, three elementary, two middle, and six high schools, were selected based on the degree of minority underrepresentation in gifted programs and AP and honors courses. We selected schools that had very high minority underrepresentation, and where possible, schools that had minority overrepresentation or little underrepresentation in these programs and courses. The goal of the case studies was to learn more about the factors that contributed to these particular outcomes.

15. This figure includes surveys returned for all public schools serving elementary grades (K–5).

16. Across the state of North Carolina, schools use either AG or AIG to refer to the gifted program, although the state Department of Public Instruction officially uses AIG. Throughout the paper I use AIG, but during interviews I generally used the term used by the informant and the particular school.

17. That is not to say, however, that the students were not aware of race, for in other cases, they did broach the subject. For example, one conversation with a group of students at Madison Elementary centered on how a "vanilla-colored" teacher left the school because "she didn't like black kids."

18. The racial ambiguity of two interviewers on the NCDPI project appeared to affect the degree to which white respondents felt comfortable discussing race.

19. Although we specifically asked the high school students whether there were any cliques or crews at their school, in most cases they began naming groups before we introduced this question. Usually, groups were mentioned in response to the question, "How well do students at your school get along with one another?"

20. See Carter (2005), McArdle and Young (1970), Neal-Barnett (2001), and Perry (2002) for a more complete list of things that students racialize.

21. This is just one of many ways in which students resist and/or dismiss the evaluations of schools in order to save face. Students are not simply passive recipients of institutional labels; they participate in the development of the student self. For example, sometimes student resistance takes the form of a resolve to prove wrong a teacher's negative evaluation (see Mickelson and Velasco this volume).

II

THE HETEROGENEITY OF BLACK IDENTITY, EXPERIENCE, AND RESPONSE

3

Shifting Images of Blackness: Coming of Age as Black Students in Urban and Suburban High Schools

Annette Hemmings

Contemporary qualitative research on black high school students' academic identity and achievement has been conducted against the backdrop of John Ogbu's cultural ecological theory (CET) of school performance (Ogbu 1978, 1987, 2003; Ogbu & Simons 1998). The theory explains persistent patterns of underachievement among black students as effects of collective identities and oppositional cultural frames of reference formed in response to historical relations with white society. The essential explanation, in Ogbu's own words, is that how "minorities interpret their history—whether they became minorities voluntarily or involuntarily, together with the impact of societal treatment or mistreatment—shapes the pattern of the collective solutions they forge for their collective problems in society at large and in education" (2003, p. 51).

While compelling, Ogbu's theory has been challenged as overly deterministic or as not going far enough in recognizing how much academic engagement is affected by individual proclivities and everyday social situations in schools (Davidson 1996; Erickson 1987). The nature of black students' schooling experiences is certainly influenced by larger social, economic, and political structures and by local community forces, but it also is very much shaped by the micro-level cultural realities of everyday life in particular school contexts. Black students are active agents who navigate these realities in strategically distinctive often inconsistent ways. Their sense of agency, as Carla O'Connor (1997) has pointed out, may be bolstered by knowledge of collective struggle against historical injustices. But it also is influenced by daily activities in classrooms and corridors as well as social interactions with teachers, peers, and others.

The significance of individual agency was evident in my own research in the 1980s on the academic identity work of high-achieving black students (Hemmings 1996, 1998). I found that the achievers' identity adaptations did not involve clear-cut choices between seemingly opposing images of being black and being a model (white) student. The manner in which students ultimately resolved whatever identity conflicts they experienced depended on two factors: how they formed and then performed their self images in *direct* relation to the formal educational criteria embodied in the model student image; and the influence of informal cultural prescriptions for what it meant to be black, especially those produced within peer groups. Black achievers' identities were constructed and, in some cases, positively transformed through individually fashioned responses to the cultural pressures confronting them within schools.

A decade later, I conducted another ethnographic study on how a diverse sample of students, including black youths, were coming of age in urban and suburban public high schools (Hemmings 2004). I did not intend to examine achievement gaps per se or to assess the validity of the "acting-white" thesis. Instead, I designed the study to explore secondary schooling as a much more comprehensive, culturally complex process of coming of age in economic, kinship, religious, and political domains of American life. The framework I developed moves well beyond the acting-white thesis by acknowledging the broader purposes of schooling, the complexity of cultural forces, and the fact that black adolescents come of age in individually creative and protracted ways.

Public high schools are recognized in this framework as institutions serving a much larger purpose than the mere facilitation of academic learning. They are established to help adolescents form viable identities and integrate themselves into community domains. As they come of age in high schools, students navigate cultural crosscurrents comprised of a myriad of conflicting discourses, including those of blackness. In their navigations, black students utilize several often inconsistent adaptations constructed in light of their historical social locations, individual dispositions, and the nature and intensity of context-specific cultural pressures, including pressures to abide by particular discourses of blackness. This framework also recognizes how coming of age is a long and variable process of individual development. Black adolescents, like all teenagers, come of age during a long stretch of years where they may stay with, change, or move back and forth in their navigational trajectories. Rather than make a simple choice between being black or acting white, many black high school students shift within and between discourses of blackness as well as other discourses flowing through cultural crosscurrents.

In this chapter, I describe my study and the coming-of-age framework in more detail. This discussion is followed by the coming-of-age stories of two black students, David North and Cassandra Sommers.[1] David was an honors student at Jefferson High, a desegregated urban public school, and Cassandra was a steadily improving low achiever who went to Ridgewood High, a public school located in a predominantly white, upper-middle-class suburb. Both had begun high school as model students who appeared to be making relatively smooth transitions to adulthood. Each then experienced catastrophic events that precipitated a developmental tailspin. By the time David and Cassandra were seniors, they had managed to (re)form or redeem themselves. As the narratives below make clear, they came of age with great hope and prospects for the future and did so by shifting through discourses of blackness.

THE STUDY

I designed the study to explore coming of age among a diverse sample of graduating high school seniors. The research framework I developed is distinctive in that it combines classic anthropological precedents with contemporary (post)anthropological perspectives. Van Gennep (1960) and Turner (1969) proposed coming of age as a normative process in which adolescents make transitions to adulthood through linear phases of psychocultural development, or rites of passage. During the first phase, adolescents undergo ritual separation, symbolically breaking with the community. These breaches are followed by a second, more turbulent phase characterized by rites that emphasize boundaries or liminality and are marked by a mounting crisis between youths and adults. Eventually, adolescents stabilize their identities and, assisted by rites of reaggregation, reenter the community as culturally integrated adults. In the 1980s, these conceptions of linear, clearly demarcated rites of passage were challenged. Spurred by postmodern/structural movements in the social sciences, a "crisis of representation" developed in anthropology (Marcus & Fischer 1986). The field's classic theories and ethnographic methods were found wanting. In particular, the certainty, clarity, and wholeness with which anthropologists had described cultures gave way to "post" perspectives that emphasized the ambiguity, relativity, fragmentation, particularity, and discontinuity of people's lived experiences.

With both classic and (post)anthropological insights in mind, I framed coming of age as a developmental yet highly fluid process of identity formation and community integration in economic, familial, religious, and political domains of American life. In examining identity, I paid particular attention to how seniors constructed a multifaceted, enduring self (Spindler & Spindler 1992, 1993). Individuals' innermost psychological orientations and culturally patterned ways of "relating to others; to the material, natural, and spiritual worlds; and to time and space, including notions of agency, mind, person, being and spirit" (Hoffman 1998, p. 326) comprise this self. It is an evolving identity, and one that includes economic, familial/sexual, religious, and political facets. Thus, I deliberately recruited students from diverse racial, ethnic, social class, and gender locations with the assumption that they were engaged in intense identity work around these facets.

Identity construction and social integration occur at the individual level, but they are shaped by larger cultural forces. In pluralistic societies like the United States, culture may be viewed metaphorically as a seascape with multilayered crosscurrents comprised of numerous discourses that envelop people and carry them off in disparate directions. Discourses are socially constructed meaning systems (language, values, beliefs, norms, and mores) that affect ways of talking and writing about, as well as acting with and toward, people and things. They are generated during the course of everyday social relations. And they exert a powerful influence on what individuals come to regard as normal or proper for them and other people to think, feel, and do in schools, homes, and other contexts. Discourses have the capacity to construct people's realities rather than simply reflect them.

Adolescents respond and adapt to multiple discourses as they strive to situate (integrate) their selves within their communities. Their integration efforts occur in institutional contexts such as schools where individuals struggle to become a specific "kind of person" (identity) while submerged in discourses that have the power to determine who they are and/or who they ought to become (Gee 2000–2001, p. 99). Ultimately, how teenagers accomplish their integration work depends on whether they end up swimming with cultural crosscurrents or against them.

I selected three public high schools (two urban and one suburban) as research sites. High schools are ideal settings for observing coming of age processes because they are places where teenagers congregate, cultural discourses converge, and adults intentionally prepare young people for adulthood. They are especially good places for observing and talking to black adolescents. As they construct their identities and integrate their emerging selves with the larger community, these students have the added task of navigating conflicting discourses of blackness—ones that may be empowering or potentially destructive.

I conducted fieldwork at Jefferson High School, a desegregated urban public school, during the 1995–1996 school year, and at Ridgewood High School, a predominantly white, suburban public school, in fall 1996. Jefferson High is located in an old, well-established neighborhood. The winding streets leading to the school are lined with small houses and apartment buildings owned or rented mostly by white working- and middle-class families. Family incomes vary widely, as adults are employed in local manufacturing firms, professional occupations, and the service sector. Black families also reside in the neighborhood, but they are a demographic minority in what for generations has been a white section of the city. A large proportion of the low-income students who went to Jefferson High in the mid-1990s were black youths bused in from distant inner-city neighborhoods as part of a desegregation plan. They did not live in the neighborhood surrounding the school, a fact that was not lost on resident white students, one of whom said that he wished "*those* black kids would go to their own school instead of ours."

Ridgewood High is located in a white, upper-middle-class suburb. U.S. census data in 1990 listed the median household income in the suburb as $46,339 and the median housing unit value as $101,900. By 1996, the year I conducted my fieldwork, a booming economy had boosted these figures to all-time highs, spawning housing developments with homes retailing at a quarter of a million dollars or more. Signs of affluence were everywhere in the places where people lived, shopped, worshipped, and entertained themselves. They also were evident in local public schools, like Ridgewood High, where interiors were beautifully designed and classrooms were state of the art.

I recruited three to four graduating seniors from each school site with the help of teachers and principals. Student volunteers represented a cross section of the school population in terms of racial, ethnic, and gender demographics and academic achievement.[2] David North, a middle-class black boy, was among the three seniors at Jefferson High who agreed to participate in the study. An only child, he lived with his mother and father in the surrounding neighborhood. He was a resident who identified to some extent with nonresident, low-income black students. Cassandra Sommers was one of four seniors who served as key participants at Ridgewood High. She lived with her widowed mother and infant son in a house at the edge of the suburb. Her mother moved there even though it was predominately white and somewhat beyond her means because, as Cassandra explained, "she wants me and my baby to have the best of everything."

I spent two months at each school, observing the cultural "shifts and changes [and] contradictions and tensions" in classrooms and corridors as I accompanied each student participant through the school day for at least two weeks (Yon 2000, p. 23). I asked the seniors questions about themselves, their past experiences, present circumstances, and future plans to elicit autobiographical stories about their identity (Munoz 1995). I also conducted semistructured, tape-recorded interviews with them, their friends, and some of their classmates. The interview guide I developed collected data on integration work through open-ended questions that elicited students' thoughts on cultural discourses in American communities and how the students were adapting to them. David North's and Cassandra Sommers's coming-of-age stories, narrated below, are based on their responses to these questions, their stories of identity formation, my fieldwork observations, and analytical insights I drew from the literature. In these stories, I begin with a detailed description of the schools. The intent of these descriptions is not to compare or analyze school contexts in relation to findings but, rather, to provide a backdrop for David's and Cassandra's remarkable navigations through discourses of blackness.

DAVID NORTH: (RE)FORMATION AT JEFFERSON HIGH

A World of Neglect

When I drove into Jefferson High's parking lot on a bitterly cold day in December 1995 to begin my fieldwork, I saw several of the yellow school buses used to transport the mostly low-income black students who lived miles away in inner-city neighborhoods. That year, the demographic composition of the student population was 54 percent black, 44 percent white, and 2 percent Hispanic, American Indian, and multi-racial. Statistics on the school's free and reduced-rate federal lunch programs for 1995–1996 indicate that 49 percent of the students lived at or below poverty level.

The exterior of Jefferson High's main building, with its neoclassical façade of pillars and roof-top spires, looked regal. Inside, the school was dismal and literally crumbling from neglect. Dimly lit, cement-gray passageways led to classrooms cluttered with piles of discarded books, broken supplies, and ancient desks covered with graffiti, profanity, and gang signs. Chairs wobbled. Clocks did not work. Windows were cloudy with grime. Among the few bright spots in the building were a state-of-the-art computer room and well-equipped labs for a technical education program that offered training for local jobs in aircraft and automotive technology, building trades, culinary arts, and "inter-city bus driving."

Neither the general public nor local school authorities seemed to show much interest in the school's plight. For several election cycles, voters had refused to approve increases in tax levies for public schools. Without the funds necessary to keep up with rising costs, school district officials felt compelled to cut building maintenance budgets, lay off teachers, eliminate programs, and limit the purchase of textbooks (already in short supply). Students were aware of the public's disinterest. Moreover, they complained that administrators and teachers did not appear to be addressing the academic and social problems that contribute to the school's high drop-out rates (officially, 17.8 percent), low standardized test scores, and mounting numbers of suspensions for fighting and other serious violations of school policy.

David North guided me through the neglected world of Jefferson High for nearly two weeks. When I met him for the first time, I thought he looked scholarly, with his wire-rimmed glasses, short-cropped hair, pullover sweater, and neatly pressed khaki slacks. I noticed that in one ear he had a small diamond earring. This adornment, he explained, was meant, "to ice any impression that I'm a total geek." After a brief stop at his locker, David led me through hallways jam-packed with hundreds of boisterous teenagers. We walked by honors students, jocks, and other kids who, I was told, were "into school." We also passed a number of disaffected students, including some of the black youths who were being bused in from the city's most impoverished neighborhoods. Some but certainly not all of the black males in this group projected what kids described as "cool" images marked by smooth, streetwise savvy and in-control toughness. Most of the other students were regarded as "normals," kids who kept pretty much to themselves and seemed nondescript in comparison to their more image-conscious peers.

We hooked up with Cory, David's best friend. Both boys were honors students who took mostly Advanced Placement (AP) and computer classes. As they walked side by side, heading toward their first-period class, they talked and laughed about things they had done, heard, or seen. At one point, David turned to me and said that due to their "overdose of the male hormone," he and Cory especially liked to compare notes on pretty girls. We all laughed at the remark. As we continued walking, David and Cory exchanged cheerful greetings and jokes with other students. As became apparent over the two weeks of fieldwork, the two boys enjoyed a high level of popularity—a remarkable achievement in a school where student relations were not always amicable.

Relations could be quite contentious, in fact, especially among students who had become submerged in a youth culture characterized by divisive discourses regarding money, respect, and difference (Hemmings 2000a, 2002). Fortunately, there also were subcultural currents that carried more positive possibilities for teenagers. Some students, including Lona Young, another senior and participant in the study, forged symbolic and social links within their cliques that enabled them to overcome adolescent opposition; repair severe breaks with family, peers, and school staff; and express a "true self" in ethical relation to others (Hemmings 2000b). Others, like David, took a different route. David's story is more about personal self (re)formation after extremely rough passages through polarized discourses of black manhood.

David's Story

"If you would graph my years in school," David told me, "you would see that I peaked in ninth grade and plunged in tenth grade and then things got better again." He elaborated:

Tenth grade was my weird year. My dad had cancer and I had a hard time with the transition to high school. I got every form of punishment they have. I was suspended twice. I was in ISS [In School Suspension] once. I skipped school and got into those fights I was telling you about. Then I got beaten up pretty bad by some guys. Everybody knew about it. It took me a couple of months to get over the pain and humiliation. But instead of going after those guys, I turned my life around. I decided that wasn't the way to go. I worked through my problems and did it by myself. Counselors didn't help me. My mother was angry and yelled at me but she couldn't tell me what to do. By the end of the year, I got a job, a car, and the weather got nicer. I turned my life around. Most important of all, I got my self-respect back.

Conflicting discourses of blackness emerged as David recounted the trajectory of his adolescence. He was an only child growing up in a middle-class family, with parents who subscribed to the black achievement ideology. This ideology is rooted in a discourse of blackness that incorporates the strong image of the respectable black man. As Gordon (1997) explains, the cultural tenets of black male respectability are derived from patriarchal African traditions and more contemporary, mainstream cultural currents of middle-class propriety. A respectable black man is someone who takes advantage of educational opportunities. He adopts the elaborated speech codes of Standard English and other conservative styles of self-presentation. He is hardworking, frugal, and economically independent. He is a good husband and attentive father. And he acts on the values of "community commitment and [political] activism, mutual help and uplift, personal responsibility [and] religious faith" (Gordon 1997, p. 41). Such a man appreciates the history of collective black struggle and regards himself as someone with a moral obligation to promote the individual and social progress of black people.

David had been quite respectable during his freshman year. Then, and again later as a senior, he regarded the mainstream work ethic as the most effective means to achieve economic success.

I think anyone in this country is in a good position to make it as long as they work hard. Like you can be from the lowest of the low and really bad off and still work hard and get lots and lots of stuff.

He also articulated a commitment to "the black community at large." While acknowledging that members of the community had made great strides in the wake of the Civil Rights movement, David recognized that much more needed to be accomplished before true equality could be attained, especially in economic and political arenas.

With regard to the economic domain, David noted that despite progressive change in the equalization of job opportunities, black people were still being shunted into "po black folk jobs."

We were janitors, garbage collectors, cleaning ladies, and stuff like that. Things have gotten better for black people but there's still this lingering thing that all black people are good for is po black folk jobs. You know, I know you know. It's waiting on people, white people.

In the political domain, David felt the issue of racial injustice, so pronounced in the 1960s, was being silenced in the 1990s:

I don't want to play the race card but race has become like a silent political issue instead of out in the open. There are people on the Supreme Court and in the Senate and the Congress who seem to be against some of the gains of Civil Rights like affirmative action. It seems like they want to go back, like what they feel is that white males, certain special interests, haven't gotten their fair shake. That's not the case, but that's what they feel. So, like, race in the 1990s—you don't talk about it. If you don't talk about it, if nobody mentions it, it's not there. It goes away, they hope.

David's outlook was a mix of cynicism and optimism. While he was well aware of the historical barriers that confronted black people, he was quite hopeful about his own economic and political prospects. His hopefulness was especially acute when he entered high school. David as a freshman earned good grades, stayed out of trouble, and otherwise projected the images of the respectable black man and model black student. Then catastrophe struck, radically altering his trajectory. David's father was diagnosed with cancer and his chances for survival were uncertain. "It was weird," David mused. "When my dad got sick, I thought I had to be *the man*, you know, the guy in charge."

I was mad at everything. I was real angry, you know, 'cause what happened to my dad wasn't fair. Nothing was fair. It went to my head to the point where I thought I had to be the man and nobody, I mean, *nobody* better mess with me.

His anger pulled him away from images of black male respectability and directed him toward what Gordon (1997) describes as the opposing "twin" image of black male reputation. Young black men with reputations adhere to a discourse of blackness that prompts them to assert their manhood by standing up to authorities (especially white authorities), showing up male rivals, and controlling women through multiple sexual conquests and harassment. Reputation also is acquired by adopting the restricted speech codes characterizing street talk. These codes for some young black men residing in impoverished urban neighborhoods not only serve as linguistic markers of dominance, but also as indicators of black American identity (Ogbu 1999).

Black teenage boys who want to build up a reputation also may follow what Anderson (1998) refers to as the code of the streets. This code arises in places where the influence of police, teachers, and other adult authority figures end and where personal responsibility for one's safety and socioeconomic advancement begins. Among the main features of the code are verbal expressions of disrespect toward competitors or people who come off as easy prey. If a man loses respect, he has no choice but to try to regain it, even if he has to literally fight to get it back.

Unfortunately, these young men may assert their reputations through hostile actions shaped by corrosive popular cultural portrayals of black males as sexually predatory, criminal, and pathologically violent (Epstein 1998). They experience enormous peer pressure to earn and keep respect in order to acquire power and dominance over one another. Under such circumstances, a young black man who wants to be *the man* must garner respect even if it means engaging in brutal acts of violence.

David bolstered his reputation by identifying with his cool black peers. In doing so, he compromised his status as a model student and directed his anger at other disaffected black youths. He got into fistfights, broke school rules, and "blew off" his schoolwork. But the consequences of such acts did not become clear to him until one fateful day when a group of boys viciously attacked him under a school stairwell. The attack not only left David physically wounded, it also seriously damaged his self-respect. "Blood was flowing," he recalled, "and I had to go to a doctor. But what hurt most of all was my pride. God that hurt."

Then David underwent another shift. He decided to (re)form his image, fully aware that he would have to confront the powerful cultural pressures that were shaping the thoughts, actions, and interactions of black boys in his school. Some of these pressures, like the reputation-enhancing ones that incited black-on-black aggression, were destructive. Others, such as those that encouraged young black men to be respectable individuals and community leaders, were more constructive. David understood that he would have to negotiate these pressures during the course of his everyday relations with parents, teachers, and peers. He could not simply walk away from them.

> I'm sittin' there thinking about going back to school and wondering what to do. I was humiliated, you know, afraid to show myself. But I had to go back even if everyone was looking down on me, you know, giving me problems. I wasn't gonna fight any more, so I had to find some other way to get through.

And get through it he did, reworking the seemingly opposing poles of reputation and respectability into a more empowering synthesis of masculine blackness. He no longer cast himself nor was he typecast by others as a dangerous black thug. Instead he adopted a friendlier, less threatening persona. He was worried that his peers would regard him as weak if he came back in the guise of a nicer, more respectable guy. That was not what happened.

> Turns out I didn't have to worry. Kids kind of, I don't know, I guess they were glad or something that I wasn't this bad dude anymore.

One reason for the acceptance was that David managed to retain his reputation even though he was no longer inclined to fight for respect with other boys. Another reason was his adeptness at code switching. This skill enabled him to express his connectedness to the black community while simultaneously reembracing the black achievement ideology. Ogbu (1999) maintains that for historical, social, and cultural reasons black students are not willing to give up the use of black dialects. Speaking Standard English is construed as allegiance to or intrusion by Whites. The dissonant beliefs that Blacks hold about language usage, Ogbu argues, have detrimental effects on their academic performance. David, however, did not appear to experience dissonance as he alternated between language codes (and behavioral norms) in his maneuverings through corridors and classrooms. As I accompanied him through the school day, he would switch with apparent ease between Standard English, local black dialect, and teenage black hip-hop slang, positioning himself appropriately for each social situation. And he did so with a cultural astuteness that not only won over his black and white peers, but also helped elevate him to an academic ranking in the top 10 percent of his class.

David's identity and integration work had repercussions for the world beyond his high school. The self he was constructing definitely positioned him as a respectable young black man with a reputation as someone who refused to be neglected or ascribed low status in the economic and political domains of American life. He cultivated an intense interest in computers, with the ambition of becoming a "computer engineer specializing in hardware and software specific operating systems." Well aware of the economic realities facing black men, David shifted his anger in a way that spurred rather than stymied his chances for success.

> The reality is that big companies and corporations are mostly white owned, like, white-operated businesses. As long as black people are minorities, we have to put up with that. It's not fair but it's reality. Sometimes I get angry, but anger for me is like a motivation to do my best even though everywhere I look I see white people.

He also altered his political orientation, situating himself to improve the status of black men by working within rather than against the dominant sociopolitical system. The system had produced policies like affirmative action that, according to David, were a "necessary step in the right direction." But black men were still being marginalized.

Politicians in the early seventies felt they could knock out two birds with one stone if they used affirmative action [to hire] black females. When you have a black female it's like you have two minorities. That leaves young black men like me out in the cold. Black men have to constantly improve themselves. That's what we're told. No one else has to improve us. You never hear they have to improve schools or bring jobs to where black men are. You never hear that.

David felt it was up to black men to define or salvage such policies and push for initiatives aimed at upgrading public schools, providing good jobs, and otherwise addressing the obstacles that kept them down. He also believed that black men must take more of an interest in politics and assume activist roles as politicians. David played his part by running for senior class president. He was elected by an overwhelming majority. "That's amazing when you think about it," he reflected. "See, kids—now kids see me as someone who can make a difference instead of the guy you better watch out for."

And make a difference he did. By the time David graduated from high school, he had made a full recovery, and for that matter, so had his father. He was an honors student who had been admitted to a major university. As far as I could tell, he was well on his way to being "the man" he had turned his life around to become. David had managed to (re)form his self by shifting toward the most positively empowering discourses of masculine blackness.

CASSANDRA SOMMERS: REDEMPTION AT RIDGEWOOD HIGH

Staying the Course

Ridgewood High was built in the 1970s on the side of a forested hill. When I began my fieldwork in fall 1996, signs of upper-middle-class suburban affluence were evident throughout the school. Hallways were covered with brand-new carpet, walls were freshly painted, and classrooms were spotlessly clean and equipped with up-to-date computers, audio-visual equipment, books, and other instructional materials. These physical attributes reinforced Ridgewood High's widespread reputation as a premier public school. So, too, did data on graduation rates and college admissions. In the school year prior to my fieldwork, 98 percent of students enrolled as seniors in October graduated in May. Eighty-one percent of graduates entered four-year colleges and universities; 3 percent (twelve of 402) were National Merit finalists; and 23 percent were awarded scholarships, including those awarded to National Merit Scholars.

One area in which Ridgewood High did not excel was diversity. The vast majority of students, about 89 percent, were white. Approximately 5 percent were Asian and Asian American, 4.5 percent were black, and 1 percent was Hispanic. Almost all students resided in the surrounding suburban community, where families were financially affluent, adults were well educated, and the cultural ethos was politically conservative and staunchly Judeo-Christian. Faculty and administrators at Ridgewood High understood that the community expected them to prepare its children to occupy similar economic, kinship, religious, and political niches. Students, in fact, referred to themselves as "preppies." They expected to go to college and assume important positions in the upper echelons of mainstream American life. School staff responded to these pressures and expectations by offering a full slate of regular and advanced college preparatory classes that were buttressed by counseling programs. The latter programs were aimed at identifying and supporting students who showed signs of not being able to stay the preppie course.

Cassandra Sommers, a black senior, was among the Ridgewood High students who volunteered to participate in my study. When we first met, Cassandra had on a baggy cardigan sweater, her hair was pulled back into a tightly bound bun, and she wore large, round eyeglasses. She looked far older and more mature than her eighteen years. As her story unfolded, I learned how Cassandra had worked to achieve her maturity, redeeming her lost sense of self-worth and importance by shaping her identity around a positive image of female blackness.

Cassandra's Story

As I accompanied Cassandra through the hallways of Ridgewood High, she moved with self-assured grace and confidence. Several black students, Asian Americans, and white boys and girls came up to her as we walked along. She spoke with each person, asking questions such as, "How are you doing?" "Is your Mom feeling better?" and other queries that probed personal problems and concerns. These encounters happened every day, making it clear that Cassandra not only was well known and liked, but also was someone students admired and turned to for advice and comfort. She projected an image of blackness other students, including Whites, looked up to.

Leading me through Ridgewood High, Cassandra described the school's relaxed social atmosphere.

Our administration doesn't have to worry about kids bringing guns to
school, fights happening everyday, and stuff like that, because basically
we get along. We're all basically preppies.

But as we continued on our way—and Cassandra continued to tell her
story—I discovered that for her, the school's atmosphere had not always
been so congenial. It had, in fact, been quite treacherous as she struggled to
come of age in a social context defined by a preppie, white-middle-class
achievement ideology. The component discourses of this ideology are similar to those promoted in the black achievement ideology. But the former are
much more forcibly driven by a pervasive fear of losing ground or "terror of
downward mobility" among middle-class Whites, whose once-solid position
near the top of the social heap grew more precarious over the closing
decades of the twentieth century (Ortner 1991, p. 176). One of the more insidious features of this ideology is that it represents historically marginalized
people, especially black people, as emblematic of that which is most feared.
Black girls in particular are positioned as "alien beings" if they give birth to
out-of-wedlock babies and engage in other morally reprehensible acts without any apparent consideration for the future (Lesko 1990, p. 116). They are
imaged as low-life women who have no rightful place in respectable white-
middle-class society.

Just as Cassandra was about to begin her freshman year, she plunged into
the darkest depths of this ideologically driven stereotype. As a result, she
spent most of her remaining years in high school trying to redeem her self-
image and her place in middle-class domains. Cassandra's downward spiral
was triggered by the loss of her father, who died shortly after being diagnosed with terminal cancer. In a slightly tremulous voice, Cassandra explained how her head got "messed up."

I kept thinkin' about what he told me before he passed. He said funny
things like "I was so happy when I walked you down the aisle at your
wedding" and "I'm so proud you graduated from college." None of that
had happened, and I was thinkin', like, thinkin' it never would.

Her problems only worsened when she met an older black boy who got
her pregnant and then left her. Not long after, he was arrested, tried for com-
mitting a crime, and sentenced to jail. At age fifteen, Cassandra was father-
less, pregnant, and, in her words, "at a low, low point."

I was like, "Why is this happening to me?" And thinkin' "What's gonna
happen to me?" I was at a low, low point and I did not know how it was
gonna turn out.

A few months later, she gave birth to a son. At that point, Cassandra experienced a profound shift in her thinking, propelled by a powerful maternal urge to take control and raise her baby. Her mother stood by her, ready to help. Cassandra felt that as a family they would rise up together, empowered by a discourse of black mother/womanhood that not only connects women in tight-knit kinship networks, but also maintains connections between living family members and deceased ancestors. The power of these connections resonated in Cassandra's words:

> My mother was the only one who I would let help raise my son. She took care of me, and I knew she could help me take care of my son. He looks like my father. It's like my dad came back with him.

As Fordham (1996a) observes, many black mothers rear their daughters to be both survivors and "ladies," embodying traits traditionally associated with middle-class female whiteness. These messages often get tangled up with opposing ones that foster resistance to such images of womanhood. Cassandra's mother successfully projected an image of female blackness that complemented, indeed improved on, white discourses without completely accommodating to them. The image she provided was of a black woman who is dignified, self-confident, occasionally outspoken, and regularly capable of holding her own in the home, at school, and in other situations. A black woman, that is, who exudes power but not in a manner that is overpowering. "My mother," Cassandra explained, "taught me how to stand up for myself without cutting other people down or letting people cut *me* down."

Cassandra also drew enormous strength and direction from her black Pentecostal church. She had not been particularly religious as a child. But after the death of her father and birth of her son, she felt God call her to faith.

> I didn't hear any voices or anything but I felt deep in my heart, in my soul, I felt Him. I felt God there and knew then and there that I believe in God. I believe in our Lord Jesus Christ. I believe in everything the Bible says. I am a Christian and I base my whole life around that 'cause all I do is pray. When you pray, God blesses you. But you gotta do right, too. You can't do bad things and keep askin' God for forgiveness. You can't do that.

She adhered steadfastly to her church's distinctively black theology and its emphasis on uplifting the downtrodden. The theology raised Cassandra to higher planes of spirituality. It also picked up women who had been beaten down financially.

[The church] makes me feel spiritual, like it carries me right up to where I feel I could almost touch the hand of God and our Lord Jesus Christ. Sometimes when the service is over it takes me a long time to come down [laughter], like, come back down to earth.

Say you're a mother on welfare. They [have programs that] will pick that woman right up off the floor and teach her how to get a job. I mean sometimes they literally pick 'em off the floor 'cause they been beaten down so far.

In addition to offering redemption, the theology provided Cassandra with empowering discursive and practical routes to the realization of her identity and ultimate integration into the community as a good, God-fearing, upwardly mobile black woman/mother.

In contrast, the atmosphere at Ridgewood High, especially among white students, furnished little support to black girls like Cassandra. When she returned to school after her baby was born, she felt alienated. "I felt like I was so bad, like as bad as anyone could get. I was this bad black girl and everyone was probably thinkin, 'Well, what else would you expect?'" Her position as an alien being was worsened by white preppie perceptions of black students as chronic underachievers. Cassandra's grades fell after the death of her father and the events that followed. But rather than be inscribed as someone who had been temporarily knocked down by terrible circumstances, she was stereotyped as another one of *those* black students who routinely slip into what Ogbu (2003) describes as "low-effort syndrome." Cassandra was viewed as a black girl who was not "good enough" to be in such a good (white) school.

I could tell, I could tell by the way kids looked at me, treated me that they thought I wasn't, like, wasn't one of them. Wasn't good, you know, good enough.

The prevailing discursive winds that worked against Cassandra also worked for her. Some of Ridgewood's white students also veered off course because of pregnancy, substance abuse, family deaths and breakups, mental illness, and what one senior described as "dysfunctional relationships." With the strong backing of parents, school counselors rescued these students through an effective peer mediation program and weekly group counseling sessions that were included in students' regular class schedules. Students who participated in these interventions were subjected to (redemptive) therapies aimed at getting them back on course, moving toward middle-class destinations.

For Cassandra, the years spent in peer mediation strengthened her relations with white and other peers. She also was a longtime participant in "grieving group" sessions established for students who had experienced the deaths of family members or close friends. I was invited to the group's weekly sessions and was struck by how Cassandra managed to redeem herself through manipulations of therapeutic discourses. She radically shifted her image as a low-life black girl by transforming middle-class-white images of black women. A striking example occurred when a white girl talked about a story she had read. She recounted how, following the death of a certain individual, a baby had been born who resembled the deceased person. Cassandra seized the moment.

> When my dad died it was a shock, such a terrible loss. I got very, very depressed. But then I found out I was pregnant, and I felt like someone new was coming into my life. I missed my dad, but I knew I would love that new life. I knew I would love that baby. The baby, my son, looks like my dad. He looks like my dad.

I observed other students in the room smiling, nodding their heads, and otherwise expressing sympathy toward and support for Cassandra. One whispered, "Wow, that's so cool," as she listened to the account. Cassandra thus firmly established her position as a good, loving black mother and did so by dispelling whatever negative impressions her white preppie peers might have had of her. And she did so with self-assured grace rather than angry scorn. This was not an isolated incident. Time and time again, I watched as Cassandra won over everyone with her words and example.

Cassandra also became a much better student. Teachers proved more than willing to provide help as long as she was willing to do her schoolwork. By the time Cassandra was scheduled to graduate, she had achieved a good academic standing. Just as importantly, she also had managed to reposition herself as a powerful role model. She exuded the black (model) student image of the good, religiously devout, mother/woman. And although her coming of age was an individually crafted process, Cassandra provided an empowering example of blackness for other students to emulate.

SHIFTING THROUGH POSSIBILITIES OF BLACKNESS

David's and Cassandra's coming-of-age stories offer compelling reasons for reconsidering prior approaches to studying the academic achievement of black high school students. Analyzing black achievement patterns as constituting "collective solutions . . . for collective problems," as Ogbu (2003, p. 51) has done, deflects attention from the fact that black students are individuals who make shifting adaptations in the midst of conflicting cultural discourses. Like David and Cassandra, who each adopted, fell away from, and then readopted images of upright black men and women and model black students, many black adolescents work with—or against—disparate discourses of blackness as they attempt to form viable identities and integrate themselves into domains of American life.

Richer understandings of black student identity and integration work require moving away from an exclusive focus on academic achievement. Coming of age must be recognized as a longer and much more comprehensive process—a transitioning into multiple domains of American life. Coming of age generally follows normative paths of psychocultural development unless disrupted by catastrophic events or blocked by insurmountable obstacles. Such events and barriers are not uncommon in the lives of young people, especially the lives of adolescents historically marginalized because of their race, class, gender, sexual orientations, or other social locations. In fact, most of the economically or socially disadvantaged students who participated in my study had experienced some kind of downfall due to terrible events or other difficulties during their years in high school (Hemmings 2004). Some, like Cassandra, were fortunate enough to attend a high school where the staff had been trained to identify students in jeopardy and steer them toward programs put in place to help them. Other students, like David, who attended schools that offered little or no assistance, felt that they were on their own. Regardless of their school environments, however, these and other teenagers fashioned a range of strategies for navigating discourses in multilayered cultural crosscurrents. That their navigations were difficult and in some cases even treacherous was evident in the stories David and Cassandra told about their high school journeys through adolescence.

Jefferson High, racially desegregated and largely working class, was rife with signs of neglect. Students negotiated the crosscurrents of seemingly opposing discourses of blackness, including those of black male respectability and reputation. David shifted up and down through these discourses until he finally settled on (re)forming his self into "the man" who could achieve economic success, political power for the sake of social justice, and other similarly positive individual and collective goals. In keeping with the black achievement ideology, he retrieved his model student image. He also synthesized black male respectability and reputation in a manner that put him in a much better position to pursue prosperity and justice in economic and political domains of American life.

At predominately white, upper-middle class Ridgewood High, the school ethos was firmly established by adults determined to make sure students stayed the middle-class course. The dominant achievement ideology contained insidious stereotypes, including that of the low-life black woman. This white-inscribed image was attached to Cassandra in the wake of the events that followed the death of her father. She spent most of her remaining years in high school freeing herself from white stereotypes of black women. She interrupted and redirected white middle-class vilifications of black women with her truly uplifting identity as a black mother/woman, an image rooted in black religious theology and black family values. Cassandra accomplished her own redemption so successfully that in addition to reviving her image as a model student, she became known as a young woman who held out hope to other "fallen" students.

Cassandra's and David's strategic adaptations led to improvements in their academic achievement. But they also opened up and held out more empowering examples of what it takes to achieve a good (black) life in American community domains. Their success does not mean black high school students can easily ignore or avoid the historical, social, and cultural forces that shape the forms of resistance to white schooling and society Ogbu describes. Nor does it excuse school personnel from providing more guidance and better support systems for black students. What these students' coming-of-age stories tell us is that like all young people, black adolescents must navigate conflicting cultural discourses as they construct their identity and integrate themselves into the community. But unlike white students, they have the added task of negotiating discourses of blackness that may pull them in different directions.

Black teenagers experience tremendous pressures from family members, peers, and others regarding their plans for the future. Nevertheless, most see themselves as active agents who can and do set their own navigational bearings. When Cassandra and David summed up their high school histories, each emphasized her or his autonomy and personal responsibility. David insisted it was he who had eventually turned his life around in Jefferson High's world of neglect. Cassandra acknowledged the help of her mother and the staff at Ridgewood High, but she also recognized that ultimately it was up to her to raise herself and her son. By the time they had become seniors, David and Cassandra had returned to their essential enduring selves: they were once again the kind of persons they had been at the beginning of their adolescent journeys. Significantly, they had achieved this positive and profoundly creative reinvention by shifting through the many possibilities of blackness.

NOTES

1. As is customary in ethnographic research, the names of people, schools, and geographic locations have been changed to ensure confidentiality.

2. I recruited ten graduating seniors to serve as key participants. At Jefferson High, they were David North (black, middle-class male), Adam Willis (white, working-class male), and Lona Young (black, working-class female). Participants at Ridgewood High were Cassandra Sommers (black, working-class female), Christina Sanchez

(Mexican American, middle-class female), Peter Hsieh (Taiwanese American, middle-class male), and Stuart Lyon (white, middle-class male). There also was a third school site, Central City High, which served low-income black students. The seniors who participated there were Monica Reese (black, low-income female), Michael Meyer (white, working-class male), and Nay Wilson (black, low-income female).

4

Intersecting Identities: "Acting White," Gender, and Academic Achievement

Prudence L. Carter

The "burden-of-acting-white" thesis is one of the most popular cultural explanations for the educational underachievement of African American, Latino, and other racial and ethnic groups. Signithia Fordham and John Ogbu's (1986) well-received and widely cited article defined the contours of a debate that continues today. They argued that African American students residing in an impoverished neighborhood in Washington, DC, came to define achievement-oriented behaviors and attitudes as "acting white" and were therefore resistant to studying hard and getting good grades. The explanatory power of this thesis and the meanings ascribed to the resistance to acting white are debatable—as the several authors in this volume point out. But a deeper problem with the burden-of–acting-white thesis lies in what it neither recognizes nor accounts for, namely, the salient male-female differences emergent *within* different racial and ethnic groups. Similarly, although Ogbu's cultural ecological theory (1978, 1991a; Ogbu and Simons 1998), especially its oppositional culture component, addresses differences *across* races, it homogenizes the academic experiences of students who are members of a single racial or ethnic group.

Explanations of minority students' school performance that focus only on race and culture overlook an important aspect of adolescence: teenagers juggle several identities, sometimes consciously, sometimes not, as they try to balance the social constructions of their race, ethnicity, gender, and sexual identities (see O'Connor 1999). Researchers need to pay attention to the intersections among these multiple identities, because they are likely to influence the extent to which students of color embrace such behaviors as

speaking Standard English, showing overt appreciation of school lessons, or
even participating in college-oriented activities, such as taking Advanced
Placement (AP) classes or enrolling in International Baccalaureate (IB) programs. As I explain in this chapter, the effects of gender on school performance are significant. Some students perceive school as a "feminine" realm
and "the street" as a masculine domain. This division is clear, for example, in
the answer Maxwell Tucker,[1] a seventeen-year-old high school senior, offered when I asked which gender he felt found it easier to thrive in school.

> Girls just smarter than boys. Girls are smarter in class work, but not
> streetwise. They fight over stupid stuff. Boys are, like, smarter than that.
> Only thing you ain't gone do is let somebody play you, or, like, put their
> hands on you.

Speaking pointedly and anecdotally throughout the interview, Maxwell
presented a picture of his high school world that was consistent with reports
from scholars, researchers, and journalists. Girls are outperforming boys in
the classroom (Jacobs 1996; Lewin 1998; Mickelson 1989). Generally, research shows that throughout their scholastic careers, girls outperform boys
in subjects that require verbal competence. Although some studies indicate
that boys do better than girls in math and science (Catsambis 1994; Maccoby
& Jacklin 1974; Nowell & Hedges 1998; Stevenson & Newman 1986), overall
girls have higher grade point averages and college attainment rates (Jacobs
1996; Mickelson 1989).

Furthermore, when disaggregating gender differences by race and ethnicity, some researchers find that African American and Latino girls receive
higher grades than their male counterparts and are more likely to be placed
in advanced academic classes (Ford & Harris 1992). Likewise, first- and
second-generation Mexican- and Vietnamese American girls do better academically than their male co-ethnic peers (Valenzuela 1999; Zhou & Bankston
1998). Ethnographic research also shows that, regardless of their level of performance, African American females are more likely to attend school regularly than are African American males (Fordham 1996a); and African American and Latino female students appear to maintain higher educational
aspirations and academic achievement compared to African American and
Latino male students (Solorzano 1992). Finally, a recent study of first-year un-
dergraduates at twenty-eight of the nation's most selective colleges and universities shows black females outnumbering black males by two to one
(Massey et al. 2003). In short, female students of color appear to exhibit
greater academic excellence and attainment than their male co-ethnics.

One way to explain these gender differences and still recognize the feasi-
bility of between-group racial analyses of academic achievement is to take a
more complex, intersectional approach and systematically examine the links

among social factors such as race (or ethnicity), gender, and class.[2] Using Ogbu and Fordham's burden-of-acting-white thesis as a springboard, I began the research I discuss in this chapter in order to try to understand these kinds of connections in the lives of African American and Latino students. I discovered that the racial and ethnic dynamics embedded in invocations of "acting black," "acting Spanish," or acting white often mask the influence of gender and social constructions of masculinity and femininity on African American and Latino youths' cross-cultural and in-group interactions, attitudes, and approaches to schooling. In other words, I found a gendered dimension to the resistance to acting white among students of color.

Boys and girls obtain specific value messages about what it means to be male and female, respectively, from close social connections, such as parents and extended family members, and also from popular culture. Hip-hop culture, for example, transmits strong notions of black masculinity (George 1998; Kelley 1994; Rose 1994), and both rap music and hip-hop culture, in romanticizing the "thug" life, have made concepts such as "hardness" and "streetwise" a common part of the cultural styles attached to masculinity in many U.S. urban areas (Anderson 1990; Majors & Billson 1992). In addition to these widely disseminated and broadly embraced cultural styles, there are ethno-specific gender messages that define, for instance, what it takes to be a "*black* man" or a "*black* woman."

Historically, what Connell (1995) calls "hegemonic masculinity" has provided males with higher social status than females, and with greater privilege and power in the spheres of the family, community, economy, and politics. For black and Latino males, however, massive unemployment and urban poverty, coupled with institutional racism, have reshaped notions of masculinity (Liebow 1967; Staples 1982). Sociologist Patricia Hill Collins (2004) suggests that males of color in America's urban areas have begun to circumvent conventional notions of masculinity based on white, middle-class models. Instead, they are emulating styles and behaviors associated with poor and working-class models. The social behaviors that accompany such changes in contemporary notions of masculinity and femininity within communities of color, including the low-income neighborhoods my research focuses on, can lead to divergent approaches to education between girls and boys.

In this chapter, using data drawn from surveys and interviews with native-born African American and Latino male and female youths, I argue that particular sets of ethno-specific behaviors that young people embrace as representing either "black" or "white" intersect and overlap with sets of gender-specific behaviors. This intersection explains in part the observed differences in educational outcomes between males and females. The findings presented here show that behaviors described by students as "masculine" and "feminine" align with language styles and codes, as well as with knowledge and orientations that are closely bound to either the school or the street. Moreover, some elements within the repertoire of social acts considered masculine render it less likely that many African American and Latino males will participate in certain activities linked to academic achievement. Most elements within the feminine repertoire, on the other hand, make it more likely that many girls will embrace activities that facilitate "book smarts," as opposed to those that support "street smarts." In sum, the cultural meanings developed by African American and Latino youth, coupled with other social factors, very likely contribute to the conspicuous gender gap in educational performance within these racial and ethnic communities.

DESCRIPTION OF THE RESEARCH STUDY

These findings draw extensively on a mixed-methods approach: I use both survey and interview data collected from a sample of sixty-eight low-income, native-born African American and Latino males and females, ages thirteen through twenty, and their parents (see table 4.1). The group of Latinos consists primarily of first- and second-generation Puerto Rican and Dominican youth, with a few of Cuban heritage; the African American youths' ancestors come mainly from the southern states and the greater New York metropolitan area.[3] The majority of the Latino males (seven of twelve) identified as "black Hispanic"; the remainder (five) identified as only "Hispanic." Among the Latinas, two identified as "black Hispanic," two as "White Hispanic," and eight as only "Hispanic." Females comprised more than 56 percent of the sample. All the participating students' families were poor and all qualified for government-subsidized housing. At least 90 percent received Aid to Families with Dependent Children funds during the period 1994–1998. Over half lived in homes with an annual household income less than $10,000, and most had a single female head of household.

The research setting, Yonkers, New York, located north of New York City, is the largest city (with a population of 189,000 in 1990) in mostly suburban Westchester County. Racially diverse and highly segregated, Yonkers's public school system faced a major challenge in 1980. The U.S. Department of Justice, the federal Office for Civil Rights, and the National Association for the Advancement of Colored People accused city officials and the Yonkers Board of Education of intentionally maintaining racially segregated schools. In May 1986, the school district (found guilty as charged) was ordered to develop a plan to ameliorate segregation in the schools. The plan the Board of Education created sought to bring about voluntary school desegregation through choice, centered on magnet schools and voluntary student transfers. In my sample, 72 percent of the students attended one of the magnet middle or high schools in the restructured school district. Fifteen percent of the stu-

Table 4.1. Sample Breakdown by Gender, Ethnicity, and Age

	African American	Latino	Ages 13–15	Ages 16–20	Total N
Female	25 (60%)	13 (50%)	17 (50%)	21 (62%)	38 (56%)
Male	17 (40%)	13 (50%)	17 (50%)	13 (38%)	30 (44%)
Total N	42 (100%)	26 (100%)	34 (100%)	34 (100%)	68 (100%)

dents had already obtained either a high school diploma or a GED, and 8 percent of this subgroup had some college experience. The remaining 13 percent were high school dropouts.

Using semistructured, open-ended interviews allowed me to inquire into the research participants' beliefs about opportunity, educational and career aspirations, school performance, delinquent behaviors, job attainment, "appropriate" gender and ethnic roles, and various cultural behaviors (e.g., speech, dress, demeanor, tastes, and peer-group interactions). To learn about the study participants' racial, ethnic, and gender identities, I asked questions such as, "In your family, are there expectations related to your [racial or ethnic and gender] background, to how you should act? What about among your friends? How do you feel about these rules? What are your feelings about the ways you're 'supposed' to behave as a [member of racial or ethnic group and gender]?"

Data gathered from three single-sex group interviews of six to eight students, each of which averaged about two hours, and all of which were conducted with the *same* research participants, complement and triangulate the data from the individual interviews and surveys. Youth who participated in these groups lived in the same housing complexes. I deliberately chose teens who knew each other so that I could observe and hear about their peer group interactions. The representation of African American and Latino youth in the groups reflected their numbers in the overall population of youth in the housing complexes where African Americans outnumbered Latinos almost two to one. The unstructured group interviews probed the same topics raised in the individual interviews and surveys. The questions explored the meaning behind beliefs, attitudes, and actions related to racial, ethnic, and gender identity; and asked about participants' beliefs regarding the opportunity structure, race relations, and means to success and achievement in American society. The interview structure intentionally allowed opinions and beliefs to volley back and forth through the group.

When I first began my investigation of acting white and its implications, I accepted at face value what Fordham and Ogbu meant by acting white and what they described as resistance to it. I set about ascertaining how actions and beliefs pertaining to this notion of resistance to acting white were manifested in the daily lives of the research participants. Early on, I decided to modify my deductive approach. Often, students did not mention acting white explicitly. They hinted at it. Sometimes, they hesitated to invoke language about race unless I mentioned it first. They did not want to appear to be too "racial" (a misnomer for their concern about appearing too racially conscious or even racist). After a handful of interviews, I decided to ask directly about "acting ethnic" or acting white any time I believed the respondent was hinting at ideas that were pertinent to these notions. Doing so often resulted in visible signs of relief on the students' part. By describing explicit and symbolic acts and meanings, including beliefs, art forms, language, gossip, dress, stories, and rituals of daily life, the study participants cataloged behaviors associated with "blackness" and "whiteness."

To facilitate analysis, all individual and group interviews were tape-recorded, transcribed verbatim, and coded systematically over a three-month period. I categorized students' responses by themes and topic areas, using a coding program developed by a graduate student colleague in the Department of Anthropology at Columbia University, Chauncy Lennon. This program allowed me to assign multiple thematic codes to each question and the responses to it. At first, I used umbrella themes (such as ones that denoted "race in school" or "gender in school") and then moved to more specific dimensional codes (such as one that denoted "beliefs about girls [or boys] and their academic ability"). Overall, I generated thirty-five thematic codes. Lennon's program also allowed me to systematically search for patterns and collate these responses by gender, ethnicity, and various other groupings, such as age or neighborhood settings.

WHITE TALK IS GIRL TALK

Within their racial and ethnic peer cultures, as well as in gendered peer subcultures, students construct idealized images, including those of blackness and whiteness, masculinity and femininity. Though I contest Fordham and Ogbu's (1986) argument that black students equate acting white with getting good grades and doing well in school (Carter 2005), I have found that black and Latino students do invoke the phrase and use it as a form of social control in within-group interactions. The actions and/or meanings students associate with acting white may be grouped into the following four categories: (1) speaking Standard English in peer spaces and emulating the speech (tone, diction, and language) of Whites; (2) sharing the dress styles of Whites; (3) having primary social interactions with Whites; and (4) acting uppity with or superior to a co-ethnic (Carter 1999). Across thirty-seven individual interviews I counted fifty-one references to the idea of (resistance to) acting white. The most frequent use of acting white was in reference to speech and language styles. This association alone accounted for close to 40 percent of all utterances of acting white.

The students' invocation of acting white was not directly related to their values about education, but it did have direct implications for the symbolic boundaries they created to spatially and performatively demark different social groups. That is, the labels acting white or "white talk" signified the cultural distinctions students made among whites, African Americans, Latinos, and other people of color. In addition, I found that as students invoked a spatial domain—typically, the "street"—they also made gender distinctions *within* racial or ethnic groups. Consistently, both girls and boys described Standard English as white talk, and boys not uncommonly emasculated white talk as they demonstrated it to me. In fact, throughout the sixty-eight interviews, all references to someone acting white were either to females, or to males who were perceived as effeminate. For instance, when I asked fifteen-year-old Adrienne Ingram, who had been accused of talking white, whether she knew of any black males who had been similarly accused, she responded this way:

Adrienne: I don't see a lot of boys who talk like me. . . . [After some musing, she continued.] Yeah, my friend Daniel. He says I act white, too. But his friends pick on him because he talks soft and stuff . . . like they call him gay or something, or they say he acts white, too.

Prudence: Just because of the way he talks? Do they say he acts white based on anything else?

Adrienne: No, just the way I talk or the way he talks.

In a separate interview, Sean Anderson, a seventeen-year-old African American male, immediately linked my explicit questioning about the meanings of acting white and acting black to questions about sexuality:

Prudence: At school, have you ever encountered or have you ever used it yourself, like someone saying somebody's trying to "act black," or somebody's trying to act white?

Sean: Nah. Mostly, somebody's trying to "act gay."

Prudence: Why would somebody try to "act gay"?

Sean: Like, not trying, but he is. You know, we shouldn't do it—it is kind of prejudice, but you see some kids and you look at 'em, the way they act and the way they walk, who they hanging with, used to look at me like they're gay, they're funny. . . . I feel men that hang with all women all the time and talk like them, that's kind of gay.

Prudence: How would he talk?

Sean: Try to raise his voice or something like that. [He raises the inflection of his voice]. "Ooooooh!" You know, something like that. You know. There's some kids like that. That's about it.

Both Sean's and Adrienne's responses signal that language and speech are neither race- nor gender-neutral social terrains. Plus, both students implicitly and explicitly equated white talk with "girl talk." The only boy Adrienne could recall who spoke in a manner like hers was perceived by others as gay because of his tone and speech patterns. When Sean demonstrated for me the "gay" way of talking that was considered a form of acting white when applied to boys, he used a pseudo-feminine tone of voice (see Mac an Ghaill 1994).

Male and female students frequently had shared understandings about speech styles and acting white. Actual negotiation of these behaviors was more complicated for males than for females, however. Sociologist Mary Waters (1996) found a similar pattern among second-generation West Indian youth in New York City: for boys, being accused of acting white often was associated with a challenge to their masculinity. Adrienne's speech styles and voice inflections made her vulnerable to the acting-white label, but when her classmate Daniel exhibited a similar style, he risked not only being sanctioned for acting white but also being emasculated or rendered gender deviant. In a society where masculinity is inextricably tied to heterosexuality, a person who possesses the requisite X and Y chromosomes but does not conform to constructed norms and cultural expectations is considered a gender and sexual deviant (Connell 1995). According to Adrienne, Daniel's sexuality was questioned because he spoke "soft," meaning that his delivery was not sufficiently forceful or deep voiced. When a boy employed a certain diction and voice inflection—higher pitched, for example, as Sean demonstrated, and when a boy had mostly female friends, he was perceived to be gay.

Perceptions of femininity worked differently. Some youths associated white speech patterns with girls, an idea that stemmed from media (particularly television) representations of white youth and their speech patterns. For instance, whenever I asked the study participants to mimic or demonstrate what talking white meant, they typically mentioned "valley-girl" speech patterns, or they spoke in a nasal voice, mimicking the way popular teen movies portray "geeks" or "nerds." With the exception of Steve Urkel, the nerdish next-door neighbor on TV's *Family Matters* (a popular 1990s series about an African American middle-class family), the characters who use these speech styles are portrayed by Whites. Valley-girl speech, a style pervasive in the 1980s, gained additional currency from the television sitcom and popular teen movie *Clueless* in which a very wealthy white girl from Beverly Hills negotiates adolescent "crises."

During an all-girl group interview, fourteen-year-old Joyelle Richards de-scribed her thirteen-year-old sister Janelle Richards as acting white. Joyelle insisted that Janelle spoke like her "rich" white friends and the wealthy, white star of the *Clueless* sitcom. Janelle, however, emphatically denied that she acted white. To prove her point about Janelle, Joyelle urged me to "lis-ten to how she talks."

Prudence: Janelle, how does it make you feel when your friends and your sister say that you act white?

Janelle: It don't hurt me!

Prudence: Do you think that you act white?

Janelle: No!

Prudence: Do you know what they mean when they say that you're act-ing white?

Janelle: 'Cause they, like—that I'm one of those *Clueless* girls.

[There is laughter from all the girls in the room.]

Prudence: Clueless girls? Like the ones on TV?

Janelle: Yeah.

Prudence: Do you talk like that?

[Janelle shakes her head no.]

Joyelle [interjecting]: Well, talk then.

Prudence: What are your [white] friends like, Janelle? Tell me about them.

Janelle: They funny. They fun. They rich.

Although Janelle and Joyelle referenced girls, they and the other girls in the interview group considered this particular speech form "white" because of the race of those they perceived as its chief practitioners.

The male study participants expressed a similar view. As we sat and chat-ted at his kitchen table, Samurai Kitchens, a fourteen-year-old ninth grader, made an explicit connection between girl talk and acting white.

Samurai: There's some black people that act white.

Prudence: Who are they?

Samurai: [They] change their tone of voice when they get around certain people. Like, maybe a black girl . . . talks like, "Oh yeah, like, where are you going?" And then when you leave and they get around certain type of person, they're like, "Come on. Oh, let's go to the mall. Let's go shopping. Come on, [raising the pitch of his voice, he imitates what he perceives as talking white] I have to be in the house by like eight o'clock." And they know they have to be in the house by ten o'clock, but they do that to impress the white people . . .

Prudence: Why is it that you decide to choose a girl in that example when I asked you what acting white was? Is it mostly girls?

Samurai: I don't know a black male that tries to act white. I don't know none. None.

Prudence: So it's mostly girls.

Samurai: They wear miniskirts to school and it's mostly girls. It's mostly girls.

Samurai's remark about miniskirts was an indirect reference to the valley-girl culture Janelle mentioned. Similarly, his references to "the mall" and "shopping" when he was imitating white talk were allusions to this subculture. (Shopping is the favorite pastime of Cher, the rich main character of *Clueless*, and her best friend and sidekick Dionne, who was portrayed by a black actress.) Samurai's comments also suggest that the notion of acting white is just that—a social *performance* in which (black) girls use an affected form of speech to impress or to be like "certain (implicitly white) people." This style of speech, Samurai maintained, was a way to move up to a more respectable status position. In making this connection, Samurai implicitly linked whiteness with respectability. The example of girls' telling their peers they have an eight p.m. curfew, when in fact their curfew is ten p.m., conveys Samurai's perception that white parents maintain tighter reins of social control over their children.

Finally, Samurai declared that among the black males he knew, none acted white. Only girls did so. Again, with the exception of two references to allegedly gay males, all of the principal characters in the fifty-one references to acting white that I heard were female.[4] Of the sixty-eight young people I interviewed, four, all female, mentioned that their peers had characterized them as acting white. Two of the four, Adrienne and Rosaria Linares, were high achievers who had enrolled in honors and AP courses in high school; the other two, Janelle and nineteen-year-old Moesha Latimer, described themselves as average students. Adrienne, Janelle, and Moesha were labeled as acting white because of the way they spoke. Rosaria said her friends referred to her as white because of her preppy dress and taste for the music of then-popular singer Michael Bolton.

Notably, Samurai (and other interviewees) conflated ideas about Standard English, slang, and the dialects of white youth subcultures. As he compared white talk to "black talk," Samurai made increasingly loose distinctions between English as a language system and slang as an informal language practice. Valley-girl talk, like black urban youth vernacular, is not Standard English. Yet, because the people Samurai, Joyelle, and Janelle heard speaking these English variants (on television) were white, they deemed them all to be white talk. In Adrienne's case, nonetheless, it was her use of Standard English that was equated with white talk:

Adrienne: Yep, like, some boys in school expect me to speak Ebonics or whatever, so they call me a "white girl." They [say] like, "Come here, white girl," 'cause of the way I talk. I tell them I'm not a thug. I go to English class; this is the way I talk. This is my grammar. I'm not going to sit here and make myself look stupid, talking about some "What up, yo." That's not English!

Adrienne classified her black peers' slang as a sign of ignorance and stupidity; she believed using Standard English was a key indicator of intelligence. Thus, she avoided and demeaned the linguistic styles of many of her peers, especially the males. She fully rejected their speech, which she dubbed as Ebonics. One consequence of her refusal to employ her classmates' speech codes was to be described as acting white.

If white talk was equated with Standard English, spoken by females, black talk became synonymous with "street talk," spoken by males. Street talk, as Anderson (1999) has noted, is imbued with a toughness associated with codes of masculinity in poor, black, urban contexts. Avery Adams, a ninth grader, spoke pointedly about the distinction between the lingo of the street and the "softer," more laid-back language of school.

Avery: Yeah, it depends on where you at. If you on the street, you gotta talk like—you know what I'm saying—like you in the street. If you in school, you got to talk like [something else] in school. It's where you at in terms of how you present yourself. You know what I'm saying?

Prudence: It's like you have to have many faces?

Avery: Yeah, we all have to do that, you know. We all gotta front. It's like when you want that job, you gonna, like, kiss a little butt. [Laughter.] It's like we all have to do that. We have thousands of faces, many different faces. When you on the job, you're not the same person. You on the street, you don't see that person [from the job]. It's obvious. You see it. Like right now, I'm with you. I'm acting pretty laid back with you, but I'm like on the street, "What up, nigger, ya'll chillin?[5] What up?"

Avery admitted he used a stronger, less "laid-back" language on the street than he did in school and on the job. He even used that more laid-back language with me, a woman in an interview setting that he considered a sphere of respectability. The street, on the other hand, was not a place where he would "kiss butt" and be deferential (another trait associated with a softer, more feminine nature).

Samurai and Avery's preference for black talk or street talk did not interfere with their strategic use of Standard English. Both clearly were aware of the latter as the dominant standard for communication in the United States. They moved back and forth freely between Standard English and slang as they demonstrated white and black talk for me. Their commentary on language suggests that they attached cultural, racial, and gender identities to particular voice inflections and trendy expressions. They used speech (and dress) to create symbolic cultural boundaries separating the spatial domains of school and the street (see also Carter 2003; Perry 2002). Speaking in certain ways, such as using a higher pitch and less forceful tone and/or using "softer" language, were associated with white talk. The softer, more deferential style of white talk, in turn, rendered it feminine. Black talk, in contrast, was tougher, "harder," and, by extension, more masculine.

These soft/hard and male/female dichotomies have some critical implications for the schooling behaviors of low-income African American and Latino students. Although each of us is socialized by our families, communities, and other social institutions to reproduce specific social roles, differences in role enactments and in gender cultures have led to some conspicuous divergences in school performances between boys and girls in low-income black and Latino communities. "Girls' just smarter than boys," was how Maxwell summed up the split. Moesha recalled, "There were, like, many more rows of girls in my graduating class." Since girls have not been shown to have greater innate intelligence than boys, what accounts for their greater academic achievement relative to boys? The next section examines some of the cultural and social behaviors that were associated with achievement differences among the youths who participated in my study.

GENDER AND SMARTS: "SOFT" GIRLS AND "HARD" BOYS

When I asked study participants whether they thought excelling in school was easier for girls or for boys, most chose the former. Objective indicators such as grades confirm their opinions. As table 4.2 shows, girls in the study reported significantly higher mean (80.12) and median (82.25) grade point averages than those reported by boys (74.61 and 75, respectively). Furthermore, girls were more than two and a half times as likely to report being "B" students, while boys were more than two and a half times as likely to report being "C" students.

Table 4.2. School Performance Patterns of Study Participants, by Gender

Performance Indicator	Females	Males
Mean grade point average	80.12	74.61**
	(23)[a]	(23)
Median grade point average	82.25	75**
	(23)	(20)
Percent reporting themselves as mainly	61	23*
"B" students	(26)[a]	(23)
Percent reporting themselves as mainly	22	58*
"C" students	(26)[a]	(23)
Percent reporting they often/sometimes	9	35**
cut an entire day of school	(26)[a]	(23)

**p< .05; *p< .10
Note: [a]The *n*'s represent those who reported grade point averages and who were enrolled in grades 8–12 at the time of the interview.

Eighteen-year-old Sylvestre Cabán and fifteen-year-old Tiara Mitchell surmised that boys and girls approach school in different ways, with girls having more ambition and drive to succeed in the classroom:

Sylvestre: I think that it will be easier for a woman. Girls and women are a little bit smarter than us. It's true. I'm serious. I see it. They think smarter than guys.

Prudence: Why do you think that they are smarter?

Sylvestre: I don't know. I know that they got a little more push, a little more drive.

Prudence: Do you as a young male feel more pressure to conform or to hang out with your partners?

Sylvestre: I think that now—I think we bored. I think, like, between the teens and the early twenties, there's, like, a phase that guys go through. Like guys just got to be guys, like, just hang out. Just be on the corner, chill. Some guys stay on the corner. And girls just say, let me think, let me get my life together.

Tiara's reasoning differed somewhat from Sylvestre's, but her conclusions were similar:

Prudence: In your opinion, in school, do you think it's easier for boys or girls to be really smart in school?

Tiara: A girl.

Prudence: Why do you say that?

Tiara: Well, boys I know are not into books. Most girls I know love to read, Whites—Blacks—all, in the library. Boys just love gym. Boys that I know just love to go to gym. But girls are not. I'm not interested in gym, but I play gym.

Tiara's observation about her male classmates' interest in sports (gym) is borne out by the sample as a whole. Fifty percent of the males played a team sport, compared to 26 percent of the girls.[6]

Prudence: Why do you think that girls perform better than boys?

Tiara: I dunno about that. Most boys just come to school to play. Boys always are in gym; that's one class that boys do not miss. I always think about that. But I'm saying, most girls, I mean, they're just in class. Most boys are always cutting. Like, when I'm going to the bathroom or something, the boys [are] in the hallway playing, rolling dice or something.

Girls, Tiara and Sylvestre imply, are more mature than boys: boys play while girls work. Both students see the differences between the sexes as significant, but neither speaker ties them to genetically defined intellectual ability. Instead, they see school effort as the critical difference between males and females. Boys follow their peers and hang out, while girls engage with school, work hard, perform better, and build on their success.

Why might some pro-school behaviors—such as motivation—become associated more with girls than with boys? Since there is no evidence of innate or essential differences in intelligence by sex in our society, the explanations for the academic gender divide must be social and cultural. More specifically, they must be tied to how gender, as a social process, is experienced, prescribed, and enforced in our society (Collins 1991; Crenshaw 1992; Frankenberg 1993; Lopez 2003). Burke (1989) suggests that certain behaviors, such as sitting still and paying attention in class, are imbued with "feminine" meaning and therefore are avoided by individuals with more "masculine" identities. Hence, the more feminine the gender identity of boys and girls, the better their school performance, as measured by grade point averages.

Maxwell, quoted early in the chapter, assigned girls and boys different spheres of expertise—girls were more "book smart" than boys; boys were more "street smart" than girls. For Maxwell, reading, going to class daily, finishing homework, and earning decent grades made one book smart, which girls, he believed, did more freely than boys. Street smarts, in contrast, included knowing how to look another person in the eye; knowing when to avert your gaze; knowing how to avoid potentially life-threatening fights and other risky encounters; knowing how to physically defend yourself; and knowing how to navigate through dangerous (i.e., gang) territories (Anderson 1990, 1999); and boys, as Maxwell claimed, embraced these behaviors more readily than girls.

Boys were under significant pressure to be the "man." High status required possessing athletic ability, coolness, and toughness (Adler, Kless, & Adler 1992). In a discussion during one of the all-male group interviews, thirteen-year-old Marcus Smith accused thirteen-year-old Michael Jones of being soft because he refused to fight. Maxwell, when we talked one-on-one, claimed a "man" would stand up and fight for himself. He emphasized that males were not supposed to back down from a physical challenge, nor were they supposed to allow themselves to be challenged in the first place ("Only thing you ain't gone do is let somebody play you, or, like, put their hands on you.") As Adrienne made clear, girls were well aware of this notion of manliness and the degree to which it proscribed being soft:

> Adrienne: It's easier for a girl to be smart, because if a boy is smart, he gets stuff from his crew or whatever, like, "Ah, man you're soft, you're soft! I can't believe you know that poetry stuff." So they'll [boys] try to hide that they're smart—that they know stuff like that. So I think that it's easier for a girl.

Adrienne's comment also is significant in its explicit description of certain aspects of school life as a threat to male students' already tenuous hold on their masculinity. Adrienne suggests that boys deliberately mask their "feminine" school-related interests to avoid being ridiculed.

Of course, not every male student is an underachiever, and the study sample included several who excelled in school. Not surprisingly, their perceptions of school and academic achievement sometimes differed from those expressed by other participants. For example, John Jamison, an eighth grader enrolled in honors classes, dismissed the notion of girls being smarter than boys as simply a stereotype. Fourteen-year-old Ramon Diaz, another high-achieving male, had his sights set on MIT; he hoped to earn a degree in a scientific area such as computer engineering. But Jeremy James, a ninth grader whose academic promise had led teachers to urge him to enroll in his school's IB program, which allows students to take college-level classes, wanted, instead, to attend the "regular" school that his friends and cousins were attending. (At the time of the interview, he had not yet convinced his mother to approve this preference; the two were still squabbling over the IB program.)

Prior research suggests that more male students follow the route Jeremy preferred—insisting on behaviors that confirm their masculinity but undermine their chances for academic success—than the one Ramon had in mind (Epstein et al. 1998; Mac An Ghaill 1994; Renold 2001). Behaviors associated with being hard and those associated with being a good student were difficult to reconcile. The former required risking reprimands and suspensions by cutting classes, being truant, fighting, and hanging out with other males (including school dropouts). My study findings also confirm the gendered nature of some aspects of school performance. Some girls admitted to practicing behaviors such as cutting school to hang out with friends, but boys were more likely to practice these behaviors. For instance, nearly four times as many boys (35 percent) as girls (9 percent) admitted to cutting school "often" or "sometimes."[7]

Moreover, as figure 4.1 reveals, males were slightly more likely to report getting a kick out of engaging in risky and dangerous behaviors (57 percent) than were females (37 percent). Two males in the study explicitly discussed their risky, dangerous, and illicit activities. Sylvestre and his next-door neighbor DeAndre Croix were small-time "street pharmacists" (a colloquial term for drug dealers). Sylvestre had dropped out of school after being suspended several times for lack of respect to school authorities (his last act, he said, had been a physical confrontation with the principal). In addition to selling marijuana, Sylvestre hauled furniture for a company—backbreaking work that he did not intend to do for the rest of his life. He fantasized about the material and status rewards of a white-collar job, working in an office, being a professional. He longed for the type of job that would bring respect and enough money to buys cars and a home, and allow him to support a wife

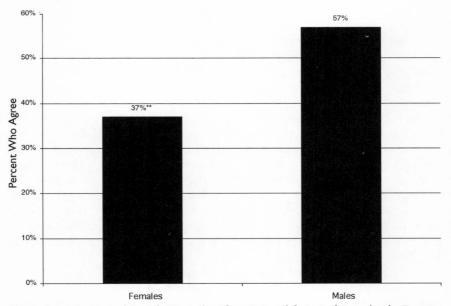

Figure 4.1.   Percent of Sample Reporting They Get a Kick Out of Engaging in Dangerous Activities, By Gender
Note: **p< .10.

and children with minimal strain. Restless, lacking a high school diploma, and thoroughly disengaged from school, Sylvestre seemed unlikely to be able to find his way to socioeconomic mobility through any conventional path.

DeAndre, on the other hand, told me he had stopped selling drugs and was now focused on getting through school (although seventeen, he was still several years from graduating). DeAndre's male identity was linked to "keepin' it real" (which, he explained, meant "that you'll be there for your man. If he fight, you fight") and rebelling against authority if he felt a school policy was unfair. Like Sylvestre, he had gotten into trouble with the school principal. In DeAndre's case, the issue was noncompliance with a school rule that prohibited students from wearing the hoods of their sweatshirts over their heads while they were in school. At the time (late 1990s), this was a popular dress style among urban black youth. However, because wearing a hood also could signify gang membership and because the style had become a code of the street, school authorities imposed a blanket ban. The school's interpretation and policy bothered DeAndre, and he claimed that the policy was one of the things he liked least about his present school.

In these boys' and young men's communities, hardness and toughness seemed to function as a coat of armor, a protection against a reopening of wounds inflicted over a long history of severe social and economic oppression. Their comments and observations also evidenced how poverty and class impair many of their dreams and aspirations for better opportunities in life. The contemporary meanings associated with masculinity stem from lives lived in inner-city poverty, where an underground economy thrives, where turf wars between gangs endanger the lives of neighborhood residents, where individuals must generate creative and often illicit life plans in order to survive, and where specialized, context-dependent systems of communication and styles of social interaction materialize (Anderson 1999; Kelley 1994; Liebow 1967; Massey & Denton 1993; Wilson 1987). Although several boys mentioned their frustration over the pervasive presence in daily life of negative stereotypes of black and Latino men, often the actual male models in their neighborhoods conformed to just such images of street corner men (Hannerz 1969; Liebow 1967). In my afternoon visits to the housing complexes where the study participants lived, I observed many men hanging out in parking lots and on corners; when I asked about these men, the young people I had come to interview would describe them either as unemployed or as "street pharmacists."

Some girls challenged the idea that the hard code of the streets provided boys with any kind of smarts. During an interview with a mixed-ethnic group of girls, one of the two female groups with whom I spoke, Teresa Anton, a young single mother with small children, led the chorus of "amen's" about how boys are raised differently. "Men don't do things right. A girl will never get caught selling drugs; men always get caught. It's the way they mamas raised them," she said. What Teresa was referring to was the differential gender socialization that occurred within the family. Others agreed with her, adding, "Yeah! Boys can stay out all night." Teresa pressed on. "That's why we're smarter," she continued. "We [are] smarter because we get less attention . . . 'cause boys, they get treated better than us, so we have to think of ways to occupy our minds. So we end up thinking for ourselves." The entire group chimed in again, "Yeah!"

These girls attributed academic differences to differential social latitude within the family. Boys get to "be running the streets and hanging with their friends," seventeen-year-old DeAndre told me, and in his opinion, you "could not blame them." "Everyone wants to do that, even if they work," he continued. Meanwhile, girls feared the reprisals poor school performance could bring from their parents. "If I don't go to school, then I can't go outside," Tiara explained. "So," she elaborated, "that's why I go to school, 'cause otherwise I can't do the things that I want to do." Research confirms that within families, girls typically face stricter rules and relatively more social control than boys (Cauce et al. 1996; Taylor 1996).

CONCLUSION

Questions about the links between racial (or ethnic) and gender identities guided the initial inquiry for the study whose results I have discussed in this chapter. I found that African American and Latino and Latina youth tended to feminize certain dimensions of acting white, particularly speech codes and personal styles associated with Whites, especially the white characters in TV programs. Previous research, articles in the popular press, and anecdotal evidence indicate that some African American and Latino males contend with accusations of acting white (Belluck 1999; Hemmings 1996), but none of the males in my sample reported being labeled this way. It was the females who were more likely to act white or to be accused of acting white, in part because of the feminized nature of the label, in part because white talk seemed to be understood as a form of girl talk, and in part because males were more likely to shy away from feminine behaviors that might allow others to attribute to them a (stigmatized) gay identity. Thus, girls appeared to have more latitude to act white: though their racial and ethnic identities were explicitly challenged, their gender identity was not.

Delving into the gendered meanings that the study participants assigned to acting white led to a further discovery. Gender identity, specifically the constructions of masculinity and femininity, also seems to differentially shape girls' and boys' orientations toward school. The cultural boundaries at least some low-income African American and Latino males constructed around masculinity and femininity had critical implications for how they approached school. Specifically, they invested less energy in academic achievement than did their female co-ethnic peers. In their efforts to balance distinctive masculine and racial/ethnic identities, many African American and Latino males in the study actively avoided behaviors that might make them appear soft. Instead, they embraced images of masculinity as hard and tough, modeling themselves after the new exemplars of masculinity for poor and working-class black men—hip-hop celebrities and professional sports figures.

Girls may share certain ethnic cultural practices with their male peers, but their responses to school differ. Even when, as individuals, girls do not thrive academically, as a group, they benefit from a gender process that renders girls more likely to exhibit educationally oriented behaviors. Low-income black and Latina girls face a triple threat of racism, sexism, and classism (King 1996), but both perform better in school than do their male co-ethnics, and thus have a higher chance of future success.

Gender expectations are inescapable. They are woven into every facet of U.S. society and affect every aspect of life, including the way individuals move, gesture, and interact. "America has defined the roles to which each individual should subscribe," wrote scholar and activist Frances Beale (1995, pp. 146–147) over three decades ago. "It has defined 'manhood' in terms of its own interests[;] [t]herefore, an individual who has a good job, makes a lot of money, and drives a Cadillac is a real 'man,' and conversely, an individual who is lacking in these 'qualities' is less of a man." Some have argued that girls do not experience the same level of estrangement from the normalized American female role as boys do vis-à-vis the normalized American male role (Fordham 1996a).

For instance, in the aftermath of the Civil Rights movement, black women have attended college in greater numbers than have black men. Since 1976, black male enrollment has dropped by 7 percent, while black female enrollment has nearly doubled, so that black female college students now outnumber black males (Benjamin 1991; Slater 1994). Moreover, perceived feminine norms of conformity and passivity, along with schools' tendency to emphasize subjects such as English and literature, may provide girls with more latitude in terms of their academic and their social identity performances. Generally, boys are drawn to and perform better in the technical and scientific subjects. Although girls do not always comply with school norms and policies (they, too, break rules), Willis (1977) has argued that the school is likely to be more complicit in than resistant to the development of female cultural forms. As Ann Ferguson (2000) has shown, school officials read certain "masculine" behaviors among black boys as signs that the boys are delinquents and troublemakers, which heightens the likelihood that they will become disengaged, be sent to detention, and eventually be suspended or expelled.

Family socialization influences male and female cultural expectations, as well. Many black and Latino parents, some sobered by the dynamics of racism, poverty, and unemployment, may socialize their sons and daughters differently in order to prepare them for an inequitable opportunity structure, one marred by both racial and gender inequality (Lopez 2003). Even within middle-class families, mothers have begun to prepare their daughters for economic self-sufficiency and higher attainment through practices that encourage more discipline and greater attention to education (Cose & Samuels 2003). Moesha was a close observer of these shifts. Echoing the theorists, she told me

> See, the girls have to get where they want to go. So . . . it's kind of easier for them to stay in school. Plus, they have fathers and mothers that push you more. [C]ertain mothers and fathers don't put so much into it, [for] the guys.

Given the late-twentieth-century shift from a manufacturing to a service economy, and given a criminal justice system that adversely and disproportionately affects black and Latino poor and working-class men, the growing educational-achievement gap between black men and black women portends a monumental shift in privilege and status. Now, college-educated black women earn more than the median for all black working men—or, for that matter, for all women (Cose & Samuels 2003). Furthermore, at every socioeconomic quartile level except the highest, black females maintain higher educational aspirations than do black males (Solorzano 1992). And these higher aspirations now correspond to a larger representation of black women than black men in professional and managerial jobs.[8]

Paradoxically, a stratified gender system underwritten by patriarchy works against many black and Latino boys. Historically, masculinity has been synonymous with social privilege. However, race and racial meanings complicate how low-income African American and Latino males' gender performances are accepted. Cultural gatekeepers in schools and in the workplace perceive the hard masculine behaviors of many men of color as troublesome and as a potential threat to proper decorum (Kirschenman & Neckerman 1991; Moss & Tilly 1996). It is essential that low-income black and Latino males create ways of moving through the world that intrinsically critique inequitable racial and economic structures. At the same time, parents, teachers, and mentors must take responsibility for ensuring that the socialization of African American and Latino boys into men does not undermine their desires and aspirations for higher education and upward mobility. The differences in these boys' socialization from their female peers correspond to observed differences in educational and occupational outcomes that currently favor girls.

Fordham and Ogbu's acting-white thesis touched off a highly contentious debate about how racial and ethnic identity influence African Americans' and some Latino ethnic groups' orientations to school achievement. The results from my study suggest, however, that the explanations for achievement differences are more complex than the acting-white hypothesis can accommodate. Students juggle multiple identities that cohere over time around a racial or ethnic identity. Within groups, gender, class, sexuality, and other sociocultural identities influence youths' schooling behaviors and their outcomes. It is all a balancing act. Placing explanatory primacy on one social identity and its relationship to the school risks oversimplifying the reasons why some students succeed and others do not.

NOTES

1. Pseudonyms are used throughout this chapter to protect the study participants' identities.

2. Though I mention class as a critical component of intersectional analysis, the effects of which others have documented thoroughly (MacLeod 1995; Pattillo-McCoy 1999; Willis 1977), here I will focus mainly on race and gender. In a few instances in this chapter, study participants make comments that allude to the influences of poverty in their lives. I provide a brief discussion of poverty and class influences in the concluding pages of the chapter.

3. Three individuals in the African American group mentioned having at least one parent who had immigrated from Africa (Liberia) or from the Caribbean (Antigua).

4. The African American and Latino girls in the study adhered to styles and tastes (e.g., in nail and hair care) that were distinct from those of their white counterparts. Many argue that African American, Latino, and white females will differ in their social and cultural responses because of the varied impact on their lives of gender, race, and class (Anzaldua 1990; Collins 1991; hooks 1984; King 1996; Rollins 1985). Parker et al. (1995) found that African American adolescent females and white adolescent females differed significantly in their concepts of beauty, body image, and ideal weight. African American females were more flexible than their white counterparts and spoke more about "making what you've got work for you." In contrast, many white females expressed dissatisfaction with their bodies and were rigid in their concepts of beauty.

5. Avery's use of the term "nigger" here is different from the historically derogatory connotation steeped in the oppressive racist experiences of African Americans. Rather, his usage signifies how many young African Americans have appropriated the term as a form of endearment.

6. The most popular career choice among boys in the study was professional athlete, followed very closely by businessman. In contrast, the girls were more likely to aspire to be doctors and lawyers. Such findings have led some commentators to assert that a fixation with excelling in school sports has replaced an interest in classroom success for minority males, particularly black males (Hoberman 1997; Solomon 1992).

7. Interestingly, although the male and female students' school-related *behavior* differed in crucial ways, both genders professed strong beliefs in the value and positive functions of education (Carter 2005; Tyson in this volume).

8. Women of color are significantly better represented in white-collar jobs than are men of color. However, for the women, there is labor market segmentation. African American, Asian American, and Latino women usually are overrepresented in clerical or administrative support jobs and drastically underrepresented in senior-level positions (Benjamin 1991; Woo 1992). Their male counterparts have a slightly greater representation in senior-level positions, though their numbers are still relatively low when compared to white men and women in the workforce. Women of color also have been shown to earn less and to be on the bottom rung of the economic ladder (see Karen Fulbright [1986], cited by Benjamin 1991). Further, Woo (1992) has shown that despite their higher levels of education, Asian American women have lower returns on education than white males and females, whose college completion rates are lower. Finally, in some spheres, males of color dominate and have more privilege (i.e., politics and senior-level professional positions), while females of color fare better in other spheres (i.e., secondary and higher education).

5

To Be Young, Gifted, Black, and Somewhat Foreign: The Role of Ethnicity in Black Student Achievement

Sherri-Ann P. Butterfield

Educational achievement, and thus social mobility, is critically important to West Indian immigrants and their children. Much of the literature on West Indians' social attainment focuses on their success relative to that of African Americans (see Bryce-Laporte 1972, 1993; Butcher 1994; Foner 1985, 1987; Kasinitz 1987, 1992; Model 1991, 1995; S. Stafford 1987; Vickerman 1999, 2001; Waters 1999, 2001).[1] In fact, qualitative, quantitative, and theoretical scholarship on contemporary black immigrants frequently argues that success among West Indians involves maintaining West Indian culture (Kalmijn 1996; Ogbu 1991a, 1992; Sowell 1978),[2] while downward mobility is a function of assimilation into the "underclass" culture of African Americans (see Gans 1992; Ogbu 1991a; Portes & Zhou 1993). Many scholars believe that for West Indians, acculturation and economic mobility are not necessarily linked in the ways they were for European immigrants at the turn of the twentieth century (Gans 1992; Portes & Zhou 1993; Rumbaut 1994).

The idea that resisting assimilation to African American culture boosts West Indians' socioeconomic status is grounded in scholarship on educational aspirations and achievement among African American students, work that deems them as educationally lacking compared to other racial and ethnic groups (Portes and Sensenbrenner 1993; Portes and Zhou 1993). Even when accounting for the diversity within the black population, both African and Caribbean immigrants achieve a higher level of education than African Americans (Logan & Deane 2003). To explain this disparity between African Americans and other racial and ethnic groups, researchers often turn to John Ogbu's (1974, 1978) cultural ecological theory (CET). CET draws important distinctions between two minority groups: those Ogbu termed "immigrant" or "voluntary" minorities, and those he labeled "castelike" or "involuntary" minorities. Immigrant minorities are those who have moved to the United States "in the belief that this change will lead to an improvement in their economic well-being or to greater political freedom" (Ogbu 1990b, p. 145). Involuntary minorities are people "initially brought into the United States through slavery, conquest, or colonization" (Ogbu 1990b, p. 145).

The theory posits that as a result of racial discrimination and limited socioeconomic prospects, some minority groups maintain culturally distinct approaches to opportunity structures. By comparing the historical, structural, and psychological factors influencing the educational adjustment problems of voluntary minorities with those of involuntary minorities, Ogbu contended, one could demonstrate why the latter "are plagued by persistent poor academic performance while the former are not" (Ogbu 1990, p. 146).[3] The legacy of slavery and racism leads many African American students to believe that high academic achievement only benefits white students. This belief prompts them to lower their own aspirations for schooling. Over time, academic achievement comes to be associated with the dominant culture, and is perceived as "acting white" (Fordham & Ogbu 1986).

There has been, and continues to be, considerable debate about the applicability of the CET framework. Some researchers argue that the Fordham-Ogbu thesis needs to more carefully consider the following issues: within-group variation (Carter 1999; Kao & Tienda 1998); class and gender (Carter 1999; Kao & Tienda 1998); specific schooling context (Hemmings 1996); and family histories, resources, and interactions (Mickelson 1990; O'Connor 1997). Other scholars posit that African American students at all socioeconomic levels adhere to the dominant achievement ideology (Ainsworth-Darnell & Downey 1998; Cook & Ludwig 1998; O'Connor 1997; Tyson 1998, 2002). As a group, these studies reveal the need for more nuanced understandings of the effects of social location on social mobility. Given the unprecedented number of immigrants of color currently in the United States, there is an additional and equally important factor not covered by these critiques, however. What is missing is an analysis of the ways in which children of immigrants, particularly children of black immigrants, complicate some of the fundamental premises of the CET model regarding achievement and perceptions of opportunity.[4]

It is important to note that Ogbu did address the unique circumstances of children of immigrants in the CET model. He asserted that voluntary minorities do not perceive or interpret learning the norms of schools "as threatening to their own language and identity (Ogbu 1987, p. 328); as a result, second-generation immigrants will follow the educational trajectory of their parents (Ogbu 1990b). According to the CET model, immigrants recognize but acquiesce to discrimination because they not only imagine themselves as "guests in a foreign land," but also imagine social obstacles (particularly those encountered in school and other social institutions) as merely temporary barriers to overcome in the pursuit of upward mobility. However, the model does not account for two important factors relevant to the children of immigrants: (1) second-generation West Indians, having been raised primarily in the United States, do not necessarily consider themselves as "guests in a foreign land"; and (2) second-generation West Indians have encountered the same obstacles confronted by involuntary minorities and do not consider social barriers, particularly those related to race, as "temporary."[5] Given that second-generation West Indian immigrants are both exposed to their parents' conception of the American opportunity structure and confronted with the challenges common to involuntary minorities, how are we to best understand their perceptions of opportunity and strategies for social mobility?

Immigration studies often present an uncomplicated picture of how individuals perceive opportunities and social mobility. For example, Portes and Zhou (1993) describe the process of "segmented assimilation," whereby acculturation may result from one of several paths: incorporation into (middle-class) mainstream culture; incorporation into the underclass; or assimilation in which individuals draw on the cultural capital of their own immigrant community. Portes and Zhou argue that immersion in the immigrant community buffers immigrant children, protecting them from prejudice and racism, in addition to allowing parents access to material resources that may facilitate upward mobility. For second-generation West Indians, this proves to be somewhat of a dilemma; as a function of race, the West Indian community is often subject to prejudice and discrimination. Conversely, assimilating to African American culture is regarded as a path leading to downward mobility (Portes and Zhou 1993). Curiously, in identifying adaptation options, the authors overlook the existence of the African American middle class and their mobility strategies. They do not consider that African Americans "might provide immigrants with a cultural framework or even a destination for assimilation" (Neckerman, Carter, & Lee 1999, p. 960).

I argue that second-generation West Indians do face racial barriers, and that they respond by employing strategies usually attributed to the African American middle class. These include family involvement, high standards for achievement set by peer groups, and the use of ethnic social networks. However, I also contend that these perceptions of opportunity and modes of mobility are not limited to the middle classes. The experiences of the second-generation West Indians in my study indicate that both low-income and middle-class youth engage in behaviors that encourage mobility for West Indians.

This chapter draws on findings from a larger study that examined the ways in which second-generation West Indians assess the process of upward mobility in relation to their social identities. The discussion presented here focuses on how the second generation navigated the educational system and what resources they mobilized to achieve school success. The analysis is grounded in data from interviews with eighty-five second-generation West Indian immigrants raised primarily in the greater New York metropolitan area. The sample includes low-income, working- and middle-class respondents, in an effort to capture possible variation in these groups' conceptions of perceived opportunities and mechanisms for achievement. Contrary to the CET model (Ogbu 1991a, 1991b, 1992, 1999), my findings suggest that perceptions of mobility (and thus educational aspirations and achievements), emerge as the second generation attempts to reconcile their racial and ethnic identities within an American classification system that is primarily based on race. The type of educational socialization they received in the home, the understandings of race and achievement they developed in their peer groups, their experiences (or lack of experiences) with discrimination in educational institutions, and their use of ethnic social networks are the factors that most significantly influence the second generation's perceptions of opportunity, and thus their pursuit of upward mobility.

Similarly to the work of Annette Hemmings (1996, 1998), I also posit that school context dramatically impacts perceptions of opportunity and strategies of mobility for the West Indian second generation. In this study, "school context" refers to the racial and ethnic makeup of the student body, the institutional racialized (and nonracialized) practices employed by agents of the school (i.e., teachers, guidance counsellors, other administrative staff), as well as the level of student interaction. My research demonstrates the multiple ways in which second-generation West Indians respond to various school contexts in order to bring about the desired result of academic achievement. Understanding that their racial barriers, in and out of school, are by no means "temporary," the respondents in this research actively worked against their negative social positioning and developed strategies that fostered high aspirations and achievement.

Employing Portes and Zhou's (1993) ideology of the utility of the immigrant community in achieving social mobility, I also investigate the function of West Indian social networks in shaping perceptions of opportunity for the second generation. Data indicate that social networks play a greater role in academic aspirations and the educational trajectory of second-generation West Indians than would ordinarily be attributed. Despite racial obstacles, the second generation has been able to gain admittance to several advanced educational programs and/or academic institutions as a result of co-ethnics positioning within the New York employment structure.

In demonstrating the ways that second-generation West Indian immigrants depart from Ogbu's CET model, the specific aims of the chapter are to (1) illustrate context-specific conceptions of achievement, focusing on peer groups in predominantly black and predominantly white institutions; (2)

demonstrate the critical role of ethnic social networks; and (3) encourage those who study the impact of social identity on achievement to conduct further work on the educational experiences of second-generation immigrants so that we may gain a greater understanding of this complex population.

THEORETICAL FRAMEWORK

The assertion that second-generation West Indians exceed the socio-economic status of their parents, and thereby surpass that of African Americans, was made initially by Thomas Sowell (1978). He argued that the socioeconomic success of West Indian immigrants relative to that of African Americans "undermines the explanatory power of current white discrimination as a cause of current black poverty" (Sowell 1978, p. 49). Sowell's work aroused heated debate that focused on verifying or disproving his initial theory, while at the same time scholars sought to explain the differential success patterns between West Indians and African Americans.

Sowell's assertion stimulated several investigations of West Indian immigrants and assessments of their success relative to African Americans, who are seen as a "natural" comparison group due to their shared racial ascription.[6] Scholarship on West Indian immigrants has documented their position in employment and housing markets (Butcher 1994; Crowder 1999; Farley & Allen 1987; Model 1991, 1995; Sowell 1978); their economic success (or lack thereof) relative to African Americans (Butcher 1994; Farley & Allen 1987; Kalmijn 1996; Model 1991, 1995; Sowell 1978; Waldinger 1996); and their reception and subsequent treatment in the United States, along with their adaptive responses to this treatment (Bryce-Laporte 1972, 1987, 1993; Foner 1979, 1985, 1987, 2001; Kasinitz 1992; Vickerman 1999; Waters 1999).

The limited but growing body of research on second-generation West Indians has investigated constructions of racial and ethnic identity in relation to racism and discrimination (Butterfield 2001, 2003, 2004a; Kasinitz, Battle, & Ines 2001; Mollenkopf, Kasinitz, & Waters 1995; S. Stafford 1987; Stepick, Stepick, & Eugene 2001; Waters 1996, 1999, 2001; Woldemikael 1985, 1989); studies also have examined whether the second generation represents continued success from the previous generation or whether members of this group undergo an alternative assimilation process leading to differential mobility outcomes (Butterfield 2001, 2003, 2004b; Kalmijn 1996; Kao & Tienda 1995; Waters 1996, 1999).[7]

Research to date has focused on "objective" indicators of educational and socioeconomic status attainment (e.g., grade-point average, income) among second-generation West Indians (Kasinitz, Battle, & Ines 2001; Stepick, Stepick, & Eugene 2001; see also Dodoo 1991). With the exception of Nancy Lopez (2003), there have been no assessments of the attitudes and belief systems of the members of this population, nor have there been examinations of how these attitudes and beliefs relate to perceived opportunities and achievement.[8] This research addresses these gaps.

Second-generation West Indians—be they high achieving or not—assimilate into a social system with a structured racial hierarchy that automatically relegates black people of all classes and ethnicities to the bottom of the racial ladder (Bashi 1998a; Omi & Winant 1994). However, for many second-generation West Indians, this positioning implies a future that is antithetical to the one they and their parents have envisioned. Contrary to the CET model, this negative social positioning compels second-generation West Indians to establish alternative strategies for achievement. The intent of this chapter is to examine the ways in which the members of the second generation defined achievement for themselves and to analyze the mechanisms they employed to reach their goals.

DESCRIPTION OF RESEARCH AND METHODS

The findings reported here are drawn from research guided by grounded theory methodology (Glaser and Strauss 1967), which allows respondents to present their personal experiences in a way that reveals how they "make sense" of their social world (Patton 1990). Data were collected via semistructured, open-ended interviews with a sample of eighty-five second-generation West Indians, aged twenty to thirty-two.[9] The respondents were part of a larger research project (see Butterfield 2001) that examined constructions of identity among second-generation West Indian immigrants living in metropolitan New York.[10] That study specifically focused on identity in relation to race, ethnicity, gender, and socioeconomic status. The interviews I report on in this chapter took place over two separate periods: I interviewed sixty-five respondents from October 1998 to August 1999, and another twenty respondents from October 2001 to February 2002. The sample was recruited using a modified snowball sampling approach. I tapped my personal network through word of mouth and also spoke with individuals I met through my ties with two West Indian community organizers. I soon had introductions to several individuals who fit the project's age and ethnic criteria. At the conclusion of the initial interview with these first respondents, I solicited each for referrals. Other respondents were recruited when they approached me after learning about the study from peers who had already been interviewed; from neighborhood associates who informed them of my work; or after they had briefly observed my research-related activities in any one of several New York and New Jersey communities.[11]

I selected respondents based on their age, gender, country of origin, and, later, their residential neighborhood. Sampling on place of residence was of particular importance to me, as different metropolitan New York neighborhoods often delineated differences in class status, level of contact with other native-born and immigrant groups, and, in a few cases, length of stay in the United States.[12] I shifted my sampling strategy over time to try to ensure that no relevant categories were missed. For example, I began specifically targeting West Indian male respondents when I realized my sample was becoming female skewed (the final sample is almost evenly split, with forty-four female respondents and forty-one male respondents).

For analytical purposes, I treat "race" and "ethnicity" as distinct concepts. Race is defined as socially constructed distinctions drawn on the basis of physical appearance, while ethnicity is operationalized in terms of distinctions based on national origin, language, religion, food, and other cultural markers.[13] I define "West Indian" to include all peoples not of Asian ancestry who are descended from those born in the Anglophone Caribbean. The thirteen Caricom member nations, the mainland countries of Guyana and Belize, the Caribbean British colonies, and English-speaking Panamanians are covered by that definition.[14] "Second-generation West Indians" are identified as those who have at least one parent who was born in the West Indies.[15]

The respondents' residences covered four of New York City's five boroughs (Brooklyn, Bronx, Manhattan, and Queens), Nassau-Suffolk County, and Newark and Irvington in New Jersey. Over the last few decades, metropolitan New York has absorbed a disproportionately large share of the nation's total West Indian population. Recent estimates put the number of West Indians at approximately 600,000, somewhat more than one-quarter of New York City's total black population (Logan & Deane 2003). Researcher Reuel Rogers asserts that "if the current immigration and demographic trends persist, first- and second-generation West Indians will soon outnumber African Americans in New York City" (2001, p. 164). Consistent with the literature on the residential patterns of West Indians in New York, the majority of respondents resided in Brooklyn and Queens (see Crowder & Tedrow 2001; Foner 1985; Kasinitz 1992; Logan & Deane 2003; Waters 1999).[16]

In addition to probing perceptions of opportunity, the interview schedule included questions about racial and ethnic self-identification; the composition and structure of social networks; the incorporation of ethnicity into household life; the negotiation of ethnic boundaries; and experiences in both school and workplace environments. Interviews averaged two hours and fifteen minutes, with the longest lasting five hours (completed in two meetings) and the shortest, one hour. The locations of the interviews varied. Some took place in the respondent's home or place of employment; others occurred in coffee shops/diners, parks, or fast-food restaurants—wherever was most convenient for the respondent.[17] Each interview was audio-taped and transcribed, then coded and analyzed using a qualitative data computer program.

It is important to note that while this chapter addresses the issue of academic achievement among West Indian adolescents, the data presented here were gathered from young adult West Indians. Researchers Robyn Fivush (1991, 2001) and Katherine Nelson (2003) have argued that memory recovery presents challenges for researchers, including subjects' intentional and unintentional lack of accuracy in recounting past events (see also Freeman 1998). It is normal for individuals to idealize the past, to reconstruct history, and to view the past through the lens of the present. "In addition, research has shown that young adults are simply in a different 'developmental place' than adolescents. This 'different place' includes their perceived 'developmental tasks,' current independence, etc., which includes 'lessons learned' upon looking back and cognitive/intellectual processing capacity" (Spencer 2004). These are important considerations. However, I argue that because the respondents are at a different developmental stage, they can be more objective about their adolescent experiences than was possible when they actually were adolescents. In addition, as young adults, the respondents are more likely to be honest about their past behaviors/histories, as they have no fear of possibly having to suffer consequences for their actions.

RESULTS

Not surprisingly, all of the respondents articulated the dominant narrative of how success is achieved in the United States—through hard work, individual effort, and education. Despite the varying levels of education represented in the sample,[18] all respondents emphasized the importance of educational achievement, coupled with a willingness to "work as hard as you have to" to succeed. The interview data, however, also suggest that the meanings respondents attribute to education and success are complicated by issues of race, class, gender, and ethnicity. Indeed, the respondents created what O'Connor (1999) refers to as "co-narratives." That is, many of them "maintained an ideological commitment to many of the fundamental elements of the dominant theory of making it, but most of them modified the character and structure of the story by incorporating mitigating factors and circumstances that mediate the efficacy of the individual and affect his or her probability of realizing particular social and educational outcomes" (1999, p. 142). In addition to constructing/negotiating their co-narratives through the lens of their social identities, second-generation West Indians shaped their attitudes and ideas in response to the impact of key social institutional milieus. Understandings of race and ethnicity in the larger social environment, peer groups, student-teacher interactions, and social networks had a significant impact on respondents' perceptions of opportunity and achievement.

The Black Divide: Tensions between First-generation West Indian Immigrants and African Americans

To understand the ways in which second-generation West Indians maneuver through educational institutions and how they interact with their African American counterparts requires first addressing the racial and ethnic attitudes they inherited from their parents. Many first-generation West Indian immigrants actively disassociate themselves from African Americans and are quick to point out what they deem as significant differences between the two groups (Butterfield 2001; Vickerman 1999; Waters 1999).[19] First-generation West Indians believe they were/are much harder working and place a higher value on education than do African Americans. These beliefs generally reflect an uncritical acceptance of images of African Americans as "preferring welfare" and being "prone to criminality," stereotypes that are widespread in the United States.[20] The first generation's apparent ease in finding employment in the United States also contributed to their belief that African Americans were "lazy." Members of the first generation were conscious that white employers preferred to hire them over African Americans, and used that knowledge to their own advantage (Waters 1999).

The responses of second-generation West Indians make clear that in communicating the importance of success to their children, members of the first generation often referred to the role of race in achieving one's goals. Children received messages about having to work "twice as hard" due to their racial identity, at the same time that they were being told they "could be and do whatever they set their minds to." The existence of this co-narrative is particularly striking as much of the literature on West Indian immigrants depicts first-generation West Indians as downplaying their racial identity in favor of their ethnic identity (Foner 1985, 1987; Kasinitz 1992; Vickerman 1999; Waters 1999). Instead, it appears that although members of the first generation often resisted identifying with African Americans, they were, nevertheless, well aware of how the American racial classification system worked and how it might impact the life chances of their children. Demali,[21] a twenty-year-old college student, elaborated:

My parents would often act like it didn't matter that I was black or not, that I could do whatever I wanted . . . which is crazy since we were so broke, but hey. . . . They never tried to limit me, but they did remind me that [I] would have to be twenty times better than white people if I wanted to get anywhere. . . . So, while we weren't necessarily caught up with being black, my family did acknowledge that we were black and would talk about it. They just didn't want us to be seen like African Americans.

Demali's comments reflect the ways in which West Indian parents construct a narrative for their children that is at once proactive in relation to future achievement and reactive in regards to perceived racial discrimination. The first generation was cognizant of the fact that racial identity often supersedes other social identities and passed this belief to their children. Nigel, a thirty-year-old assistant principal at a public high school, recounted:

> I don't know why people keep talking about how much better West Indians are than African Americans . . . cuz my dad would always say that to white people, we were only one step above black Americans. He told me that white ladies clutch their bags just as easily around us as they do them [African Americans]. So my parents constantly harassed us about how we dressed, spoke, and made sure that school was our top priority. They thought if we looked the part, and had a good education, we would be less likely to be discriminated against.

As these quotes make clear, the social identity conferred by race-tempered conceptions of opportunity and strategies of mobility given West Indians' placement in America's inequitable social structure. All of the respondents disagreed with their parents' opinions of and behaviors toward African Americans (which I will address in depth in the following section), but they appreciated their parents' honesty about the power of race in shaping their future.

The tensions between these voluntary and involuntary minorities are in many ways just as Ogbu's cultural ecological theory would lead us to expect. But what conclusions are we to draw regarding the children of these two categories of immigrants and their relation to educational institutions and to their peers? Both first-generation West Indians and African Americans have passed their attitudes on to their children, who now confront one another in school. In what ways are social constructs such as race, blackness, and community defined and redefined in school settings? More importantly, how do these social constructs require us to reevaluate the distinctions that Ogbu has drawn between voluntary and involuntary immigrants in relation to how they interpret and respond to social mobility and educational norms for success? The next section examines how peer interactions affect both perceptions of opportunity and educational attainment for the second generation.

PEER GROUPS: FRIENDS OR FOES?

The literature on school achievement notes the importance of peer influence on attitudes toward and behaviors in school (Carter 1999; Lew 2004; MacLeod 1995). For the second-generation respondents, peer groups were sources of both pride and ridicule at different points in their school careers. They recalled being accused of "dressing and talking funny," "listening to crazy music," and not being familiar with "black" culture. This section examines the second generation's experiences in predominantly black and predominantly white school settings and tracks the respondents' efforts as adolescents to be both academically successful and "authentically black."

The Battle of the Ethnic Groups: Predominantly Black School Settings

Half the respondents in the sample had attended predominantly black elementary and high schools. Many talked of initial struggles with African American students around issues of culture, such as language and style of dress. Aubrey, a thirty-year-old paralegal recalled:

> I got jumped the first day of school when I started the third grade. People thought I talked funny, and then my mom put me in these crazy clothes. The clothes would have been fine for Guyana, but not for central Brooklyn. . . . I thought that everything would have been cool because we was all black, but clearly that was not the case. Needless to say, I told my mom to stop putting me in country clothes and shop at the stores that other people's parents went to. Oh . . . and I lost my accent right quick.

Sociologist Prudence Carter has found that low-income African American youth "set boundaries to acquire status among themselves to ward off outsiders . . . as they laid these symbolic boundaries, they also evaluated which of their co-ethnics was most worthy of "black" cultural membership based on their use of specified resources" (2003, p. 142). The data in this study reveal a similar phenomenon during initial interactions between African American and second-generation West Indian youths. The African Americans used particular cultural cues, such as speech patterns and tastes in food and music, to draw boundaries between themselves and the West Indians. In these moments, second-generation students attempted to lose their cultural markers so that they could fit in with the larger student body and be regarded as authentically black. This did not necessarily entail compromising their academic ideals or performance in any way. When I asked Aubrey how trying to adapt to American culture had affected his schoolwork, he replied thoughtfully:

> One thing doesn't have anything to do with the other. I knew that no matter how I dressed or spoke, I still had to do well. . . . I wasn't stupid. . . . I knew who I had to go home to at the end of the day, and what was expected of me. Plus, you forget, everybody in there was black, so

what, we weren't going to work hard? A lot of us worked our butts off!
I mean, somebody had to get good grades . . . and years before that my
mama told me that was going to be me!

Aubrey's comments reveal the factors he saw as essential to his performance
in school: his interactions with his mother and her conceptions of achievement and the fact that black students in the school did not regard good
grades as undesirable.

Aubrey was on the older end of the sample's age range. He and his parents had migrated to New York in 1971. The family settled in the Bedford-
Stuyvesant area of Brooklyn, where Aubrey was one of only a few West Indian children in the neighborhood.[22] He mentioned that when he began his
education, his school was not only predominantly black, but also predominantly African American. Brooklyn has long been understood to be home to
multiple West Indian ethnic enclaves, but as Aubrey's experiences reveal,
time, place, and space play key roles in racial and ethnic group interactions.

The student body was more racially and ethnically mixed at the high
school level. Colin, a twenty-two-year-old college student who attended the
same high school as Aubrey had, remembered the atmosphere:

> When I got to that school, there were mad West Indians up in there. I
> heard it used to have only African Americans, but we wrecking shop over
> there now. It's crazy though . . . when I first started over there, kids were
> split . . . you know, African Americans on one side, West Indians on the
> other, and then the Haitians—who knows where.[23] [Laughs] . . . Lunch
> was always battle of the bands because the African Americans would be
> playing rap and hip-hop, and we'd be blasting reggae and soca.

The critical mass of West Indian immigrants in Bedford-Stuyvesant did
more than change the ethnic composition of the student body at Colin and
Aubrey's high school. It also changed the ways in which blackness came to
be understood. The "unified" West Indian group in the cafeteria also reveals
how a group with similar experiences yet different backgrounds often will
come together for the sake of real (or perceived) competition.

Colin went on to explain that when African Americans were not their reference point, the West Indian students spent their time arguing with one another about who came from the "better" island and had the "better" music.
However, when confronted with a group deemed as culturally different from
their own, the second generation reverted to a "survival of the fittest" attitude. Colin recalled that "the real competition was in class":

> You know, West Indians got so much damn pride that they would try to
> get the best grades to make the African Americans look bad. Then the

African Americans stepped their game up because they didn't want us to make them look like shit. I guess it worked out for everybody in the end.

For these students, academic achievement was reinforced through ethnic competition. It was evident to both West Indians and African Americans that "doing well" was something open to all students rather than just to members of a particular racial or ethnic group. In fact, according to Colin, students who did not at least strive for good grades often were stigmatized and accused of belonging to the "other" ethnic group:

[I]f fools didn't even study or anything, we would accuse them of acting like an African American, and they would do the same to us . . . nobody wanted dead weight.

Of course, not all students engaged in this kind of one-upmanship, but Colin's recollections indicate that the school provided an environment where the definition of blackness included high academic performance. Generally, Colin understood "blackness" as simply a function of skin color and the ability to trace one's heritage back to the African continent. However, he also argued that for nonblack people, and specifically for white people, blackness carried a host of other images and impressions, including inherent laziness, poverty, and most of all, lack of intelligence. Educational achievement was one way to actively fight against stigmatization.

In addition to altering perceptions of achievement, the presence of a large number of West Indians at the school compelled all students to revise their constructions of blackness to include multiple ways of being. Sheila, a twenty-four-year-old private secretary who also had attended a predominantly black high school, remembered the point at which she had realized the fundamental differences between West Indians and African Americans:

When I got to high school and learned about the Civil Rights Movement . . . you know, beyond MLK . . . I didn't know much about it before I started class. All my African American friends had some knowledge about it, and some of their parents had participated in the marches. . . . I always felt like I missed something really important to my history as a black person in this country. . . . So when my African Americans friends say that they do not have an ethnicity, I tell them that yeah, they do. . . . We are all black, but we are not all African American. . . . There is still a southern culture that I am trying to learn about in the same way that they are learning about the history of the Caribbean.

Sheila's comments capture some of the ways in which the second generation's conceptions of themselves in relation to African Americans differed from their parents' attitudes. "Black" became an umbrella term, encompassing all persons of African ancestry. It also came to imply

> a particular kind of struggle that goes with living in this racist society . . . which is why we always got to do our best, so they don't have more reason not to like us.

At the same time, Sheila's invoking of "they" and "us" suggests the ways in which members of the second generation reinforce the lessons they learned from their parents: perceptions of success often remain mediated by race.

"Us" vs. "Them": Predominantly White School Settings

One-third of the sample had attended predominantly white schools.[24] These respondents, like those who attended predominantly black institutions, were confronted with issues of achievement and "authenticity," albeit in a starkly different manner. Second-generation students in predominantly white schools encountered issues of race almost immediately upon entering school. Mervis, a twenty-six-year-old teacher at a private suburban high school, recounted her first impressions:

> By the second week of school, I noticed that all the black kids were in the same classes, and they were all low-level classes. Actually, I remember walking into my honors history class and the teacher telling me that I was in the wrong room. Ol' girl hadn't even asked me my name yet, she just knew that I wasn't supposed to be there by looking at me.

Numerous respondents told me stories similar to Mervis's. From their perspective, the teachers' racist ideology was evident not only in the tracking process, but also in their interpersonal interactions with black students. Teachers frequently made erroneous assumptions about black students' intellect. As one of two students (out of an entering class of 500) who had won academic scholarships to the school, Mervis was especially indignant about the treatment she had received from her teacher. Her outrage at the teacher's behavior is still apparent:

> [W]hat, do black girls not take honors classes? I don't know what pissed me off more . . . that someone challenged MY intelligence or the fact that they had stigmatized the entire race.

Second-generation West Indians in predominately white schools frequently found themselves trying to cope with situations similar to the one Mervis described. For school agents, students' racial identity seemed to take precedence over all else, including their academic performance. Many respondents noted that they had been tracked into the wrong courses, often without ever having had the opportunity to take a placement exam. Others recalled having been held to harsher grading standards than their white counterparts. Some, such as Everald, a twenty-seven-year-old computer programmer, continued to be steered away from high academic performance, even while taking college-track courses. Everald had been encouraged to follow the stereotypic path of the athletic black male.

> I know that the teachers didn't think we were capable of getting good grades. More than one teacher asked me if I was considering a basketball career because I was so tall. Were they asking the white boys that? Hell no!

His experiences clearly illuminate the ways in which "schools and school personnel serve as a location and means for interracial interaction and a means of both affirming and challenging previous racial attitudes and understandings" (Lewis 2003, p. 4).

The circumstances second-generation West Indians faced in school might reasonably have prompted them to modify their conceptions of achievement. The respondents, though, seem to have taken a different tack. Everald described their common strategy this way:

> I knew that they were going to make me work harder for my grades than the white students, but I decided to take them up on it. Cuz who was going to tell my mother that the reason I wasn't doing as well was because my teacher was racist? I wasn't even sure that she would believe me.[25] So, I got together with the some of my black friends and we formed a study group and studied like you wouldn't believe. Teachers found it hard to argue with a perfect paper or a hundred on a test. But then again . . . a few of us were suspected of cheating.

That some of the high-achieving black students were suspected of cheating reveals how deeply ingrained the racist ideology was at Everald's school. Intelligent black students were not even considered the exceptions that proved the rule; they were perceived as simply not capable of attaining such high scores. Everald contended that none of the high-achieving white students was ever accused of cheating. "Because we were black," he surmised, "more than one of us at a time couldn't possible know the right answer."

Interestingly, Everald's strategy of forming a study group was a more common response than I would have initially predicted. Other respondents who had taken similar steps attributed their action to "doing what they had to" to ensure their own academic success. Some respondents had consulted older black students and received advice and/or tutoring on how to maneuver through the school.

Respondents such as Everald viewed their struggle with white teachers and white peers as fighting against the widespread stereotypes of black students as low- and underachieving. Their efforts to redefine others' conceptions of "authentic" Black students demonstrate that many different attitudes about achievement exist within the black community, much as they do in the white community. The proactive approach to their education these students took was particularly striking because the black portion of the school's student body consisted of both second-generation West Indians and African Americans. In the predominately black high school Aubrey and Colin attended, the West Indians and African Americans had used competition with one another as incentives to do well. In the predominantly white context, the groups overlooked their ethnic differences and aided one another in the quest for academic achievement. The competitive factor was still there. Only the reference group changed. Mervis, recalling the competition, commented:

> I don't know if they [the white students] knew it or not, but we [the black students] were always competing with them. . . . There were five people that I hung with, and we would always try to get higher grades than the white kids in our classes . . . if all of us didn't get the top grades, it had to be at least one of us. I know it wasn't right, but hey, . . . it made us better students, I think. What's funny is that after a while teachers and students just accepted that we were smart . . . but I knew there were still limits. For example, some white boys would always try to get some of us to cut class with them. We were cool and all, but I knew that there were still some things that I couldn't get away with because of what I looked like.

As this quote shows, peer interaction can facilitate school achievement. The second generation entered school with a belief in the dominant ideology of success. When they encountered racism and prejudice, contrary to the conventional wisdom, they did not abandon their beliefs but instead clung to them even more passionately. Certainly, not all black students engaged in "retaliatory" achievement strategies, but neither did those who chose other responses make any effort to discourage their classmates from pursuing high performance. Everald recalled an explicitly supportive atmosphere:

> Sure there were a lot of black kids who did not want to be down with the study groups or tutors. I guess they were happy with the grades that they got. But they were mad cool about us trying to get our work done. . . . When the honor rolls came out every term and some of us we on them, the rest of the folks would be cheering for us and yelling at us that

we were "representing" for the whole group . . . you know how it is
. . . we were cool . . . for nerds, anyway.

Everald's statement belies the argument (Fordham and Ogbu 1986) that
black underperforming students disparage black high-achieving students for
acting white. This example illustrates the importance of context in the applicability of the acting-white hypothesis. In addition, Everald's use of the word
"nerd" implies an identity inherently linked to academic performance, but
with no specific racial connotation. Anyone can be a nerd.

IT'S WHO YOU KNOW: ETHNIC SOCIAL NETWORKS

Immigration research has documented the impact of ethnic networks on employment within Asian and Latino communities (Portes 1995; Portes and
Rumbaut 2001; Portes & Zhou 1993; Rumbaut 1994; Tuan 1998) and on educational achievement, most especially among Asians (Lee 2004; Lew 2004;
Louie 2004a, 2004b; Portes and Rumbaut 2001; Zhou 1997; Zhou and
Bankston 1994, 1998). With the notable exception of Bashi (1997, 1998b), little attention has been focused on how ethnic social networks serve West Indian immigrants and their children in regard to either employment or education. Respondents in my sample, particularly those of low income,
reported that ethnic social networks provided resources that were critically
important in helping them navigate the educational terrain.

Demali, the twenty-year-old college student quoted earlier, recounted
how her father's social network had provided her with crucial academic
help:

If my dad didn't have that friend from work whose son went to Brooklyn Tech,[26] I wouldn't even known about it. My dad just came home one
day talking about how I should go there because it was a good school.
I remember that I asked one of the counselors at school about it, and
she told me that it wasn't for me . . . which was crap because I knew that
I had the grades. After that, I had my father have his friend introduce me
to his son. It worked out great cuz he sat me down and told me about
the entrance exam, how to study for it, and what to expect when I got
there.

Demali's educational trajectory would have been very different had her father not befriended a fellow Jamaican at work. Her story also highlights the
fact that black students' aspirations for achievement are sometimes hostage
to factors beyond their control. Respondents frequently mentioned that as
students they (much like their African American counterparts) had been

steered away from certain high schools/colleges by teachers and/or guidance counselors.

Other low-income respondents spoke of learning about educational programs through social networks outside of school. Typically, this happened when a family member was a teacher or knew of a teacher who had access to information about programs for city kids. Aubrey elaborated:

> When I was in high school, I remember going to this program in advanced math and science at City College. Now, I lived in Brooklyn, so what was I doing up in Harlem every Saturday morning for a month, you may ask? Yeah, that's right, every Saturday morning nine to eleven when other kids was in they beds. . . . My mom heard it about it from my aunt who taught up in Harlem. They decided that even though the program was only supposed to be for kids who went to school in Harlem, I needed to be there. . . . At first I hated going because I hated getting out of bed, but the classes were so hard that it became a challenge for me to pass the course . . . and in a good way. I can honestly say that I still use some of the things that I learned in that class today.

Aubrey is only one of many respondents who mentioned utilizing programs in New York City to further their education, a course of action that often involved sacrifice (e.g., less time for sleep, less time with friends).

Middle-class members of the second generation also made use of their social networks, but they did so more systematically than did the low-income respondents. Alecia, a twenty-five-year-old law student, explained how her family's network functioned:

> I don't remember what started it, but in my junior year of high school my mother and I started spending a lot of time with her Caribbean friends and their kids. I wasn't sure what the point was, but we went to museums, libraries, Broadway shows, and the movies together. It was kind of cool to do that, even though I didn't always feel like going. The best part of those ladies was that once they had some college student . . . another Jamaican, of course, come by and tell us about different colleges, how to apply, what admissions committees looked for . . . you name it . . . everything we needed to know done in about three sessions. . . . Now that I think about it, she even tutored me for my SATs.

Given that Alecia was from a middle-class background, she would likely have had access to resources for pertinent college information. However, the presence of the Jamaican college student was a concrete way to reinforce the viability of academic achievement. In addition, the other second-generation West Indians in the group served as a support network during the college application process. What is most striking about this narrative is how closely the behaviors of this informal group of families resemble those of the African American organization, Jack & Jill.[27] Adult members of that organization similarly employ the particular resources at their disposal to facilitate upward mobility for their children.

For both low-income and middle-class respondents, ethnic social networks provided the second generation with access to opportunities for mobility. While these networks did not necessarily buffer the respondents from instances of prejudice and discrimination, they did offer ways to circumvent racism's negative effects.

CONCLUSION

This research addressed second-generation West Indian immigrants' perceptions of opportunity and the mechanisms of achievement that they used. Although the study was based on a small regional sample of second-generation West Indian young adults, the findings do raise questions about the current state of knowledge about West Indian students' relationship to academic institutions, the experiences of voluntary versus involuntary minorities, and the dominant view of black students in general as culturally opposed to academic achievement. The data presented here also demonstrate the ways in which social constructs such as race, blackness, and community are defined and redefined in school settings.

While John Ogbu's (1974, 1978) cultural ecological theory (CET) suggested that children of voluntary immigrants would follow in the path of their parents and acquiesce to racial prejudice and discrimination, the present study suggests that the opposite is actually occurring. Armed with messages from their parents about the significance of their racial identity while confronting various racial barriers, second-generation West Indians are utilizing multiple academic coping strategies. Context-specific conceptions of achievement, particularly peer groups located in predominantly black and predominantly white institutions, as well as ethnic social networks, play a central role in the development of attitudes toward achievement. The study indicates that the second generation developed a variety of individual and collective strategies to stave off the negative effects of discrimination. The combined influence of peer groups, student-teacher interactions, and ethnic social networks facilitated high aspirations and educational achievement. This would imply that a conceptualization of attitudes toward achievement is part of a social, contextual process rather than a specifically cultural one delineated by (im)migration status. Therefore, while the CET model as it relates to voluntary and involuntary minorities has some merits, it appears to be less useful for explaining the experiences of children of black immigrants.

The respondents presented in this study shared common attitudes toward education and articulated similar approaches to academic achievement, regardless of their class status. Given the heterogeneity of the West Indian population, however, this study makes no claim to have captured ideas and experiences shared by all members of the second generation. There are those for whom positive academic outcomes have not been attainable. Under what conditions can some individuals actualize their goals, but others cannot? The concept of acting white and its associated burdens did not resonate with any respondent in my study, but this notion may nevertheless be valid for other students, in other contexts.

Important research still needs to be conducted with this population. Future research questions should consider the following: Given that immigrant children and children of immigrants currently constitute the majority population in several metropolitan New York public schools, how does this translate into perceptions of opportunity? Do these conceptions of achievement carry over into later (i.e., college) years? What are the ways in which perceptions of opportunity change over time? How are any changes in attitudes toward achievement related to confrontations with racialized barriers? Additional research needs to further explore the ways in which social identities, familial experience, and collective group consciousness interact with institutions to shape narratives of opportunity and academic engagement for both voluntary and involuntary immigrants. Considering that immigration is continuing at a rapid rate, studying the experiences and attitudes of second-generation immigrants in relation to academic achievement may provide a lens by which to better understand how schools can serve current and future students.

NOTES

I thank the following for helpful comments and suggestions on earlier drafts of this chapter: Josette Banks, Edward Fergus, Rosamond King, Jamie Lew, Lorelei Vargas, and the contributors to and editors of this volume. Support for the research presented here was provided by grants from the Joseph C. Cornwall Center for Metropolitan Studies and the Institute on Ethnicity, Culture, and the Modern Experience of Rutgers University, Newark.

1. I use the term "African American" to refer to U.S. native-born Blacks whose mother and father also are U.S. native-born Blacks.

2. In these studies, "culture" is defined as constituting a way of life of an entire group that includes codes of manners, dress, language, rituals, norms of behavior, and systems of belief.

3. For a more extensive treatment of CET, see Ogbu (2003) or O'Connor, Horvat, and Lewis's introductory chapter to this volume.

4. Numerous studies address the impact of ethnicity on immigrant youth's educational aspirations and achievement (e.g., Kao, Tienda, & Schneider 1996; Matute-Bianchi 1986; Mehan, Hubbard, & Villanueva 1994; Portes & MacLeod 1996; Suarez-Orozco & Suarez-Orozco 1995). However, none of this research specifically investigates the experiences of black immigrant youth. Kasinitz, Battle, and Ines (2001) and Waters (1999, 2001) examine the educational experiences of West Indian youth, but they do not focus on achievement and perceptions of opportunity.

5. In fact, my data suggest that even first-generation West Indians do not view racial barriers as temporary in any way, but something that can be mediated with a good education and other forms of cultural capital.

6. I would argue that a more valid comparison would pair West Indians with another immigrant group (of color) rather than with a native-born group. The selectivity of migration skews the findings in favor of West Indians when the comparison group is native born. It is only recently that researchers have begun assessing West Indians in relation to another black immigrant group—Africans (see Dodoo 1997; Logan & Deane 2003). Interestingly, African Americans continue to be included in these analyses.

7. Most scholarship on the second generation has been speculative (Foner 1978, 1985; Gans 1992; Portes & Zhou 1993) because it is only recently that children of post-1965 immigrants have reached an age where it would be appropriate to analyze their mobility paths.

8. It is important to note that sociologists Alejandro Portes and Ruben Rumbaut (2001) have conducted in-depth studies on the attitudes and belief systems of the second generation in relation to opportunity and achievement, but they primarily focused on the Latino and Asian adolescent second generation.

9. The upper end of the age range of the sample was set at thirty-two because this was the oldest a child born to post-1965 immigrants could have been at the time the larger study (of which the work reported here is a part) began. The lower end of the age range is meant to capture those now coming into full adulthood and thus primarily responsible for their own lives (younger respondents may still rely on parents or guardians). This age category also encompasses individuals who, although still young, have experienced some socioeconomic advantages and/or disadvantages in the labor market (Mollenkopf, Kasinitz, & Waters 1995).

10. The metropolitan New York area served as my research site due to its absorption of a disproportionately high percentage of the nation's West Indian immigrants. (Census estimates indicate that nearly 40 percent of the city's black population is of West Indian ancestry.) Given the number of West Indian immigrants, in addition to the large numbers of other immigrants of color, and combined with an already significant African American and native White population, New York provides a unique context by which to explore interracial and interethnic interaction. West Indian immigrants and their children have been transforming, and are being transformed by, New York's system of race and ethnic relations. Their presence underscores the way blackness is being renegotiated in an increasingly multiethnic black community both locally and nationally. Moreover, because West Indians are closely identified with, and often live in neighboring areas to, African Americans, examining their experience in New York illuminates the complex ways that West Indians utilize their ethnicity in various contexts.

11. One of my initial respondents was a Brooklyn party promoter and DJ who used his connections to aid me in recruiting additional respondents. This approach helped me reach communities of people I would not likely have had access to through my own networks.

12. For more on the importance of neighborhood location and composition for West Indian immigrants and their children, see Crowder and Tedrow (2001).

13. My examination of ethnic identity and its significance for second-generation West Indian immigrants (Butterfield 2001) looks at the ways in which West Indians define themselves; how these identities influence their social behavior, networks, and attitudes; and how they define the membership boundaries of their group (Barth 1969; Nagel 1994; Waters 1990). In evaluating the salience of ethnic identity, I also use measures drawn from other studies, including preferences for and use of home country language/style of speech, preference for doing business with co-ethnics, church membership or religious affiliation, participation in voluntary organizations, and participation in events and activities sponsored by such organizations (Alba 1985; Nagel 1994; Waters 1990).

14. Almost half of the Panamanian immigrants to the United States are of Jamaican descent (Waters 1999).

15. I also included those respondents who immigrated to the United States before the age of twelve—the group Rumbaut (1991) classified as the "1.5 generation."

16. Specifically, those who lived in the City resided in central Brooklyn, northern Bronx, the upper west side of Manhattan (mainly Harlem), and southeast Queens.

17. Regardless of the site of the interview, I used a one-to-one, interactive interview format with each respondent.

18. Fifty-four percent of the sample had either a college degree or some college experience. The high level of education among the sample can be attributed to the relatively easy access to college provided by the City University of New York. Immigrants and their children predominate in the CUNY system's student body (Mollenkopf, Kasinitz, & Waters 1995).

19. For the first generation, this is true regardless of socioeconomic status; this pattern of attitudes and behavior is not unique to West Indians, however. Many immigrants view their native-born counterparts as "too Americanized" and as not sufficiently hardworking.

20. Ironically, West Indian immigrants are increasingly coming to be identified as having these same negative traits (Butterfield 2001).

21. All names and any identifying characteristics that might compromise the respondents' anonymity have been changed.

22. Aubrey's experience contrasts significantly with that of respondents who grew up in the Flatbush section of Brooklyn during the 1970s, where incoming West Indians quickly outnumbered African American and white residents. The uniqueness of Flatbush is further confirmed by older respondents who grew up in the Bronx, Queens, Long Island, and Newark, all of whom described their families as being one of the few West Indian families in the area during their childhood.

23. As respondents reflected on their educational pasts, it became clear that Haitians were the group most frequently maligned by both West Indians and African Americans. I asked follow-up questions, but no one seemed able to provide a definitive reason for this targeting.

24. All respondents who had attended predominantly white institutions had gone to parochial schools. The remaining 17 percent of the sample had attended racially and ethnically heterogeneous schools. That 17 percent of the sample is not included in the analysis presented in this chapter.

25. Versions of Everald's comment were independently articulated by many other respondents. Parents seem to have initially blindly trusted the schools to operate in the best interest of their children. If students were doing poorly in school, their parents would accuse them of not trying hard enough. Several respondents noted, however, that after they had recounted multiple stories of the unequal treatment they received in school, their parents had, more often than not, interceded with the teachers and/or principal.

26. Considered one of the city's finest high schools, Brooklyn Technical High School is one of three specialized public high schools in New York. It is known for placing its graduates in some of the best colleges in the country. Competition for admission is quite fierce.

27. Jack & Jill is an organization for middle- and upper-class African American children. It facilitates exposure to other African Americans through a variety of social and service activities.

III

THE STRUCTURING OF RACE AND MATERIAL INEQUITIES

6

Reconsidering "Material Conditions": How Neighborhood Context Can Shape Educational Outcomes across Racial Groups

James W. Ainsworth and Greg Wiggan

In the late 1970s, John Ogbu (1978) shifted the debate about school performance. He argued that students from historically oppressed groups engage in a kind of agency by resisting the achievement ideology *because of* racism and racial stratification in the social and economic system.[1] These students, he theorized, perceive their limited access to education, employment, economic opportunities, and social advancement as due to racial barriers. He noted, as well, that in addition to a racialized political system characterized by hegemony and white domination, neighborhoods and residential patterns create resistance in students. Drawing attention to the link between structure and agency at the individual level was a major contribution. Over time, however, Ogbu's prescriptions (and their implications for policy) have attended less and less to the need for structural changes in the social system. Rather, his recent solutions focused primarily on getting students and their parents to acquire the attitudes and habits that white Americans value. For example, in his latest book he advised black families to "assume a proactive role to increase the academic orientation, effort, and performance of their children," noting that "the academic achievement gap is not likely to be closed by restructuring the educational system or by what the schools . . . can do for black students" (2003, p. 274).

Ogbu posited that students with an involuntary minority status respond to racial discrimination in the opportunity structure and the reward system in racialized ways. The students' behaviors are a reaction to perceived racial discrimination; cumulatively, they form what Ogbu calls an oppositional identity. Students' reactions contribute to a culture that is both anti-achievement and anti-intellectual. Ogbu focused on what he viewed as the negative culture of black students, bringing his thesis very close to a culture-of-poverty argument (Lundy 2003). Because he perceived low achievement as resulting from students' own actions (i.e., their embrace of oppositional culture), Ogbu directed his prescriptions toward the students themselves, rather than linking his recommendations to larger social structures.

Research by others shows that African American high school students, contrary to Ogbu's oppositional culture theory, tend to have more positive school-related attitudes than white students (Ainsworth-Darnell & Downey 1998; Cook & Ludwig 1997; Downey & Ainsworth-Darnell 2002). However, these positive attitudes are associated with less positive school-related behaviors than those exhibited by white students. Ainsworth-Darnell and Downey (1998) point to differential "material conditions" as the cause of variations in school-related behaviors and individual outcomes across racial groups. In this chapter, we discuss how one dimension of material conditions, neighborhood context, may lead to racial differences in educational performance.[2] Drawing heavily on William Julius Wilson's (1987, 1991, 1996) social disorganization/social isolation theory, we identify five neighborhood mechanisms: collective socialization, social control, social capital/social networks, limited occupational opportunity, and institutional characteristics. We then examine how each can shape educational outcomes across racial groups. Lastly, we encourage new directions and perspectives in neighborhood research and offer suggestions for policymakers.

RECONSIDERING OGBU'S OPPOSITIONAL CULTURE THEORY: POSITIVE AGENCY AND MICRO-MACRO LINKAGES

Our proposed theoretical alternative to oppositional culture theory incorporates both positive and negative agency into students' perceptions of school success, and emphasizes prescriptions that link structure and agency (see figure 6.1). Rather than assuming that black students will have a negative reaction to racial discrimination in the social and economic system, this approach views student resistance as positively related to achievement, where students view school success as a means of social mobility. Ainsworth-Darnell and Downey (1998) found that black students had more pro-school attitudes than their white counterparts. Furthermore, Cook and Ludwig (1997) found that black and white students had equally high educational expectations. These empirical findings are consistent with other research, which indicates that black students engage in positive agency by giving greater educational effort (Hilliard 1995; Lundy 2003; O'Connor 1997; Perry, Steele, & Hilliard 2003). While some students may resist school success, this behavior may be the result of differences in social class and material conditions, rather than being the racialized reaction Ogbu proposed.[3]

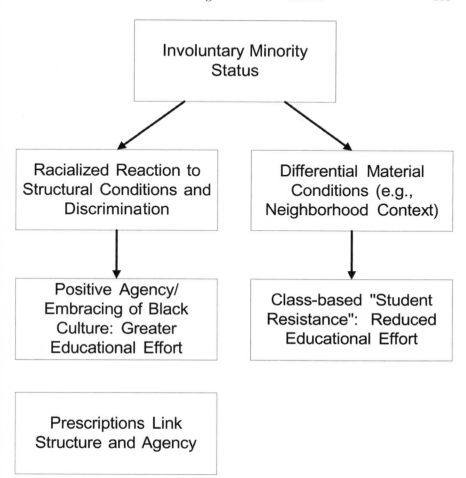

Figure 6.1. Theoretical Alternative to Ogbu's Oppositional Culture Theory

Ogbu's argument, despite its popular appeal (which further increased when he and Fordham [1986] articulated the notion of the "burden of acting white"), is problematic on several counts. MacLeod (1995) shows that resistance to the ideology of achievement is not unique to minorities; poor white students are similarly resistant. Tyson (2002) finds that black students are achievement oriented, that the varying school experiences of black students shape the development of school-related attitudes (rather than all Blacks responding to school in a similar fashion), and that oppositional culture theory is "less useful for explaining the underachievement of middle-class Black students" (p. 1184). Carter (2003) provides evidence that acting white is more closely related to speech, dress, musical tastes, and styles of interaction than it is to academic achievement. Furthermore, Lundy (2003) argues that rather than rejecting academic success, many black students see high achievement as cultural agency and resistance to white supremacy. Similarly, O'Connor (1997) concludes that some African American students, armed with knowledge of how a collective black struggle can combat racial oppression, develop the agency necessary for engaging successfully in school.

These and similar studies demonstrate that students' awareness of structural inequalities (e.g., racism, discrimination, sexism, etc.) that place minorities at a social and economic disadvantage does not necessarily result in anti-achievement dispositions. Rather, students may engage themselves in school with the hope of producing positive change (Hilliard 1995). These findings diverge from Ogbu's arguments that students disengage from schools and other institutions that reflect or contribute to racism and social inequality. Ainsworth-Darnell and Downey (1998) and Ainsworth (2002) argue that minority students generally report high levels of pro-school attitudes. In addition, they note that oppositional peer culture is not specifically related to school achievement. It may be, as Carter (2003) has found, invoked when minority students adopt the language, music, and attire of the dominant group.

The relative influence of micro- and macro-level processes, agency, and structure on students' performance continues to be hotly debated in the literature on achievement. Ogbu's arguments and those of researchers in the same tradition, like McWhorter (2000), have a mass appeal, perhaps because they seem to hold students responsible for school failure without reaching back to implicate the social structures that create inequality in the educational system. The aim of this chapter is to help bring structure back into the student achievement debate by looking at neighborhood processes as a structural condition that affects students' performance.

NEIGHBORHOOD CONTEXT AS ONE ASPECT OF MATERIAL CONDITIONS

Research suggests that concentration of poverty in urban areas intensified during the 1970s (Massey & Eggers 1993; Wilson 1996) and became extreme during the 1980s (Coulton, Pandey, & Chow 1990; Kasarda 1993; Krivo et al. 1998). By 1990, two in five urban census tracts had at least a 20 percent poverty rate, and one in seven had poverty rates over 40 percent (Kasarda 1993). This disturbing trend has prompted renewed interest in the effects of neighborhood-level conditions on individual-level outcomes. A prominent concern is that high levels of neighborhood poverty, combined with race and class residential segregation, promote a wide variety of negative behaviors and attitudes (Massey & Denton 1993; Massey, Gross & Eggers 1991; Wilson 1987, 1996). As Massey, Gross, and Eggers (1991) argue, "since people who occupy the same space are likely to interact frequently and intensely, neighborhoods have a profound effect on the values, beliefs, and knowledge of the people who grow up and live within them" (p. 398).

One dramatic way in which neighborhoods may affect social mobility and quality of life is through their influence on the educational outcomes of young residents. Dropout rates in severely distressed neighborhoods are more than three times higher than those in nonpoverty-stricken neighborhoods, and jobless rates for young high school dropouts in distressed urban neighborhoods often are over 80 percent (Kasarda 1993). Although numerous studies have detailed the causes of concentrated urban poverty and explored its association with behavioral outcomes (Fainstein 1986–1987; Farley 1988; Hughes 1989; Jargowsky & Bane 1991; Massey & Denton 1993; Wilson 1987, 1996), empirical research generally has neglected the processes through which neighborhood disadvantage influences individual and group behavior (for recent notable exceptions, see Ainsworth [2002], South & Baumer [2000], and Turley [2003]), let alone how these processes may differ across race. Unless we consider both structural and individual factors and their relationship to one another, our understanding of educational processes will remain incomplete, and our directives for bringing an end to chronic school failure will never achieve their goals. Fleshing out the degree to which neighborhood characteristics influence educational outcomes is key to understanding the processes that reproduce social inequality in general, as well as across racial groups. To this end, we delineate some neighborhood characteristics that influence educational outcomes, identify mechanisms that mediate these associations, and assess the degree to which students' race conditions the impact of neighborhood context.

WHICH NEIGHBORHOOD CHARACTERISTICS AFFECT EDUCATIONAL OUTCOMES?

Although Wilson (1987, 1996) provides several theoretical reasons why neighborhood context should affect educational outcomes, until recently little empirical work had tested these connections. Steinberg (1989), for instance, reported that systematic studies of the relationship between families, neighborhoods, and education were "virtually nonexistent." A year later, Jencks and Mayer (1990) reviewed the literature and found only two studies, Datcher (1982) and Corcoran et al. (1987), addressing school and neighborhood effects on educational attainment and cognitive skills. Both studies report that positive neighborhood characteristics are related to gains in educational attainment.

Since Steinberg's assessment and Jencks and Mayer's review, a number of researchers have begun examining the impact of neighborhood characteristics on educational performance (Brooks-Gunn et al. 1993; Catsambis & Beveridge 2001; Chase-Lansdale, & Gordon 1996; Chase-Lansdale et al. 1997; Connell & Halpern-Felsher 1997; Connell et al. 1995; Crane 1991; Dornbusch, Ritter, & Steinberg 1991; Duncan 1994; Duncan, Brooks-Gunn, & Klebanov 1994; Ensminger, Lamkin, & Jacobson 1996; Entwisle, Alexander, & Olson 1994; Garner & Raudenbush 1991; Halpern-Felsher et al. 1997; Klebanov et al. 1997; Spencer et al. 1997; Turley 2003). One conclusion these empirical studies consistently support is that some aspects of the neighborhood influence educational success. Beyond this broad statement, however, determining the relative importance of neighborhood characteristics has been difficult because of inconsistencies in terms of which neighborhood characteristics are examined.

Most commonly, researchers look at indicators of neighborhood socioeconomic composition. Several studies find that children living in neighborhoods with affluent residents benefit educationally regardless of their own family's socioeconomic status. For example, the presence of high-status neighbors is associated with a lower probability of dropping out of high school (Brooks-Gunn et al. 1993; Crane 1991), an increased likelihood of school completion (Duncan 1994 [for all groups except black males]; Ensminger, Lamkin, & Jacobson 1996 [among male adolescents]), and higher test scores (Turley 2003). Moreover, high socioeconomic status neighbors are associated with positive school- and cognitive-related outcomes among young children (Brooks-Gunn et al. 1993; Duncan, Brooks-Gunn, & Klebanov 1994; Klebanov et al. 1997).

Other studies, focusing on negative neighborhood characteristics, conclude that the presence of low socioeconomic status neighbors has a negative effect on students' educational and other related outcomes. For example, the presence of poor neighbors is a significant predictor of dropout status, although the size of this detrimental effect is considerably less than the beneficial effect of affluent neighbors (Clark 1992). In addition, the presence of poor neighbors is related to behavior problems among young children (Duncan, Brooks-Gunn, & Klebanov 1994). Moreover, poor neighborhoods and neighborhoods with high levels of male joblessness are associated with less cognitively stimulating home environments (Klebanov et al. 1997).

Despite these gains in understanding in recent years, neighborhood research has yet to resolve many important issues related to the effects of neighborhood context on individual educational performance. Questions remain about which neighborhood characteristics matter most in terms of educational performance. Other issues, such as *how* neighborhood context affects educational outcomes, and whether neighborhood processes vary across racial groups, continue to be underinvestigated.

VARIATION IN NEIGHBORHOOD EFFECTS ACROSS RACES

While much of the neighborhood literature discussed above has focused on individual-level outcomes in general, the intent of Ogbu's oppositional culture theory is specific. It is meant to address *racial* differences in educational performance. Therefore, the questions we need to ask and answer are: Are children from different racial groups affected similarly by the neighborhood context in which they live?; and Do the mediating processes different for various racial groups?

Several studies suggest that neighborhood effects are stronger for white children than they are for black children (Brooks-Gunn et al. 1993; Datcher 1982; Duncan 1994; Halpern-Felsher et al. 1997). Some report, for instance, that white teenagers are more likely to benefit from the presence of affluent neighbors, in terms of staying in school (Brooks-Gunn et al. 1993) and educational attainment (Datcher 1982), than are black teenagers. Similarly, Halpern-Felsher et al. (1997) find that among early adolescents, white males demonstrate fewer educational risk behaviors when living in neighborhoods with a higher proportion of middle-class neighbors, and that among middle adolescents, all but black males benefit from high socioeconomic status neighbors in terms of number of years of schooling completed and educational risk behaviors.

Alternatively, some research suggests that Blacks are affected more strongly by neighborhood context than Whites (Chase-Lansdale & Gordon 1996; Duncan 1994; Halpern-Felsher et al. 1997). For instance, black males are more likely to drop out of high school if they live in a neighborhood that has a high proportion of black residents (Duncan 1994), and Blacks also are more likely to complete school when positive role models are present in their neighborhoods, but only if those role models are also black (Duncan 1994; Halpern-Felsher et al. 1997; Turley 2003). Furthermore, higher levels of behavior problems are reported among Blacks, but not Whites, in neighborhoods characterized by high rates of male joblessness (Chase-Lansdale & Gordon 1996).

Studies also support the position that Blacks and Whites are influenced by their neighborhood context, but the specific effects on each group vary because the two tend to reside in different types of neighborhoods. Dornbusch, Ritter, and Steinberg (1991) argue that Blacks and Whites are affected similarly by neighborhood problems, but that Blacks face more of these problems because they live in more disadvantaged neighborhoods than Whites. Klebenov et al. (1997) also suggest that racial differences in neighborhood effects vary depending on the type of neighborhood. Whites living in resource-poor neighborhoods receive greater returns from having high quality home environments, in terms of their verbal IQ scores and instances of behavioral problems, than do Blacks. Furthermore, Klebenov et al. suggest that such results stem from the fact that black children, on average, live in poorer neighbor-hoods than do Whites.

Overall, the neighborhood literature suggests that Whites are more likely to benefit from living in advantaged neighborhoods, and that Blacks are more likely to suffer from living in disadvantaged neighborhoods. But are these types of racial differences the result simply of differences in the racial distribution across neighborhood types, or are neighborhood level processes racialized? The picture is muddled because there is a serious lack of empiri-cal data that examine whether the processes through which neighborhoods shape individual level outcomes differ across racial groups. Even more lim-ited is theorizing on this topic. Our focus on material conditions is not meant to deny that race and racism persists as important features in American life. They do. What neighborhood researchers have yet to address is how and why structural factors might differentially affect youth from different racial backgrounds.

NEIGHBORHOOD CONTEXTUAL EFFECTS ON EDUCATIONAL OUTCOMES

Wilson (1987, 1996) argues that the social isolation and disorganization ex-perienced by inner-city residents (who are disproportionately black) results in major social problems, including a prevalence of delinquent subcultures, a weakening of basic institutions, and a lack of social control. These prob-lems, in turn, contribute to residents' high rate of educational failure. Ac-cording to Simcha-Fagan and Schwartz (1986), socialization processes medi-ate neighborhood effects on individual outcomes to a large extent. This suggests that the common strategy of considering only direct effects of so-cialization should be rethought. Wilson and others have described five in-terrelated mechanisms through which neighborhood characteristics affect educational achievement: collective socialization, social control, social capi-tal or social networks, differential occupational opportunity, and institutional (i.e., school) characteristics. We examine these processes and assess the de-gree to which they differ across racial groups.

Collective Socialization

According to Wilson (1996), neighborhood characteristics influence col-lective socialization processes by shaping the type of role models youth are exposed to outside the home. He believes that neighborhoods where most adults have steady jobs foster behaviors and attitudes conducive to success in both school and work. Working adults display such behaviors and atti-tudes as the association of effort with rewards, a stable daily routine, and personal responsibility for one's actions. Children who live in this kind of environment are more likely to value education, adhere to school norms, work hard, and stay out of trouble because that is what they see modeled for them by neighborhood adults.

In neighborhoods where most adults do not work, Wilson argues, life can become "incoherent" for youths, due to the lack of structuring norms normally modeled by working adults (1991, p. 10). The specifically school-related behaviors and attitudes of youth in disadvantaged neighborhoods are likely to be conflicted because of the competing influence of mainstream ideological imperatives and structural constraints resulting from a lack of opportunity that prevents youth from reaching their goals (Anderson 1999). Wilson (1996) argues that the typical inner-city "ghetto" culture includes many elements of mainstream culture, including an achievement ideology that hard work in school will pay off in terms of a good job. The contention that "ghetto" residents adhere to the basic values of American society is also consistent with the findings of ethnographic studies (Anderson 1978, 1999; Hannerz 1969; Liebow 1967; MacLeod 1995; Rainwater 1966).

What sets residents of disadvantaged neighborhoods apart from other Americans is their inability to realize such ideals through legitimate means. Restricted opportunities and other social constraints stymie these residents' upward mobility (Massey & Denton 1993; Massey & Fong 1990; Wilson 1996).[4] According to Merton's strain theory (1938), the inability to access legitimate means for socially desirable ends is likely to produce innovative or structurally adaptive behaviors that are inconsistent with the values inner-city youth hold. For example, Anderson (1990) describes how black youths "grit" or "go for bad" as a defense mechanism to protect themselves from situations they perceive as dangerous. According to Anderson, "many black youths, law-abiding or otherwise, exude an offensive/defensive aura because they themselves regard the streets as a jungle" (p. 173). Thus, while some residents of disadvantaged neighborhoods may gain status by adhering to the mainstream ideology and by putting down their neighbors who do not (Wacquant 1996), others are likely to scorn conventional American values (Anderson 1990). As Massey and Denton (1993) put it,

> In response to the harsh and isolated conditions of ghetto life, a segment of the urban black population has evolved a set of behaviors, attitudes, and values that are increasingly at variance with those held in the wider society. . . . As a result, an alternative status system has evolved within America's ghettos that is defined *in opposition to* the basic ideals and values of American society. [pp. 165–167, emphasis is original]

Structurally adaptive behaviors and attitudes that discourage success in school and work are examples of divergent values that may emerge in disadvantaged neighborhoods (Hannerz 1969; Swidler 1986; Wilson 1996).

Specifically, in neighborhoods with weak labor force attachment, youth may perceive unemployment or underemployment as normative (Ricketts & Sawhill 1988; Wilson 1991). They are less likely to develop educationally beneficial skills (e.g., the ability to rationally plan their future) and attitudes (e.g., associating hard work with success), because neighborhood adults do not demonstrate these behaviors and beliefs. Moreover, with few real-life examples to confirm that hard work translates into success, children in disadvantaged neighborhoods are likely to feel powerless to control their own fate. They may lack confidence in their abilities or may judge the structural constraints too great to be overcome (Wilson 1991).[5]

Ainsworth (2002) concludes that collective socialization processes account for more of the neighborhood effect on educational performance than the other four mechanisms discussed below. Whether black and white students are affected similarly by neighborhood-level socialization remains open to debate, however. Two studies address this question directly. Turley (2003) finds that white students' test scores and behaviors improve as a result of living in neighborhoods with high proportions of high-status residents, but the same is not true for black students. Black students benefit only when the high-status residents were also black. South and Crowder (2000) found evidence of racial differences in socialization processes related to the timing of first marriage. They contend that residing in disadvantaged neighborhoods propels white residents into first marriages. African Americans who live in disadvantaged neighborhoods delay marriage.

Social Control

Neighborhood levels of social control, or the monitoring and sanctioning of deviant behavior, may indirectly influence local youths' educational performance. Wilson (1996) argues that inner-city black neighborhoods have experienced a recent exodus of middle-class and stable working-class families and an increase in single-parent families (also see Kasarda 1993). Such trends are apt to increase the child/adult ratios in these neighborhoods. With fewer adults per child, there is a greater risk of social disorganization (i.e., an inability to adequately monitor youth activities) because single parents tend to be less involved in neighborhood organizations such as schools. Thus, this change contributes to both social disorganization and a weakening of social control.

Steinberg (1987) cites three reasons why increased numbers of single-parent households result in less supervision of youths: there are fewer adults to monitor the activities of youths in general; working single parents may spend less time monitoring their own children's activities; and some adults in the most disadvantaged neighborhoods may rationally choose to isolate themselves from their neighbors because they believe that interacting with them could be dangerous. The falloff in adult monitoring of youth activities in turn leads to an increase in deviant behavior because young peoples' problem behaviors are not sanctioned.

Neighborhoods with fewer adults also are likely to have fewer people involved in organizing community activities for neighborhood youth (Anderson 1990). Children in such communities have fewer choices about how to spend their time in constructive ways and therefore are more likely to take part in deviant activities (Wacquant 1996). With limited adult supervision, peer-group influences may become stronger relative to parental influence. If so, subcultures that resist mainstream (adult) culture—including school norms —are more likely to develop. Brody et al. (2001) provide supporting evidence for this perspective. They report that in small towns and rural areas, deviant behaviors resulting from structural problems are similar to those found in inner-city neighborhoods. Brody et al. maintain that children who live in disadvantaged communities, whether urban or rural, have a higher probability for antisocial behaviors. South, Baumer, and Lutz (2003) argue that neighborhood disadvantage impedes educational attainment because youth are placed into social networks that do not value academic achievement. Alternatively, Stewart, Simons, and Conger (2002) contend that living in a violent neighborhood does not produce violent children; in their view, micro-level effects of family, peers, and individual characteristics are more important considerations.

Social Capital/Social Networks

A third mechanism through which neighborhood context can influence educational outcomes involves the amount and quality of social capital (habitus and social networks) in a given community (Wilson 1996). Van Haitsma (1989) argues that all else being equal, larger social networks should be more beneficial than smaller social networks. Shaw and McKay (1942) postulate that informal local friendship networks are a key dimension of community organization; these networks increase the likelihood that community members will recognize strangers and exert social control over deviant behavior. Sampson and Groves (1989) provide support for this, noting that communities characterized by sparse friendship networks have higher crime and delinquency rates.

It follows that children who live in advantaged neighborhoods are more likely to be exposed to helpful social networks, or to adults who can provide resources, information, and opportunities that may be educationally beneficial (e.g., the use of personal computers or other technology, job opportunities, or help with a science fair project), than are children from disadvantaged neighborhoods. For example, Horvat, Weininger, and Lareau (2003) find that middle-class parents are more likely to react collectively to effectively use information, expertise, and authority to promote advantage for their children in school.[6] Furthermore, involved neighbors may act as positive role models for other neighborhood adults by encouraging them to support and mentor neighborhood children. Such adult involvement is likely to integrate children into mainstream culture and promote their academic success by exposing them to positive, pro-school role models and by limiting their involvement in anti-school peer-group cultures. Finally, social networks in this type of neighborhood are likely to transcend family effects, because adults outside the home help monitor neighborhood children (Wilson 1996). The social capital provided by neighborhood adults who support pro-schooling and pro-work norms will benefit local youths' educational outcomes.

Alternatively, individuals in impoverished neighborhoods may be disadvantaged not only by smaller social networks (Wacquant & Wilson 1989), but also by networks that are less beneficial, owing to the relatively low social position of their members (Sampson & Groves 1989). Ties to groups or individuals with few resources could be disadvantageous because those ties may represent obligations rather than opportunities to draw on each other's useful information and resources (Van Haitsma 1989). The importance of neighborhood context is further supported by Wilson's (1996) argument that in impoverished neighborhoods "children are disadvantaged because the social interaction among neighbors tends to be confined to those whose skills, styles, orientations, and habits are not as conducive to promoting positive social outcomes as are those in more stable neighborhoods" (p. 63).

Finally, in neighborhoods with widespread resistance to mainstream norms, strong social networks could prove detrimental to children's educational attainment because such neighborhoods would provide negative, anti-school role models and limited monitoring and sanctioning of problem behaviors. In such cases, intentional family-level social isolation may be an adaptive strategy to counteract negative neighborhood effects.

Limited Occupational Opportunity

Wilson (1996) also emphasizes the importance of occupational opportunity in structuring the lives of neighborhood youths. Several researchers have argued that perceptions of occupational opportunity positively affect educational outcomes (Ainsworth-Darnell & Downey 1998; MacLeod 1995; Ogbu 1978; Willis 1977). While most students, regardless of their neighborhood type, are taught that anyone can be successful if they work hard enough, the degree to which this ideology is supported by adolescents' concrete experiences may vary by neighborhood context (Massey, Gross, & Eggers 1991; Turner et al. 1991; Wilson 1987). Lewin-Epstein

(1985) and Osterman (1980) report that labor markets for youths correspond closely with their neighborhood. The jobs available in a neighborhood thus shape adolescents' early occupational opportunities. Moreover, Neckerman and Kirscherman (1991) find that youth from disadvantaged neighborhoods are more likely to face employment discrimination. They report that employers use a youth's residential address as a marker of reliability, productivity, and even race. Residential location alone thus can limit youths' chances for employment, regardless of their work ethic or positive employment track record. If students are motivated to succeed in school because they believe education will result in better employment, residence-based discrimination may erode or even eradicate this belief and undermine their academic effort.

Youth in disadvantaged neighborhoods are also more likely to have poor work histories. Typically, the few jobs available to them do not have starting salaries and working conditions that would encourage employee stability; most openings are for service-sector positions that have high turnover (Kasarda 1989; Petterson 1997). Moreover, Wilson (1996) argues that the weak informal employment networks in disadvantaged neighborhoods reduce the chances that neighborhood youths will gain important human capital skills, making them unattractive to employers offering better jobs, regardless of the youths' abilities or motivation to succeed. In addition, the cost of commuting keeps inner-city Blacks from working outside their neighborhoods (Kasarda 1988; Wilson 1996). Lastly, if youths living in disadvantaged neighborhoods perceive no difference in the occupational prospects of their older peers who completed high school and those who dropped out, they are likely to become discouraged and stop putting forth academic effort. In a study supporting this theoretical position, Bellair and Roscigno (2000) conclude that the absence of work and the presence of low-paying service industry job are precursors to delinquency. It is logical that the same process could lead to poorer educational performance.

Institutional Characteristics

The last of the five mechanisms through which neighborhood context can influence educational outcomes is the neighborhood's effect on institutions, particularly the local schools. School quality varies with neighborhood context. Neighborhood schools in disadvantaged neighborhoods are unable to recruit and retain quality educators (Jencks & Mayer 1990). Wacquant (1996) argues that students from disadvantaged neighborhoods are more likely to attend inferior schools that spend less time on teaching and learning. In support of this position, Wilson (1996) states that inner-city residents are more likely to complain about uncaring and unqualified teachers and lack of school resources. Similarly, Simcha-Fagan and Schwartz (1986) claim that neighborhood effects on an individual's association with delinquent peers are primarily indirect and mediated through weak attachment to school. Institutionally based mediation of neighborhood effects seems likely, but it has received relatively little theoretical or empirical consideration in the neighborhood literature.

On the other hand, Welsh, Greene, and Jenkins (1999) find unwarranted the assumption that poor communities produce bad schools, where bad schools are associated with violence and poor school performance (see Sheley, McGee, & Wright 1995; Sheley & Wright 1998). Instead, they assert that individual-level factors like student beliefs and practices have the most significant effect on school misconduct and performance. They conclude that a "school is neither blessed nor doomed entirely on the basis of where it is located" (Welsh, Greene, & Jenkins 1999, p. 108).

In summary, few studies have specifically addressed the mediating mechanisms (i.e., collective socialization, social control, social capital/social networks, limited occupational opportunity, and institutional characteristics) that link neighborhood context and educational outcomes. Several studies have pointed out the need for such research, however (Connell & Halpern-Felsher 1997; Datcher 1982; Duncan 1994; Ensminger, Lamkin, & Jacobson 1996; Garner & Raudenbush 1991). Connell and Halpern-Felsher (1997) propose that an "enormous gap in our empirical representation of processes mediating neighborhood effects on adolescent outcomes" (p. 197). The question of how neighborhood context influences individual outcomes (e.g., educational performance) is arguably the most important unanswered question in neighborhood research. As we learn more about how neighborhood-level processes shape school performance, the literature may recapture a focus on Ogbu's original contribution, namely, the link between material conditions and individual-level achievement.

CONCLUSION

The goal of this chapter was to encourage researchers who study racial difference in educational performance to look beyond the debates concerning oppositional culture theory and the burden-of-acting-white hypothesis and instead reconsider Ogbu's important insight into how structure shapes agency. Specifically, we urge systematic attention to the different material conditions that black and white students face. We contend that the relatively poor school-related behaviors demonstrated by some black students (Ainsworth-Darnell & Downey 1998) do not stem from poor school-related attitudes, as is commonly claimed by proponents of the oppositional culture theory. Instead, these student behaviors reflect different structural conditions.

We examined existing findings regarding the effects of one such condition, neighborhood context. However, other interrelated structural factors (e.g., broader local labor market context or school/school district characteristics) also likely shape disparities in educational performance. Thus, we believe a multidimensional approach is needed in order to adequately explain the complex process of educational achievement. An ideal starting point is the work of William Julius Wilson. Although his social isolation/disorganization theory (1987, 1996) represents the leading view regarding the causes and consequences of concentrated poverty in U.S. cities, overspecialization in the field of educational research has tended to obscure this structural perspective. We hope that future researchers will incorporate structural factors more systematically in their studies of educational performance.

One difficulty associated with such a shift in perspective is that it presents new challenges for policymaking. Bringing about significant change in structural conditions is not easy. Since public policy cannot quickly ameliorate the problems associated with living in a disadvantaged neighborhood, understanding *how* neighborhoods affect individual level outcomes may be an important way to inform social action. We described five potential mediating mechanisms between neighborhood context and educational outcomes. Developing educational policies that target collective socialization, social control, social capital/social networks, limited occupational opportunity, and institutional characteristics may improve Blacks' academic performance relative to Whites.

On the other hand, some potential strategies that would target these mediating mechanisms could be misguided. For example, policymakers might find the idea of building social networks among parents an attractive solution —inasmuch as it does not cost money and it puts the onus on parents. But this strategy is likely to do little to resolve the educational problems of children in disadvantaged neighborhoods. When parents lack access to valuable resources and information, social networks may be less helpful and the benefits associated with enhanced social networks may not impact the education of some of the most needy students, namely, those who are poor and members of racial minorities (Horvat, Weininger, and Lareau 2003). If poor students and minorities, particularly poor blacks, are excluded from white-dominated social networks, then fostering parental links will not affect many of the social problems associated with neighborhood disadvantage.

Ultimately, targeting mediating mechanisms addresses the symptoms rather than the root causes of racial achievement disparities. In our view, the foundational causes of racial disparities in education—such as discrimination in housing (which leads to racial residential segregation), unequal funding of schools through local property taxes, racial inequality in school quality, and the lack of stable legitimate employment in urban centers—must be addressed if we are to eliminate the problems of school failure and low student achievement.

174   *Chapter 6*

NOTES

Direct all correspondence to James W. Ainsworth, Department of Sociology, Georgia State University, University Plaza, General Classrooms 1063, Atlanta, GA 30303 (socjwa@panther.gsu.edu). The authors wish to acknowledge Douglas Downey, Lauren Krivo, Vincent Roscigno, and the other authors/editors of this volume for helpful comments. This research was supported by a grant from the American Educational Research Association, which receives funds for its AERA Grants Program from the National Center for Education Statistics and the Office of Education Research and Improvement (U.S. Department of Education) and from the National Science Foundation under NSF Grant #RED-9452861. Opinions expressed are the authors' and do not necessarily reflect those of the granting agencies.

1. During a gathering at a national conference a few years ago, a late-career sociologist pulled the first author aside to talk about the impact of oppositional culture theory. He said that when Ogbu's ideas were first presented, they reshaped the landscape of thought related to race and educational inequality. At that time (1978), highly individualistic explanations of racial inequality (such as the culture-of-poverty thesis) held sway; Ogbu's theory brought the connection between structure and agency into the discussion. Suddenly, racial inequality in schooling had to do with broader structural conditions, such as occupational opportunities and related racial discrimination. This was a monumental contribution. Unfortunately, the educational inequality literature increasingly has ignored the structural aspects of Ogbu's ideas. This chapter aims to help refocus the discussion on broader social structures and how they shape student performance.

2. "Neighborhoods" are both conceptually slippery and difficult to operationalize. For the purpose of this conceptual discussion, neighborhoods are defined as socially constructed geographic areas with boundaries that are generally, although not necessarily universally, agreed upon. Neighborhoods may or may not have names, promote a sense of membership, form organizations, or be defined as such by residents and outsiders; but neighborhoods are seen as shaping the lived experience of residents through interactions and institutional mechanisms.

3. A theoretical distinction between social class and "material conditions" is useful here. In this discussion, "social class" refers to family level characteristics such as parental occupational prestige, education, income, and wealth. "Material conditions," on the other hand, refers to a broader set of factors both within the family and beyond. For example, family-level material conditions aptly refer to family structure, number of siblings, and the like. However, our conception of material conditions is much more expansive, and includes dimensions such as neighborhood context, school characteristics, and labor market conditions. In short, material conditions and those structural factors, largely beyond the control of the individual student, that shape their experience and constrain their opportunity.

4. Gans (1996) discusses the negative aspects of American culture's greater encouragement of high aspirations, and even expectations, among the poor relative to other societies. He argues that poor Americans who do not reduce their aspirations have a higher risk of depression and other mental illnesses.

5. We recognize that role modeling occurs within homes as well as within neighborhoods. Our emphasis on the latter is not meant to downplay the importance of parental role modeling. Rather, we are simply arguing that youths consider neighborhood role models when making evaluations about their own life prospects. Neighborhood context, therefore, affects the development of skills, attitudes, and norms over and above the effects of household influences.

6. Horvat, Weininger, and Lareau (2003) did not find substantial differences between Blacks and Whites with respect to the effective use of social networks.

7

Whiteness in School: How Race Shapes Black Students' Opportunities

Amanda E. Lewis

Ogbu's cultural ecological theory (CET) incorporates both structural and cultural explanations for black students' school outcomes. For example, the theory is premised on a recognition that educational policies, treatment of black children within schools and classrooms, and the ways in which society does or does not reward Blacks' educational accomplishments all influence school performance. The theory also posits that discrimination alone is not enough of an explanation for minority school outcomes; we must also pay attention to the cultural aspects or the attitudes, beliefs, and behaviors of children, families, and communities. Fordham and Ogbu's "acting-white" hypothesis is an example of one part of the "cultural" in CET. As Ogbu (1990a, p. 53) summarized it, "[Involuntary minorities] appear to avoid adopting serious academic attitudes and persevering efforts in their schoolwork . . . partly because they have internalized their groups' belief that such attitudes and behaviors are 'White,' and partly because they are uncertain of acceptance by Whites even if they succeed in learning to 'act White' and subsequently lose the support of their group." Thus, the theory goes, black students develop oppositional culture to school, which depresses their performance.

As outlined in the introduction to this volume, and irrespective of Ogbu's intentions, the structural or ecological part of his theory has received far less attention in recent years than the cultural aspects. Moreover, discussion of the cultural aspects of the theory, which specifically blame black students, their peer cultures, or their communities for their lack of school success, often take place absent any discussion of the larger context or the structural aspects of CET. That is, focus has been on the values and attitudes of black children and families, rather than on the extent and adequacy of their educational opportunities. While Ogbu's original theory might have offered a multilevel framework for understanding minority school success, the greater attention to a select aspect of this theory is not only theoretically problematic but practically, undermines our ability to develop public policy that will actually improve black students' schooling experiences.

The theory of race embedded within the acting-white hypothesis and related oppositional culture theories is one in which race fundamentally operates at the level of the cultural. Though structure is implied as the "origin" or source of opposition, the problem is defined as one that resides in the hearts and minds and social networks of black students. Thus, the solution is for them to get their collective act together. This fundamentally confuses causal ordering and is doomed to never provide a successful solution to the real problem of racial inequality and inadequate educational opportunity. In a parallel example, when we try to understand the alarmingly high rates of asthma among inner-city black children, it would be absurd to suggest that the problem is that they do not value proper breathing techniques. Neither is it particularly effective over the long run to address the symptoms by prescribing inhalers and other medications to each individual child. Rather, a real solution requires confronting the larger set of factors that are producing the problem in the first place including, for example, the high level of environmental pollutants in their neighborhoods (Bryant 1995; Bullard 2000; Cole & Foster 2000; Pulido 2000). Appropriate action would include eliminating the pollutants and preventing the continued dumping of such toxins into poor neighborhoods filled with disenfranchised people of color. In this way, interventions attempting to change black students' attitudes, never mind the growing body of research questioning whether there is actually a problem with those attitudes, addresses only the symptom of a much larger problem.

An abundance of research has demonstrated that U.S. public schools, from the national level to particular districts and individual sites, have not served the majority of black students well, either in recent times or in the past (Anderson 1988; Walters 2001; Watkins 2001; Weinberg 1977). These educational institutions exist within a broader social context that actively and passively supports both racial inequality and racial ideologies that disparage Blacks (Bobo, Kluegel & Smith 1997; Bonilla-Silva 2001; Feagin 2000; Forman 2004; Gould 1999). These larger dynamics penetrate schools explicitly and implicitly, fundamentally shaping black students' school experiences. Most black students attend schools that are essentially "white" institutions in terms of the interests that define them structurally (e.g., housing segregation, school funding structures) and culturally (e.g., dominance of individualism, ideology of meritocracy, and Eurocentric traditions).

In this chapter, I make a case for turning our attention to the many contributors to black students' school experiences that are downplayed or ignored in discussions of black students' "oppositional culture." Focusing on the way race is a part of everyday school life, I attempt to demonstrate the ways that structures are manifest in large and small ways and include the micropolitics of daily practice. Specifically, I use findings from observations and interviews I conducted with members of three different school communities to explore how whiteness is implicated in black children's educational opportunities and outcomes. Recent studies have noted the influence of school community members' ideas about blackness on African American student outcomes (e.g., A. Ferguson 2000), but few have examined the potential role of whiteness in shaping these same outcomes. Here, I understand whiteness not only as racial ideas and ideologies but also as embodied social locations that impact (among other things) access to resources and perspectives on the social world. Defined this way, the concept of whiteness is the foundation of white supremacy. As Bonilla-Silva (2003a) puts it, "whiteness, then, in all of its manifestations, is embodied racial power" (p. 271). Some might contend that white supremacy is not an appropriate descriptor for the current racial order in the United States. Mills (1997, 2003), however, has made a strong case for its use in understanding both the global and the national social system. He argues that conditions in the United States meet Francis Lee Ansley's definition of white supremacy, namely,

> A] political, economic, and cultural system in which whites overwhelmingly control power and material resources, conscious and unconscious ideas of white supremacy and entitlement are widespread, and relations of white dominance and non-white subordination are daily reenacted across a broad array of institutions and social settings. [Ansley, as quoted in Mills 2003, p. 37]

Several components of white supremacy are incorporated into everyday life in schools. These include historic white control over major institutions and the resulting institutionalization of white understandings and practices as normative (Doane 2003; Rasmussen et al. 2001). White dominance does not, of course, explain all facets of contemporary social life; white supremacy operates in a context in which capitalism and patriarchy also are at play. The influence and effects of race, class, and gender overlap and intertwine. For example, as Oliver and Shapiro (1995), Conley (1999), Shapiro (2004), and others have outlined, the cumulative consequences of several centuries of systematic racism in the United States has left some communities collectively with far more wealth than others.

The parallel developments of white supremacy and capitalism in this country meant that even after emancipation, black workers were limited to the worst and lowest-paying jobs, were blocked from access to union jobs, and, when admitted into unions, were often the first fired in bad times because they were the last hired (Marable 1983; Takaki 1993). Urban black communities forged in the context of virulent segregation were devastated by urban renewal programs, redlining, and other public and private practices (Drake and Cayton 1962; Massey & Denton 1993; Segrue 1996). One result of this is that today, even controlling for income and education, Blacks on average have far less wealth than Whites (Oliver and Shapiro 1995).

It is impossible to separate the realities of class from those of race. We cannot understand why so many black children are living in poverty without reference to their blackness. We cannot understand why so many black (and Latino) students are struggling in school without attention to racial dynamics. Race, gender, and class matter also for understanding heterogeneity within black students' experiences. Thus, in trying to understand why many black students are underperforming, we must also ask, as contributors to this volume do, why black boys and girls are succeeding at such different rates, and why middle-class black students are not doing as well as their middle-class white peers. My aim in this chapter is to reinsert into the discussion of black students' school outcomes an understanding of the complex ways in which race shapes everyday school experiences. If we are to understand black students' school outcomes, we need to renew our attention to the ecological aspects of Ogbu's CET model and pay attention to the ways white supremacy continues to shape educational experiences, including white dominance in economic and political spheres, white privilege in everyday social interactions, and white cultural hegemony.

RACE, WHITENESS, AND SCHOOLS

Our national school system has been deeply shaped by the color line (Anderson 1988; Chesler, Lewis, & Crowfoot 2005; Litwack 1998; Woodson 1997). Before Reconstruction, black children were subjected to a "system of compulsory ignorance" (Weinberg 1977, p.11) in which white interests in maintaining a subordinate class of black slaves and laborers led to a systematic denial of access to education. White dominance of schooling is less overt today but no less real. Intergenerational transmissions of racial resources provide Whites in the United States far greater access to quality education. I refer to these as "racial" resources because they were originally accrued largely through a combination of discriminatory private practices and the operation of racist federal, state, and local laws in the past (Feagin 2000; Feagin and McKinney 2003; Lipsitz 1998; Massey & Denton 1993; Quadagno 1994). The benefits resulting from this racial injustice continue to be passed on to successive generations. This enduring legacy includes powerful social networks, wealth accumulated in homes purchased before fair housing laws, seniority accrued in previously segregated employment sectors, and alumni status (which provides advantages to offspring as "legacy admits") at previously all-white colleges and universities.

Such resources are concentrated within particular communities not by accident but as a result of centuries of formal, state-supported racial domination in all arenas, including education. According to Walters (2001), "racial inequality in educational funding and other forms of educational opportunity were explicit policies of the state throughout the country" (p. 35). And as Mickelson (2003b) points out, though less obvious than during periods of slavery and Jim Crow, state participation in the production of unequal education continues:

> State actors site schools and draw attendance zones that assist or hinder deseg-regation; they design and operate systems of ability grouping and tracking; they operate schools and school systems so as to permit middle class white parents to activate their race and class privileges . . . they generate reforms—such as high stakes testing—whose harsh accountability outcomes affect whites, Blacks and Latinos disparately, in part because these state actors often fail to ensure eq-uitable distribution of opportunities to learn the materials covered on the tests. [p. 1070]

Thus, even when not directly or explicitly involved, the state enables elite groups (Whites) to resist efforts to curtail their relative educational advantages. Today, Whites are the most segregated racial group in our country's educational institutions, attending schools with the highest level of resources (Kozol 1991; Mickelson 2003b; Orfield & Gordon 2001; Orfield & Yun 1999). Overall, majority minority schools have less-qualified teachers, less access to technology, less access to advanced curricula (e.g., AP Courses), lower-quality facilities, and less availability of instructional materials (Darling-Hammond 2003; Institute for Democracy, Education, and Access 2004; Mickelson 2003b; Oakes 2003).

The culture of schools also contributes to making many of them white places (Delpit 1995; Ladson-Billings 1994; Nieto 2001). "School problems," Mickelson (2003b, p. 1067) asserts, "are linked to the failure of white-controlled educational institutions to incorporate non-dominant cultures into school culture, curricula, pedagogy, or structures." Raced and gendered ideas (e.g., stereotypes about inherent ability, criminality, and family dysfunction) penetrate deeply into schools and fundamentally shape everyday encounters between school personnel and students and their families (A. Ferguson 2000; Lareau & Horvat 1999; Lewis 2003a). Educational anthropologists have documented the ways in which dominant cultural frameworks read students of color as deficient (Au and Jordan 1981; Cazden 1988; Cazden, John, & Hymes 1972; Philips 1972). A. Ferguson's (2000) work demonstrates how school personnel interpret similar behaviors by male students differently, depending on whether the boys are white or black. Lareau and Horvat (1999) and Roscigno and Ainsworth-Darnell (1999) show that resources children and families bring with them to school are differentially valued by teachers.

These conditions reflect in part the institutionalization of dominant forms of whiteness. Gould (1999) explains:

> When the major institutions in society are constructed within the culture and in the interests of one group instead of another, even when the subordinate group is included within those institutions, its performance will be, on average, less proficient than the dominant group. Organizations may systematically favor the culturally constituted performances of one group over the developmentally equivalent, substantively different, performances of another group. [p. 172]

Black students who attend schools that appear on the surface to be culturally neutral but that, in fact, privilege certain cultural attributes and devalue others, thus are systematically disadvantaged. White cultural hegemony, including the institutionalization of white cultural norms and the demographic dominance of white middle-class teachers in schools, sets the context for much of what takes place in public schools (Delpit 1995). Cultural differences in styles of interaction, modes of expression, and ways of handling conflict (Kochman 1981) have significant effects on students' school experiences (Delpit 1995; A. Ferguson 2000; Fordham 1996b; Ladson-Billings 1994; Lewis 2003a; Nieto 2001).

In addition to the impact of the material and cultural components of whiteness on educational outcomes, white skin itself provides certain advantages. This kind of "symbolic capital" has been documented across a range of social institutions (e.g., health care, employment, service industry, criminal justice), and is one form of what DuBois (1999) terms the "wages of whiteness." To suggest that white skin privilege persists does not mean that all white children in all schools are guaranteed success or are assured of being treated well at all times. It does mean, however, that some children (and adults) more often receive the benefit of the doubt, a second chance, a few extra seconds to answer a question. In a racialized social system, racial thinking and stereotypes shape *all* social actors and lead us almost unconsciously to assume we know something about a person before he or she speaks or acts.

The role of whiteness in shaping schooling experiences is, in some cases, mediated by class and gender. For example, while most major social institutions are subject to white cultural dominance, this is not equally true in all places nor does it necessarily benefit all those defined as white. Moreover, there are many forms of whiteness, including some that are devalued within mainstream institutions (Lewis 2003a). Heath (1983), for example, describes working-class white children who struggle to make sense of the middle-class sensibilities that dominate public school. Regardless of their skin color, those who deviate from hegemonic whiteness are likely to suffer some consequences (e.g., reduced access to job opportunities, educational sanctions) unless they have access to alternative, buffering resources.[1] Finally, although people who are not "white" can attempt to perform whiteness (e.g., by embracing certain cultural forms, defending institutional practices, protecting particular interests), unless they can "pass," these individuals continue to be denied the symbolic capital of white-skin privilege.

To make clear how these components of whiteness shape black students' educational experiences, I provide below examples of whiteness in day-to-day life in three different school communities. These site-specific patterns are connected to the larger dynamics of housing and school segregation and differential funding structures, but they are also important in their own right. They show how whiteness shapes daily practice and meaning making and, thus, how white supremacy, white cultural hegemony, and everyday manifestations of white privilege routinely affect Blacks' schooling experiences.

OVERVIEW OF THE RESEARCH SETTINGS

The examples I provide below are drawn from a larger ethnographic study of three public elementary schools in a large metropolitan area in California (Lewis 2003a). During one school year, I spent approximately seven hours a day in one or more of the schools (e.g., attending a preschool staff meeting at one school and then spending the rest of the school day at another). At each site, I was located primarily in one fourth/fifth-grade classroom, but I spent a great deal of time in other classes. I also observed activities in the schoolyards, lunchrooms, and main offices. I attended staff meetings, PTA meetings, and other school events before and after school and on weekends. I conducted formal and informal interviews with school personnel, teachers, parents, and students, and I colleted site documents from each school.

I selected the three sites—West City, Foresthills, and Metro2—with several criteria in mind. I wanted a fairly typical and diverse urban school (West City); a fairly typical and homogeneous suburban school (Foresthills); and a structurally and culturally nonwhite (or at least bicultural) school (Metro2).[2] By *bicultural* or *nonwhite*, I mean more than the racial composition of the student body; these terms also reflect the racial composition of the staff, the explicit and implicit focus of the curriculum, and the school's culture and expressed values and goals. In this way I looked for a school where the current racial formation and racial meaning systems would potentially be subject to challenge. Metro2 was a Spanish-immersion school in which Spanish was deemed the official language of all school interactions, except for the percentage of each days' instruction specifically required to be conducted in

English.[3] At Metro2, the student body and staff were demographically diverse. West City had a diverse student body and predominantly white staff, while the entire Foresthills community was predominantly white. All sites were small-to-midsize elementary schools (230–450 students) and were neither the best nor the worst schools in their respective districts. The sampling technique I used was intended, if anything, to underestimate the effects of race; I purposefully selected places that had good reputations among parents and district personnel (teachers, principals, central administrators), both on academic dimensions and in terms of race relations.[4]

The examples I discuss below illustrate some of the ways in which whiteness works in everyday school life; they are not meant to represent how whiteness works for all people, or in all places. Context will change what is relevant and how racialization works. By racialization I mean the assignment of bodies to racial categories and the association of symbols, attributes, qualities, and other meanings with those categories (which then are understood to belong to those bodies in a primordial or natural way). Racialization processes include (1) how people get racially categorized; (2) how boundaries between racial categories are formed, negotiated, and interpreted; and (3) how those first two processes (racialization and boundary formation) affect interactions and opportunities. Through these processes racial categories are being made and remade daily rather than existing forever in some fixed way. What does not vary is that race is a part of what is going on in every context within a racialized social system (Bonilla-Silva 2001).

WHITENESS AS POWER: METRO2

At Metro2, white (or Anglo, an alternate label often used within this school community) parents and children represented only about one-third of the school community but have a much larger impact on key school policies and everyday practices. This group's powerful position clearly reflected overlapping race and class effects—that is, almost all white families in the school were middle-class—but racial differences often were utilized as quick and easy signifiers of those who did or did not have the "right stuff," including access to important school resources. At issue here was the convergence of differences in culture, concerns, and priorities with differences in power and resources. Some families in the school had more control than others.

School power struggles unfolded both in relation to schoolwide politics and in terms of classroom practices. When I began my observations, parents were already somewhat divided over one issue and about to split over a second. The first issue initially arose several years earlier. A number of Latino parents had raised the topic of school uniforms. According to teachers who related the story to me, white and middle-class parents thought uniforms were too regimented and would likely quash their children's creativity. For Latino parents, the issue was one of reduced cost, greater equity, and firmer discipline. In the end, the uniform initiative failed. In what the principal called "a pretty weak compromise," the school instead introduced "spirit days." On Mondays and Fridays, students were encouraged (but not required) to wear school t-shirts.

The other divisive issue at Metro2 emerged not long after I began my observations there. At the beginning of the year, teachers adopted a new policy of assigning third-, fourth-, and fifth-grade students who had not completed their homework to "detention" during recess. A very heated discussion of the subject arose during Back to School Night. As a Spanish-immersion school with a large number of Spanish-speaking parents, Metro2 had a policy that all schoolwide events were to be bilingual. Translation was supposed to occur continually so that all parents could participate equally. As a teacher explained, however, when a "brouhaha" developed over detention, English (and English-speaking parents) took over. He described the dynamics involved this way:

> It's definitely Anglo parents over, over Latino parents. I don't mean "over." It's not like they're squashing them down, although maybe—I think they are in—well, you saw the Back to School Night. What happens is, like, this brouhaha develops in English. And it becomes just, like, this growing wave, and it's hard to fight it in Spanish. It's hard to keep the Spanish part in place. So, yeah, it is run by English, run by Anglo parents . . . generally it is, I think they're the ones that—well, they tend to be middle class. But not all of them. I mean there's more middle-class Anglo people than there are middle-class Latino people, right?

As the teacher alluded to above, these conflicts involved important race and class dimensions. It was true at the school that more, though not all, white families were middle class. It was also true that more, though not all, Latino families were working class. These patterns are, of course, not accidents but reflect larger patterns of differential access to power and resources more generally. As represented by the Back to School Night discussion, what these patterns meant for the school was that white, middle-class, English-speaking parents often silenced Latino, working-class, Spanish-speaking parents, both literally and symbolically. This is one sign of power—the ability to control a space even when, as at Metro2, it has been organized to minimize power differentials. As the meeting unfolded and voices became heated, it was impossible not to notice that only those seated in part of the room were speaking and that only English was being spoken.

Issues of race and power came up not only in how the meeting progressed —with Spanish-speaking parents increasingly marginalized—but also in what different groups thought of the detention policy. The silence of Latino parents at the meeting was not reflective of a lack of opinion on the policy. While one group, composed almost entirely of white parents, strongly opposed the policy, calling it Draconian and a likely violation of school district policy, most Latino parents, in contrast, were supportive. For example, after the meeting a Latino father I spoke to firmly endorsed the policy and laughed at the other parents' "sensitivity" (some of those in opposition were afraid their children would have their "feelings hurt" by the public punishment). He understood, however, that the other parents were likely to hold sway. As he put it, "It's gonna be just like the uniforms thing," meaning that the white parents would again dominate the debate and determine the result.

Eventually, to try to capture a wider set of opinions than those that had been voiced at Back to School Night, teachers took a poll about the new detention policy. Almost all the forms filled out in Spanish supported the policy, while almost all those in English were against it. Detention was ended within the first month of school. As the Latino father had predicted, the power of the different parent groups led white concerns to dominate school policy. In a close vote, white middle-class parents' threats to appeal the policy to the district as a potential violation of district rules, along with their reputation for vigorous and regular intervention on behalf of their children, were likely as significant to the final decision as the tally of votes. Teachers' willingness to abandon their new policy so quickly, despite support from a large segment of the parent population, also spoke volumes about the pressure they felt to keep particular constituencies in the school happy.

Although, as one mother put it, Metro2 was full of "political people . . . like the white sort of left-leaning people" who want their children to learn Spanish, who appreciate a diverse learning environment, and who value multicultural curriculum, this was no assurance of harmony. At moments like those surrounding school uniforms and a detention policy, we see not merely cultural differences at play, but differences in resources and power. Here the confrontations involve different understandings of discipline and different priorities. A white liberal commitment to individual freedom of expression was pitted against concerns about cost, discipline, and equity. School battles like these are in the end not won or lost based on principle—clearly both sides of the issue were taking what they believed to be a principled stance—but on power. The question is whose principles, whose priorities dominate school life. In this case, white and biracial or bicultural middle-class families pursued what they believed was in their children's best interests and the priorities of lower-status, predominantly Latino families lost out. This is especially noteworthy at a school like Metro2 where, unlike schools most white students attend, they are numerically in the minority.

Within the classroom, the relatively empowered white middle-class students had access to certain kinds of knowledge, skills, and cultural capital that paid off. By cultural capital I mean not just that knowledge held valuable in high-class cultural circles but instead, sets of knowledge and skills valuable in a particular field or social setting (Bourdieu 1977; Bourdieu & Passeron 1990; DiMaggio 1982; Lamont and Lareau 1988). This includes a general facility with interacting appropriately in various contexts, knowledge of and facility with the rules of engagement in particular settings, general cultural knowledge relevant for and held in esteem in a particular situation, and ownership of certain kinds of possessions or credentials.[5]

Quite inadvertently, some curricula rewarded those who already possessed particular cultural knowledge. One day, for example, as an introduction to a new unit on U.S. geography, the class played several rounds of a game called USA Bingo. The teacher read clues about a state and students raised their hands to answer. Prizes were awarded for those who correctly named the state and for those who got Bingo (not related to answering questions). The teacher went through twenty to twenty-five cards before someone won the game. Of the over twenty students playing, only two Latino students even raised their hands to guess. Many white and middle-class students who answered talked about the states as places they had traveled to or as places where relatives lived or where their parent(s) had gone to college. While a Latina was the one to eventually call out "Bingo!" she, along with many of her Latino peers, had otherwise been silent for twenty minutes. This classroom episode provides a clear example of the ways knowledge from nonschool sources provides school benefits. In this case, unlike with a standardized test, students were not directly penalized for not having the necessary cultural information. They did, however, lose out indirectly, as their peers who had those resources received benefits in the form of prizes and/or increased teacher expectations.

Knowledge that students brought to the classroom from their homes was important in other ways as well. Sometimes, these effects were beyond the school's control. On more than one occasion, white students talked about help a parent had given them with their homework. One day, for instance, four white or biracial/bicultural (white/Latino) boys were the only ones who had completed a long, complicated math assignment; all four talked about getting some assistance from a parent. In contrast, Marlyn, a working-class Latina, arrived with a note from her mother that read, "Dear teacher: we were unable to do the homework. My daughter she didn't understand and also me, I've tried but I couldn't explain it to her." While Marlyn was not penalized, the boys were rewarded for their completed work. Obviously, schools cannot fix home-based resource imbalances. They do have some control, however, over how often and in what ways those resources are rewarded in classrooms.

Since Metro2 was a Spanish-immersion school, one might expect that Spanish-dominant children's language skills would secure them some advantage. Yet, when teachers described their best students, they spoke about the cultural resources in Anglo homes. One teacher referred to Spanish-speaking students' language skills as a resource only in the context of their serving as language models for others:

> Yeah, I think the kids that do best are the kids that, the kids that come from bilingual or Anglo homes that are very involved and that are warm, nurturing places where they get a lot of extra help . . . kids coming from, I don't even know if I think the kids coming from Spanish-speaking homes do that well—in a lot of ways, I don't think they do nearly as well as some of the higher-end English-dominating kids—because ESL is a major element that is missing from this program. So, it's almost like Spanish-speaking kids serve as models [for Anglo students], and then they don't get the support when it comes time for them to acquire their English, not in later years or even in their earlier years.

While in many ways the teacher's description of "bilingual or Anglo homes" would be indistinguishable from a standard description of a "middle-class home," it is noteworthy that racial descriptors are used to capture who does or does not come from a "warm, nurturing" home. Class status is obviously implicated in families' differential access to resources, but such differences were often talked about in terms of race or ethnicity and led to broader assumptions about group differences that mattered in daily classroom life. Also noted in this teacher's discussion is the relative absence of a strong ESL program at the school. At Metro2, as elsewhere, the school structure is much more supportive of Anglo acquisition of Spanish than it is of Latino acquisition of English (Valdes 1997). Thus, white students tend to graduate with much greater dual-language proficiency than do Latino students for whom Spanish is the first language. This imbalance has multiple potential ramifications for future school success.

In addition to these formal curricular advantages, white students seemed to be better positioned informally as well. They were more likely to have spontaneous and informal interactions with staff. For example, white students were more often in the classrooms before or after school helping out; talking to a teacher at recess; or corresponding with teachers from previous grades via email. These interactions brought subtle benefits. When I asked one white teacher whether she thought her race had any impact on her relationships with students, she hesitated before answering. Stumbling through her reply, this otherwise articulate teacher explained that her stronger connections with Anglo students were not necessarily how she *wanted* it to be but the way it *was*:

> Well, I guess, um, I don't know, no. I don't know, maybe it could be . . . I think I'm pretty fair to all the students. I mean at least I try to be as

fair as I can to all the students. I would not deny, though, that I definitely have more conversations with, or the kids that seek me out more tend to be the more Anglo kids. And I think that it's two things. One is, their English is strong, and I'm their English model and so they feel like, you know, whatever. Two is, I think it's a personality thing—that they really identify with me or whatever and they reach out to all their other teachers as well. We have, like, a certain group of Anglo kids that are always very verbal. So yeah, I guess in some ways, it does.

Given the multiple demands on her time and energy, this teacher did not seem to have much energy left to worry about who was stopping by to chat. Linked here are issues of who most easily "identifies" with her, who attaches themselves most easily and readily, and who in connection with this kind of informal relationship gets read as being more "verbal."

Arguably, these types of informal interactions have effects that spill over into formal classroom interactions. Relationships with individual students can impact teachers' expectations of these children. I had an opportunity to see how this teacher's estimation of some children as more "verbal" than others could shape her overarching view of their skills and abilities. One day, two white female students stopped by before school to chat and ended up helping organize books in the classroom. Before they arrived, the teacher had been telling me about her class. Now she whispered to me, while gesturing toward the girls, "You'd be amazed at the intellectual capacity of some of these children. It blows me away sometimes." Student ability at the school, she continued, ranged very widely, "from LEP kids to middle-class white kids like them." Particularly in a Spanish-immersion program, limited skill with English should not be an automatic referent for low school performance. LEP is supposed to denote a skill level—English language proficiency—not a measure of academic ability or proclivity. Yet, as this teacher's comment demonstrates, terms such as LEP, Spanish, and English often were used as shorthand designations of status that signified much more than language mastery.

In sum, race mattered at Metro2. It resulted in group-level differences in who students of different races spent time with, it shaped the amount of class participation across groups, and it influenced teachers' relationships with and attitudes toward student groups. In each case, racially correlated differences in access to power, cultural capital, and skills produced school outcomes that benefited white students.

WHITENESS AS SOCIAL CONTROL: WEST CITY

West City was a small elementary school with a large black and Latino student population and a predominantly white staff. White structural and cultural dominance was present in many ways. For instance, the school was not exempt from our society's pervasive racist notions about African Americans generally and black males in particular (Hopkins 1997). I was startled one day in the lounge when some teachers who were trying to get me to apply for an opening at the school quite seriously commented to one another that I would be an excellent choice because I "wasn't afraid of the kids." Later, when I joked with Mr. Ortiz, the only Latino teacher in the school, about the idea of being afraid of eight-year-olds, he offered this interpretation of his colleagues' comment:

> Well—it's like—I'll give you an example. You put on a news program— CNN, ABC, NBC, CBS. Look at the news. And you'll see increasing numbers of aggravated assaults by youngsters. I think it gets translated back, saying, "I heard in the news last night that a twelve-year old was arrested for aggravated assault with a weapon. And I have eight year olds, but one of those eight-year olds is a little larger than the rest. . . ." So, I believe that that adds to the apprehension. And then I think that again we're going to come back to race, because I think that some teachers, they hear, "Oh, African Americans. I'm not gonna get involved with their families." "Latinos, I'm not gonna get involved with their families." Why? Because they hear in the news about gang shootings, drive-bys, carjackings. Again—I mean, I may be way off—but I really feel more and more that what individuals see and hear then gets translated and it gets convoluted. Because I agree with you—it's a thirty year old [who's talking about being afraid of an] eight year old.

Mr. Ortiz's comments capture the ways in which news coverage of crime and violence are part of a larger constellation of cultural phenomena that shape our understandings of others. In conversations with staff of color in the school, all at one point or another suggested that fear influenced how black students were treated by school personnel. During a conversation in the hall, Ms. Harrison, a first-grade teacher and one of West City's two black teachers, told me she had "even seen teachers who, even on the kindergarten level, you know, are very fearful of African American boys." These ideas about black students generally and black boys in particular had a clear impact on school practice. As has been documented in many other settings (e.g., A. Ferguson 2000; Hopkins 1997; McCadden 1998), black boys at West City were disciplined more often and more harshly than other students. While they were less than 20 percent of the student body, they represented over 80 percent of the disciplinary referrals.

Unfortunately, except for the few people of color on staff (such as Mr. Ortiz and Ms. Harrison), teachers were neither very skilled at nor very interested in talking about racism or racial patterns in school outcomes. The issue of race did surface in certain situations, but as Ms. Sullivan, a white third-grade teacher, explained, that happened only when people of color on the staff raised what were perceived to be "their" issues (as, for example, when Mr. Ortiz "comes up with 'the Hispanics' stuff"). In fact, Ms. Sullivan was one of the few teachers I spoke to who wanted more of this kind of discussion. She recognized that the school would profit from more explicit talk about race. But even Ms. Sullivan could imagine such conversations taking place only if another black person was hired to fill an open slot for the upcoming year. At West City, discussions about race seemed to be understood as neither white teachers' responsibility nor their area of expertise. The presumed "nonracialness" of Whites meant that the few staff of color were left with the burden of raising difficult or complicated issues.

When I asked in various ways whether race ever was talked about in relation to children, achievement, or curriculum, Ms. Sullivan said such discussions generally were limited to the obligatory incorporation of specific racial and ethnic holidays within the core curriculum.

Well, only like, you know, like Martin Luther King Day, and then African American month is next month. I don't understand why it's not with Martin Luther King month—Ruby [the secretary] did that, I think. And then we have the Lunar New Year next week, so we'll have to, you hear me, "gotta make sure that we get the Chinese thing touched upon." I don't like it isolated so much. I don't know. I think sometimes if we make it too much an issue, heritage, you know, like foods, customs, on holidays and stuff—to hear all of that is really cool, but to make it like an isolated, "gotta make sure I get in the Chinese book next week," you know, that's not right.

Ms. Sullivan was not the only white teacher I spoke to who said the subject of race did not come up unless a person of color on staff raised it. Although she favored more frequent and more open discussions of race, other teachers expressed quite different opinions. One teacher, as she described one of the few meetings where lack of diversity on the staff was raised, angrily asserted, "It's okay to criticize white people all the time, and I'm sick of it." In fact, there had been no direct criticism of anyone at the meeting, but this teacher had interpreted the emphasis on diversifying the staff as an indirect criticism of the (white) teachers currently working at the school.

Later, I questioned Ms. Harrison about the meeting. She offered the following analysis:

The thing is, is that teachers in general feel like no one really appreciates us. And if you put on top of that, that white missionary type vibe, like—"I'm trying to help these poor kids! I spend [so many] hours here!"—and then there's issues of power—of, like, "What, me give up mine?" I mean, the bottom line is, when you talk about diversity of staff, it's like, "What—me give up my shit? *That ain't gonna happen!*" And it's not going to happen, you know. I mean, it was an interesting discussion. Yeah, when Sara [Ms. Sullivan] leaves, we might get a person of color, but no one else is going to leave here, nor is anyone going to step up and say, "I feel committed to [diversity]; it should be a diverse staff, and I'm willing to give up [my spot]." *No one's* gonna do that, and that makes all the difference in the world. [Ms. Harrison's emphasis]

Though she was disappointed that discussion of hiring a single additional person of color would cause a fuss, Ms. Harrison admitted that she "was not surprised." Her experience at West City led her to believe that part of the problem was the white teachers' puzzlement (or, in some cases, angry frustration) over why their presence at the school and the personal sacrifice it represented was not received with more open appreciation. Ms. Harrison found this "missionary type vibe" infuriating in its condescension, but even more difficult to take was its coupling with a stubborn refusal to give up the "mission" for principles of diversity. The same teachers who claimed to be sacrificing themselves for the good of the children would not yield their power or position for that same worthy cause.

This progressive (or missionary) narrative also may have contributed to the enormous difficulty teachers had in discussing the school's everyday racial reality. Being there "for the good of the children" was hard to reconcile with the reality of mediocre or poor student outcomes. Moreover, the teachers' narrative expresses a particular kind of power and privilege—one that supports silencing conflict and/or facilitates silence about uncomfortable subjects. Thus, a teacher like Ms. Harrison found it difficult, if not impossible, to draw attention to a practical and visible reality that challenged the image of teachers helping, making sacrifices for, and ultimately saving children. The less defensive staff members might have agreed that the teaching staff's current racial composition when compared to the racial profile of the student body, was troubling. Still, no one was going to voluntarily surrender her or his job at West City. Similarly to the pattern of white attitudes identified by Wellman (1993), Blumer (1958), and others, Ms. Harrison's experience of her white colleagues was of people who were, in important ways, unwilling to yield their power. As she put it, "that ain't going to happen!"

Ms. Harrison also contended, contrary to Ms. Sullivan's report, that staff talked about race all the time; they just did not do so explicitly. Race informed many everyday conversations in which the (white) staff projected cultural deficit models onto their students and their students' families. As Ms. Harrison explained during an interview, staff might not have known they were talking about race, but the code words were clear.

Lewis: When issues of race come up, like in the lunchroom or in meetings and staff meetings, how do they usually come up? What usually
brings them up?

Harrison: I think that they come up in an informal way. And I think it's
because some of those people are very unconscious that they're talking
about race. But I hear discussions and comments. . . . When we're talking about, in particular, African Americans, this kind of automatic assumption comes up that these kids live in a dysfunctional family. I think
that all teachers don't want to feel that they can't do something for children. So, I think that blaming the children happens quite a bit. Or blaming their family or blaming that they came to us in this broken condition
and we just don't have enough resources to fix it.

The kind of language Ms. Harrison refers to is not uncommon in contemporary racial discourse. Essed (1991) and others have pointed out a shift in
ways of talking about race in the United States (Bonilla-Silva 2001; Bonilla-
Silva & Lewis 1999; Edsall & Edsall 1991; McCadden 1998; Omi & Winant
1994). While "the traditional idea of genetic inferiority is still important in the
fabric of racism, the discourse of black inferiority is increasingly reformu-
lated as cultural deficiency, social inadequacy, and technological underdevelopment" (Essed 1991, p. 4). Racial ideologies that perpetuate common-
sense understandings of racial groups as different (and inferior/superior)
have not entirely fallen by the wayside, but they are expressed less in terms
of innate characteristics and more in terms of "cultural" attributes, often manifested through the use of code words such as "urban," "inner-city," "welfare," and "crime."

On numerous occasions, staff used these and other local variations of
code language to talk mostly about black students and their families. Staff referred to the "project kids," "eastside" folks (even in reference to those who
did not live in public housing or on the east side), or some other variant in
referring to children or families who were perceived to be missing something, taking up too much of a teacher's energy, or causing problems. Many
of the staff would deny that they were talking about race in their diatribes
about various families, but their assumptions about families and children
were very specifically focused on African American families and drew on
common racial stereotypes (e.g., families were dysfunctional, chaotic, did
not value education, and/or were disorganized). Such families were constructed as deviant or deficient vis-à-vis a (white) normal family. As Ms. Harrison offered, some of these remarks were intended to deflect blame for
school failures from teachers and the school onto children and families.

While teachers were correct that neither they nor the schools could "do
everything," it did not necessarily then follow that children and families were

solely to blame. Moreover, having this particular excuse ready and available not only made the school's low scores on standardized tests easier to explain, and thus reduced the pressure to initiate change and improvement; but the excuse itself could be seen as one potential cause of failure, as it inhibited the potential for families and schools to work together. On multiple levels, interactions between teachers and students and teachers and parents included more than just the minutiae of the specific interaction. These encounters were rife with the larger ideas and assumptions in our society that lead to both subtle and explicit benefits for some students.

FORESTHILLS: WHITENESS AS RACELESSNESS

From the very beginning of my time at Foresthills, a predominantly white school in an almost all-white suburb, it was clear that people were not sure why I wanted to conduct my research there. When I first contacted the school principal to inquire about including the school as a research site, she seemed puzzled by my request. "You understand that this is a pretty homogeneous school," she asked, and then immediately elaborated, "We don't have much diversity here." This principal (as well as other suburban administrators) believed the absence of students of color (or the presence of only white children) at a school would make it a less-than-interesting place to conduct research on race. People also seemed very concerned that I not misinterpret anything I saw. On my first day in the classroom, the teacher, Mrs. Moch, took me aside before the children arrived and explained that there was one mixed race (black/white) student in her class. Sylvie, Mrs. Moch said, was "dealing with a lot of fourth-grade girl stuff," but tended to play "the race card" a lot. Even as she explained that Sylvie was misreading the significance of race in her daily experience at the school, Mrs. Moch described her own practice of going to get the school's one black staff member to explain this point to Sylvie. Finally, when parents and other members of the school community talked about race, it tended to be in relation to "others"—people of color, primarily Blacks. So, for example, when I asked a student's mother (during an interview) what the school did in terms of educating the children about diversity and multiculturalism, she responded:

> Well, I think that a certain part of that they don't have to deal with, because the school's not extremely multicultural. You know. It's not . . . uh, there's not a . . . a lot, a lot, a lot of black people that go there. So, I think maybe they don't have to address it too much.

These three encounters were early signs of what became clear throughout my time at Foresthills: members of the school community had complicated and conflicting understandings of the relevance of race. At Foresthills, the salience of race was downplayed, trivialized, or challenged: The principal was unclear about why I would want to do research on race in her white school; a teacher explained to me that the one black child in her class was misreading what she was experiencing as being racial (either innocently or because the student knew it would bring attention); a parent explained that multicultural education was not necessary, because the school had so few black students.

Generally, people verbally expressed the idea that "everybody is human," just as they expressed, in various forms, beliefs in group-level racial differences. Despite explicit claims to not see color, for better or worse, racial differences mattered to the Foresthills community—they shaped where they chose to live, whom they wanted their children to marry, whom the children chose to play with in the schoolyard, what television shows they liked to watch, and how they understood gaps in achievement. These ideas were not part of contrived arguments to defend privilege; they were simply what the speakers took "to be true," the result of a "natural" instinct to be around people who are "like [our]selves" or reflective of "cultural differences" in values. In fact, almost none of the white people I spoke to ever thought consciously about their own "racialness." In response to questions about what impact they thought race had had on their lives, they answered much like Mrs. Grant, the mother of a fifth grader, "I haven't been around it very much." These patterns are emblematic of a color-blind ideology gaining dominance more generally (Bonilla-Silva 2001; Crenshaw 1997; Forman 2004; Lewis 2003b), in which Whites continue to live their lives in multiple, racialized ways and simultaneously deny the salience of race generally and ignore the fact of their own whiteness, failing to see themselves as racial actors.

That those living in this white suburb, situated within a multiracial metropolis, fail to understand their social space as racially coded belies the wider reality of the racialized history of suburbanization (Lipsitz 1998; Massey & Denton 1993; Oliver & Shapiro 1995). No one I interviewed articulated race as the primary factor for choosing to buy a home in the suburbs, but many individuals offered only slightly veiled racial explanations for why they had chosen not to live elsewhere. A strong commitment to colorblind racial narratives makes it possible to exist with the contradictions of living in racialized ways while ignoring or refuting whiteness. These narratives provide a seemingly progressive discourse for avoiding race generally ("we are all colorblind; race doesn't matter") and supply a seemingly nonracial language (racial code words) for those occasions when it is necessary to express racial preferences or to explain one's behavior.

The reliance on colorblind narratives at Foresthills could have significant implications for the school's (few) students of color. For instance, the mother of Sylvie, the child Mrs. Moch described as "playing the race card," described her daughter's early experiences at school this way:

> I mean, it started from the very beginning, you know . . . an incident happened where somebody used the "N" word with her. And she waits until she's going to bed to tell me these things, so of course I run to the phone and leave this scathing message to the principal, who avoids me . . . and then when I talk to her, she says she'll talk to Sylvie. Well, I keep asking Sylvie [who says], "No, I haven't talked to her, haven't talked to her," so I'm just getting angrier and angrier. And then it turns out that she's trying to get Sylvie to confront this boy, and deal with this. And I'm thinking to myself, why does Sylvie have to deal with this? This is the teacher's responsibility . . . or the principal's. Sylvie shouldn't have to deal with this. This is, you know, she has to be protected. And then I find out that . . . she keeps . . . she won't discuss it. Her grades are getting worse, and everything and. . . . And then, finally, we have a sitdown, with the teacher and the principal, and find out that the teacher dealt with it. Sylvie had been avoiding the meetings with the principal, with understandable, valid reasons, you know. But nobody was communicating with *me*. So, I—I'm not very happy with the way things are handled like that. It just—I shouldn't have to bug the principal, force a meeting, to get . . . to get some answers. And, just this week, she had two other incidences . . . middle-school boys out on the playground during the after school care, calling her "Blackie"—which [the school] said they couldn't do anything about, 'cause it wasn't one of the school kids. And then a little kindergartner [used a racial epithet]. . . . And, you know, I tried to explain to her, the kindergartner's, like, trying out a cuss word, you know, but it's—and I told her, I said that the sad thing is that he heard it somewhere . . . but it's just the idea that she knows that this is gonna come up over and over and over again.

Sylvie's mother recounted how her daughter's grades dropped, how she did not want to go to school, and eventually, after making one good friend, how she began to rebound. Clearly, Sylvie was dealing with a stressful situation. Conversations with other students in the class provided independent confirmation of Sylvie's reading of the world. In response to generic questions about why some kids do not like to play with other kids, over half of the children acknowledged that kids did not want to play with Sylvie at first because she was "different."

In fact, blackness was not the only skin color that carried negative connotations, and Sylvie was not the only student to confront racial hostility at the school. One day while I was outside observing schoolyard play, Angus, one of three biracial fourth-grade boys (Angus, Cedric, and Michael each had one parent who was either a Latino or an Asian) who often played together ran over to me. He asked, "Is it illegal to call someone something because of their race? I mean, can you sue them?" I asked him what he meant. He explained that Ricky, a white fifth grader, had just called Cedric a "black boy," and he wanted to know if they could sue. I asked Cedric what had happened, and he told me that Ricky called him and Michael "you brown boy." I looked around the yard, but I could not find Ricky. I talked to their teacher (Mrs. Moch), who told me where to look. We brought all the boys together. After giving each side a chance to relate their version of events, Mrs. Moch told Ricky not to use "derogatory names." Ricky then headed back to his classroom. I talked to him later, hoping to get some understanding of what he thought he had been doing out on the schoolyard. I asked him why he had used those terms:

Ricky: Just because.

Amanda: Is it okay to say that to people?

Ricky [Looking down at the ground and speaking slowly]: Nooo.

Amanda: Why?

Ricky: Because of racism.

Unfortunately, the bell rang and cut off our conversation. But the exchange made it clear that Ricky had purposefully used a designation of color, of racial otherness, as a put-down. In truth, Cedric, a fairly dark-skinned Filipino, is a "brown boy." But it is telling that in this setting, the mere allusion to color substituted as a racial epithet. These students and their teacher seemed to understand that, in this case, in this context, to "see" and/or acknowledge race (particularly to identify a person as black or brown) was negative or, as Mrs. Moch put it, "derogatory."

As these examples of racial logic in operation at Foresthills show, school personnel's limited interventions or downplaying of such incidents did little to address the anxiety and unhappiness of those who were the victims of the hurtful behavior. Nor did it go far to address the ignorance or hurtful behavior of the white perpetrators. What this way of handling racism did do was demonstrate the pernicious effect of trivializing racial incidents. Foresthills teachers seemed to be at least moderately aware of these kinds of incidents among the students, but the teachers interpreted them as relatively unimportant and tended to deracialize them:

Mrs. Moch: I don't see a lot of racism in the class, I mean occasionally a remark's made . . . but frequently what I find with the remarks, is that they aren't as clearly defined as racist as they are . . . kid put-downs.

And, that they kind of—sometimes just can get lumped into everybody else's put-down kinds of things. So I haven't seen much here.

Glossing over racist put-downs—defining them as not really about race but instead as just one of many normal taunts children exchange—is problematic. Essed (1997) points out that deracializing incidents where racist slurs are used implies that they are like regular, everyday conflicts in which both parties may be held equally responsible; such an approach to racist events makes it seem as if the victim rather than the perpetrator is the one with the problem, as if the victim is making "a big deal out of nothing." This brings about an atmosphere of tolerance for racist slurs—implying they are like other put-downs and just happen to be racial. These kinds of micro events crystallize "the structural and experiential differences between the two parties; one party enjoys the safety of dominant group protection, whereas the other experiences the unsafe conditions of his 'race,' a group subjected to violence and discrimination" (Essed 1997, p. 140). Even seemingly minor events like these can reinforce the victim's sense of being an outsider and thus are experienced as more than mere put-downs. For example, the very fact that a child would question whether you could sue someone for calling him a "brown boy" suggests that the experience goes beyond regular or everyday schoolyard banter. Obviously, race did matter at Foresthills. It not only shaped the everyday school experience of students of color; it was also an important underlying reason for why the school was almost all white.

CONCLUSION

Examples from three very different schools illustrate the many ways whiteness penetrates everyday school practices and meaning making. It shapes who ends up in particular school buildings, how students within those schools are understood, what kinds of expectations staff have for students, how children interact with one another, and which groups triumph in power struggles around contested school policies. The impact of white supremacy and its related dynamics on black students extends from places in which they are dominant to places in which their numbers are small. Beyond the large impact of race on which schools black students attend, embodied white power clearly shapes their lives within particular schools and classrooms. There is vast complexity in how Blacks take up this array of social constraints and opportunities. As O'Connor (2001), A. Ferguson (2000), Perry, Steele, and Hilliard (2003), and others (Steele 1999; Wells & Crain 1997) have documented, the processes of constructing social identities and school orientations are shaped but not determined by power inequities, historical and social context, local places, and cultures. What I have argued in this chapter is that we cannot truly understand black academic achievement or black orientations toward education without paying close attention to the larger racial context within which black students are trying to make sense of the world and achieve in school—a larger context still dominated by whites and structured to maintain the status quo.

Obviously, there are individual teachers, schools, and school practices that are not hostile to black students (e.g., see Foster 1997; Ladson-Billings 1994). We can use such examples to learn about how to help black students succeed within a world that too often is not structured to help them do so. It is, of course, also true that there are black students who manage to succeed and thrive despite the barriers, but these students are not the rule. It is their success that needs explaining, not the fact that so many other black students are not living up to their full potential. Not only are there many reasons for questioning the explanatory value of Fordham and Ogbu's acting-white hypothesis (in fact, several authors in this volume challenge its key premises head-on); the very fact that it has become so popular is illustrative of the exact dynamics that facilitate the perpetuation of the larger racial hierarchy—that we continue to successfully blame the subjects of racial exclusion for their own situation. Not until African American students have equal educational opportunities—including such things as access to preschool, schools with highly qualified and culturally competent teachers, all necessary instructional supplies, functional technology, and safe facilities—can we begin to talk about black students' attitudes as relevant for explaining their overall school performance. Until then, such conversations serve as ways to avoid having to make tough choices about how to fundamentally change social and schooling arrangements more generally.

NOTES

1. Hegemonic whiteness is that set of embodied racial practices that occupies the dominant position in a particular racial formation. These forms are not fixed but vary over time. In fact, hegemonic whiteness is that which successfully manages to occupy the empty space of "normality" in our culture. It is that seemingly "neutral" yardstick against which cultural behavior, norms, and values are measured.

2. By "typical," I mean a school that is generally similar to the kind most white or most nonwhite students attend, and thus one that offers a fairly typical experience. Most students of color in the United States, particularly Latino and African American students, attend urban public schools with primarily nonwhite student populations and predominantly white staff. Most white students, on the other hand, attend schools whose student and staff populations are all or almost all white. In selecting schools, I was careful to pick those that, if anything, would yield an underestimate of effects. Thus, I limited my selection of urban schools to those that were not in the lowest tier for performance, disciplinary problems, or socioeconomic status. In se-

lecting a suburban school, I looked among districts that were neither particularly wealthy nor particularly working class and whose student populations were between 80 and 90 percent white. I also limited my focus to districts that were part of the same metropolitan area as the urban schools.

3. The specific ratio of instruction taking place in Spanish versus English instruction was designed to shift as students moved through the program. The ratio began at 90/10 in kindergarten and eventually transitioned to 50/50 by fourth and fifth grades. For more on the politics of such programs, see Valdes (1997).

4. School reputations are inherently relative, and what constituted a good academic reputation within the city would not have been seen as adequate in the suburbs. Thus, West City was known for being much better than many other of the city schools, even though its standardized test results were low.

5. All students have very important cultural resources, acquired in their home and neighborhood lives, which serve as valuable assets in those settings. Problems arise when the students enter new fields (e.g., school, where these skills and knowledge sets are not rewarded). When, in these different settings, other forms of cultural resources are the currency of exchange, then students not only have trouble accessing resources but may be penalized for trying to put other understandings to work.

Afterword

Education has always been a key site of struggle in the African American quest for freedom, equality, personal dignity, and self-determination. Under the American creed and ideals of meritocracy, schools were to be the great levelers. Within the American democracy, schools were to provide equal opportunity for all without regard to race, gender, ethnicity, nationality, region, language, or class origins. On the American democracy's level playing field, open, fair competition and merit would determine who won society's choicest rewards—prestigious jobs, high salaries, fine homes, the good life.

In fact, it has not quite worked out that way: a great chasm separates ideals from reality. As a treasured, scarce resource, education has not been equally available to all children and families in the society. Educational opportunities have been most accessible to the privileged, to the powerful, and to Whites. Throughout their long history in this country, African Americans have been denied equal educational opportunity. During slavery, Blacks risked life and limb simply to learn to read and write. Later Jim Crow, de jure racial segregation, and persistent de facto racial discrimination blocked black access to education. As a consequence, African Americans have invested education with great symbolic and pragmatic significance. For us education became the hotly pursued, highly contested Holy Grail that would somehow solve the problems of black exclusion and inferiority in American society.

A generation after the Supreme Court overturned the legal basis for racial segregation in the epic case *Brown v. Topeka Board of Education* (1954), a reasonable question arises: "How well are African Americans doing in contemporary society?" Competing assessments present two radically different and contradictory narratives. One perspective argues that African Americans have achieved full equality, parity. Major media beam a parade of popular, successful African American icons to confirm that the American Dream is alive and well. These achievements are presented as undeniable proof that America has embraced Dr. King's "Dream." Yet, in terms of educational achievement, workforce participation, wealth accumulation, incarceration, and health status, African Americans continue to be significantly disadvantaged compared to Whites (Brown et al. 2003). In short, this counternarrative argues that America continues to be a racially stratified society, separate and unequal.

RACIAL SEGREGATION AND EDUCATIONAL ACHIEVEMENT

In the United States, geographic residence and educational opportunities are inextricably linked. Students are legally required to attend schools in the districts where they live. Since school district budgets are largely based on property taxes, schools located in communities with expensive homes and thriving businesses are better funded. Due to unequal funding patterns, the economic resources of schools vary dramatically across districts, states, and even neighborhoods in the same city. Schools in wealthy, mostly white districts routinely spend more per student than do schools in poor, nonwhite districts. These pronounced differences in resources produce disparities in the quality and quantity of education dispersed. Given economic inequities by race in the United States, black, Latino and Native American parents are less able to afford living in the expensive neighborhoods served by wealthy school districts. Thus, their children's educational opportunities are automatically restricted.

Residential patterns in the United States have been historically and continue to be highly segregated by race. Residential segregation is associated with extreme racial/ethnic disparities in poverty levels, housing quality, public services, crime, employment, health, and education. Residential segregation operates to deny educational opportunity and to diminish greatly educational access and success for black, Latino, and Native American students (Kozol 2005). Schools with majority black and Latino populations are more likely to be characterized by extreme poverty levels and low academic achievement. Schools with high poverty rates have substandard facilities, more social problems, outdated learning materials, lower test scores, weaker courses, less-qualified teachers, and lower graduation rates, and send fewer students to college.

Research shows an accelerated trend toward racial segregation in American schools. After peaking in 1985, the percentage of black students attending white majority schools dropped to the lowest levels since 1970. In both

1970 and in 1996, the average black student attended a school that was over two-thirds nonwhite. For Latinos, the level of racial segregation in schools steadily increased from 1970 to 1996. In 1970, most Latino students attended schools where the nonwhite students were slightly over half (56 percent). By 1996, most Latino students attended schools that were well over 70 percent nonwhite. At the very moment when the United States is becoming more racially diverse and more multicultural due to immigration and demographic shifts, the nation's schools are defying these trends and becoming increasingly resegregated by race (Frankenberg, Lee, and Orfield 2003).

The segregation of black, Latino, and Native American students is driven by racial, historical, social, political, and economic factors. Racial segregation in American schools has profoundly negative educational consequences for nonwhite students. Low-income students of color are forced to attend schools with fewer educational resources, where they likely receive substandard, inferior educations (Kozol 2005). As a result, these students are ill equipped to compete on equal footing with Whites for advanced education and training or jobs. The overall effect is to reinforce historic racial disparities in education and economics. The vicious, circular cycle repeats: non-Whites are poor because they lack education and training; they are denied education and training opportunities because they are nonwhite; and without education and training, they and their children are doomed to poverty. Although the society cynically pretends that all racial barriers have been removed, Blacks, Latinos, and Native Americans continue to be denied equal opportunity to participate fully in this society. It is no coincidence that Blacks, Latinos, and Native Americans are disproportionate among the nation's poor, the incarcerated, the unemployed, those with higher morbidity and mortality rates, and those who experience the poorest quality of life. Racial prejudice and racial discrimination operate in tandem with blocked educational opportunity and economic deprivation to disadvantage Blacks systematically in all areas of American life. Current policies, such as the diversion of funds from public schools to voucher systems and the increased usage of "high stakes" standardized tests, pose additional barriers to educational equality for Blacks, Latinos, and Native Americans.

BLACK EDUCATIONAL INEQUITY: DILEMMA OR DESIGN?

Written during the Great World War, which promised freedom and democracy for all mankind, Gunnar Myrdal's *An American Dilemma* (1944) examined the status, problems, and prospects of racially oppressed African Americans. He concluded that African Americans presented this nation with a moral dilemma since legal segregation and the racial caste system were inconsistent with the American Creed and its embrace of freedom, equality, and democracy. Myrdal optimistically concluded that the inherent tension between the reality of black second-class citizenship and the ideals defining America as the land of opportunity for all would eventually be reconciled by the acceptance of African Americans as full members of this society. The years have proven Myrdal partly correct but, on too many points, disturbingly wrong. Racism, racial discrimination, racial prejudice, and racial stereotypes have been shown to be intractable elements of the American cultural ethos (Bell 1992). Without a doubt, there have certainly been substantial progress and many victories; nevertheless, the empirical record demonstrates unequivocally that Blacks continue to be disadvantaged, dominated, and discriminated against in the land of their birth (Brown et al. 2003; Farley and Allen 1989).

Unless we acknowledge and discuss race and this country's racial history squarely, we are helpless to confront racial stereotypes or to dismantle the elaborate, discriminatory machinery on which black subordination *and* white supremacy are built. We also risk failure to comprehend a racial stratification system anchored by Whites at the apex and Blacks at the very bottom—conceptually, if not always accurately or completely in reality. Black progress has always helped fuel the progress of other groups in this society since the reality is that social expectations and norms continue to view Blacks as the underclass group and to place us at the very bottom of the racial hierarchy. Put another way, American ethics of justice, fairness, and equity require that "what we would do for the least of us, must certainly be done for the rest of us." The hot rhetoric about racial preferences and reverse discrimination aside, little evidence sustains the view that African Americans are somehow privileged in a society that systematically and unremittingly devalues blackness (Bonilla-Silva 2003b).

Myrdal was correct in pointing to an American dilemma; however, he misconstrues this as a moral dilemma. Rather, the dilemma with which America wrestles—and has wrestled for centuries—is how best to reconcile the practical morality of American capitalism with the ideal morality of the American creed (Ellison 1973; Marable 2002). Can an inherently exploitative system accommodate both the rhetoric and reality of equality? The historic and continuing subjugation of Blacks in America results from conscious, willful, determined actions designed to achieve this end. The power of this volume lies in its systematic illumination and interrogation of these factors and forces. The challenge this volume places before the country is "Will America commit to change and to a new, more democratic future or will the country continue to cling to its self-destructive heritage of racial exploitation, discrimination, and oppression?" Not only is the "black-white Achievement Gap" implicated and interrogated here, but also the very soul of the nation. How America answers the questions these authors raise will ultimately be the truest measure of the nobility of this country's unique experiment with democracy and our hope for survival and prosperity as a truly egalitarian, multicultural, caring society.

Walter Allen
David Lemmel

Bibliography

Adler, Patricia A., Steven J. Kless, and Peter Adler. 1992. Socialization to gender roles: Popularity among elementary school boys and girls. *Sociology of Education* 65(3): 169–87.

Ainsworth, James W. 2002. Why does it take a village? The mediation of neighborhood effects on educational achievement. *Social Forces* 81(1): 117–52.

Ainsworth-Darnell, James W., and Douglas B. Downey. 1998. Assessing the oppositional culture explanation for racial/ethnic differences in school performance. *American Sociological Review* 63(4): 536–53.

Akom, A. A. 2001. Racial profiling at school: The politics of race and discipline at Berkeley High. In *Zero tolerance*, ed. W. Ayers, B. Dohrm, and R. Ayers, 51–63. New York: New Press.

Alba, Richard, ed. 1985. *Ethnicity and race in the U.S.A.: Toward the twenty-first century.* Boston: Routledge and Kegan Paul.

Allen, W. R., and A. D. James. 1998. Comparative perspectives on Black family life: Uncommon explorations of a common subject. *Journal of Comparative Family Studies* 29(1): 1–11.

Anderson, Elijah. 1978. *A place on the corner.* Chicago: University of Chicago Press.

———. 1990. *Streetwise: Race, class, and change in an urban community.* Chicago: University of Chicago Press.

———. 1998. The code of the streets. In *Crossroads: The quest for contemporary rites of passage*, ed. Louise Carus Mahdi, Nancy Geyer Christopher, and Michael Meade, 91–97. Chicago: Open Court.

———. 1999. *Code of the street: Decency, violence, and the moral life of the inner city.* New York: Norton.

Anderson, James. 1988. *The Education of Blacks in the South: 1860–1935.* Chapel Hill: University of North Carolina Press.

Ann Arbor Public Schools. 1998. Indicators of Student Progress. Ann Arbor, MI: Board of Education.

Anzaldua, Gloria, ed. 1990. *Making face, making soul: Haciendo caras.* San Francisco: Aunt Lute Foundation Books.

Attaway, N. M., and B. H. Bry. 2004. Parenting style and black adolescent achievement. *Journal of Black Psychology* 30(2): 229–247.

Au, Kathryn, and Cathie Jordan. 1981. Teaching reading to Hawaiian children: Finding a culturally appropriate solution. In *Culture and the bilingual classroom,* ed. H. Trueba, Grace Pung Guthrie, and K. Au, 139–52. Rawley, MA: Newbury House.

Barth, Frederick. 1969. *Ethnic groups and boundaries: The social organization of culture difference.* Boston: Little, Brown.

Bashi, Vilna. 1997. Survival of the knitted: The social networks of West Indian immigrants. PhD diss., University of Wisconsin, Madison.

———.1998a. Racial categories matter because racial hierarchies matter: A commentary. *Ethnic and Racial Studies* 21: 959–68.

———. 1998b. Hubs, spokes, and a culture of reciprocity: Elements of an immigrant social network. Paper presented at the annual meeting of the American Sociological Association, San Francisco.

Beale, Frances. 1995. Double jeopardy: To be Black and female. In *Words of Fire: An Anthology of African-American Feminist Thought,* edited by B. Guy-Sheftall, pp. 146–55. New York: The New Press.

Belk et al. v. Charlotte-Mecklenburg Schools. 99-2389. 1999.

Bell, Derrick. 1992. *Faces at the bottom of the well: The permanence of racism.* New York: Basic Books.

Bellair, Paul, and Vincent J. Roscigno. 2000. Local labor-market opportunity and adolescent delinquency. *Social Forces* 78: 1509–38.

Bell-Scott, P., and R. Taylor. 1989. The multiple ecologies of Black adolescent development. *Journal of Adolescent Research* 4(2): 119–24.

Belluck, Pam. 1999. "Reason is sought for lag by Blacks in school effort." *New York Times,* July 4, p. 1.

Benjamin, Lois. 1991. *The Black elite.* Chicago: Nelson-Hall.

Bernstein, B. 1977. Social class, language and socialization. In *Power and ideology in education,* ed. J. Karabel and A. H. Halsey, 473–86. New York: Oxford University Press.

Bloom, B. S., A. Davis, and R. Hess. 1965. *Compensatory education for cultural deprivation.* Chicago: University of Chicago Press.

Blumer, Herbert. 1958. Race prejudice as a sense of group position. *Pacific Sociological Review* 1: 3–7.

Bobo, Lawrence, James R. Kluegel, and Ryan A. Smith. 1997. Laissez faire racism: The crystallization of a 'kinder, gentler' anti-Black ideology. In *Racial attitudes in the 1990s: Continuity and change,* ed. S. Tuch and J. Martin, 15–42. Westport, CT: Praeger.

Bonilla-Silva, Eduardo. 2001. *White supremacy and racism in the post-civil rights era.* Boulder, CO: Lynne Rienner.

———. 2003a. 'New racism,' color-blind racism, and the future of whiteness in America. In *White out: The continuing significance of racism,* ed. A. Doane and E. Bonilla-Silva, 271–84. New York: Routledge.

———. 2003b. *Racism without racists: Color-blind racism and the persistence of racial inequality in the United States.* Lanham, MD: Rowman & Littlefield.

Bonilla-Silva, Eduardo, and Amanda Lewis. 1999. The new racism: Racial structure in the United States, 1960s–1990s. In *Race, ethnicity, and nationality in the United States*, ed. P. Wong, 55–101. Boulder, CO: Westview.

Bourdieu, Pierre. 1977. Cultural reproduction and social reproduction. In *Power and Ideology in Education*, ed. J. Karabel and A. H. Halsey, 487–511. New York: Oxford University Press.

Bourdieu, Pierre, and Jean-Claude Passeron. 1977. *Reproduction in Education, Society and Culture.* London: Sage Publications.

Bowen, W. G., and D. C. Bok. 1998. *The shape of the river: Long-term consequences of considering race in college and university admissions.* Princeton, NJ: Princeton University Press.

Bowles, S., and H. Gintis. 1976. *Schooling in capitalist America: Educational reform and the contradictions of economic life.* New York: Basic Books.

———. 2002. Schooling in capitalist America revisited. *Sociology of Education* 75(1): 1–18.

Brint, S., and J. Karabel. 1989. *The diverted dream: community colleges and the promise of educational opportunity in America 1900–1985.* New York: Oxford University Press.

Brody, Gene H., Xiaojia Ge, Rand Conger, Frederick X. Gibbons, Velma McBride Murry, Meg Gerrard, and Ronald L. Simons. 2001. The influence of neighborhood disadvantage, collective socialization, and parenting on African American children's affiliation with deviant peers. *Child Development* 72: 1231–46.

Brofenbrenner, Urie. 1979. *The ecology of human development: Experiment by nature and design.* Cambridge, MA: Harvard University Press.

Brooks-Gunn, Jeanne, Greg J. Duncan, Pamela Kato Klebanov, and Naomi Sealand. 1993. Do neighborhoods influence child and adolescent development? *American Journal of Sociology* 99: 353–95.

Brown v. Board of Education of Topeka. 347 U.S. 483. 1954.

Brown, J. 1995. "Author puts a happy face on racism." *Tampa Tribune*, October 8, metro edition, p. 4.

———. 2000. "Mirror reveals difficult truths," *Tampa Tribune*, September 24, final edition, p. 4.

———. 2003a. "Civil rights pioneers strove to close gap," *Tampa Tribune*, January 19, final edition, commentary, p. 6.

———. 2003b. "Failing students too often lack motivation." *Tampa Tribune*, July 6, final edition, commentary, p. 6.

Brown, Michael K., Martin Carnoy, Elliott Currie, Troy Duster, David B. Oppenheimer, Marjorie M. Schultz, and David Wellman. 2003. *Whitewashing race: The myth of a color-blind society.* Berkeley: University of California Press.

Bryant, Bunyan. 1995. *Environmental Justice: Issues, Policies, and Solutions.* Washington, DC: Island Press.

Bryce-Laporte, Roy S. 1972. Black immigrants: The experience of invisibility an inequality. *Journal of Black Studies* 3: 29–56.

———. 1987. New York City and the new Caribbean immigration: A contextual statement. In *Caribbean life in New York City: Sociocultural dimensions*, ed. C. Sutton and E. Chaney, pp. 54–73. New York: Center for Migration Studies.

———. 1993. Voluntary immigration and the continuing encounters between Blacks: The post quincentenary challenge. *Annals of the American Academy of Political and Social Science* 530: 28–41.

Bryk, A. S., V. E. Lee, and P. B. Holland. 1993. *Catholic schools and the common good.* Cambridge, MA: Harvard University Press.

Bullard, Robert D. 2000. *Dumping in Dixie: Race, Class, and Environmental Quality.* Boulder, CO: Westview.

Burke, Peter J. 1989. Gender identity, sex, and school performance. *Social Psychology Quarterly* 52(2): 159–69.

Butcher, Kristin F. 1994. Black immigrants in the United States: A comparison with native blacks and other immigrants. *Industrial and Labor Relations Review* 47(2): 265–83.

Butterfield, Sherri-Ann P. 2001. Big tings a gwaan: Constructions of racial and ethnic identity among second generation West Indians. PhD diss., University of Michigan, Ann Arbor.

———. 2003. Something in between: Locating identity among second-generation West Indians in New York City. In *Mighty change, tall within: Black identity in the Hudson Valley*, ed. Myra B. Armstead, 232–61. Albany: State University of New York Press.

———. 2004a. Challenging American conceptions of race and ethnicity: Second generation West Indian immigrants. *International Journal of Sociology and Social Policy* 24(7/8): 75–102.

———. 2004b. 'We're just black': The racial and ethnic identities of second generation West Indians in New York. In *Becoming New Yorkers: Ethnographies of the new second generation*, ed. P. Kasinitz, J. Mollenkopf, and M. Waters, 288–312. New York: Russell Sage Foundation.

Campbell, J. R., C. M. Hombo, and J. Mazzeo. 2000. NAEP trends in academic progress: Three decades of student performance (NCES 2000-469). Washington, DC: U.S. Dept. of Education.

Capacchione et al. v. Charlotte-Mecklenburg Schools. Civil Action No. 3: 97 CV 482. 1997.

Carter, Prudence. 1999. Balancing 'acts': Issues of identity and cultural resistance in the social and educational behaviors of minority youth. PhD diss., Columbia University, New York.

———. 2003. 'Black' cultural capital, status positioning, and schooling conflicts for low-income African American youth. *Social Problems* 50(1): 136–55.

———. 2005. *Keepin' it real: School success beyond Black.* New York: Oxford University Press.

Catsambis, Sophia. 1994. The path to math: Gender and racial-ethnic differences in mathematics participation from middle school to high school. *Sociology of Education* 67(3): 199–215.

Catsambis, Sophia, and Andrew A. Beveridge. 2001. Does neighborhood matter? Family, neighborhood, and school influences on eighth-grade mathematics achievement. *Sociological Focus* 34: 435–57.

Cauce, Ana M., Yumi Hirage, Diane Graves, Nancy Gonzales, Kimberly Ryan-Finn, and Kwai Grove. 1996. African American mothers and their adolescent daughters: Closeness, conflict, and control. In *Urban girls: Resisting stereotypes, creating identities*, ed. B. J. R. Leadbeater and N. Way, pp. 100–116. New York: New York University Press.

Cazden, Courtney B. 1988. *Classroom discourse: The language of teaching and learning*. Portsmouth, NH: Heinemann.

Cazden, Courtney B., Vera P. John, and Dell Hymes. 1972. *Functions of language in the classroom*. Prospect Heights, IL: Waveland.

Cenzipur, Debbie. 2001. "New standards hit minorities hard." *Charlotte Observer*, December 17, A7.

Charen, M. 1997. "The answer to racial discrimination cannot be more discrimination." *St. Louis Post-Dispatch*, December 14, five-star edition, editorial, B3.

Chase-Lansdale, P. Lindsay, and Rachel A. Gordon. 1996. Economic hardship and the development of five- and six-year-olds: neighborhood and regional perspectives. *Child Development* 67: 3338–67.

Chase-Lansdale, P. Lindsay, Rachel A. Gordon, Jeanne Brooks-Gunn, and Pamela K. Klebanov. 1997. Neighborhood and family influences on the intellectual and behavioral competence of preschool and early school-age children. In *Neighborhood poverty: Context and consequences for children*, ed. Jeanne Brooks-Gunn, Greg J. Duncan, and J. Lawrence Aber, 79–118. New York: Russell Sage Foundation.

Cheng, Simon, and Brian Starks. 2002. Racial differences in the effects of significant others on students' educational expectations. *Sociology of Education* 75(4): 306–27.

Chesler, Mark, Amanda Lewis, and Jim Crowfoot. 2005. *Challenging racism and promoting multiculturalism in higher education*. Lanham, MD: Rowman & Littlefield.

Clark, B. R. 1960. The "cooling out" function of higher education. *American Journal of Sociology* 65(6): 569–76.

Clark, Reginald. 1983. *Family life and school achievement: Why poor Black children succeed and fail*. Chicago: University of Chicago Press.

———. 1992. Neighborhood effects on dropping out of school among teenage boys. Mimeographed. Washington, DC: Urban Institute.

Cole, Luke, and Sheila Foster. 2000. *From the Ground Up: Environmental Racism and the Rise of the Environmental Justice Movement*. New York: New York University Press.

Coleman, James S., et al. 1966. *Equality of educational opportunity*. Washington, DC: U.S. Dept. of Health, Education, and Welfare.

College Board, The. 1999. *Reaching the top: A report of the national task force on minority high achievement*. New York: The College Board.

Collins, Patricia Hill. 1991. *Black feminist thought*. New York: Routledge.

———. 2004. *Black sexual politics: African Americans, gender, and the new racism*. New York: Routledge.

Conley, D. 1999. *Being black, living in the red: Race, wealth, and social policy in America*. Berkeley: University of California Press.

Connell, James P., and Bonnie L. Halpern-Felsher. 1997. How neighborhoods affect educational outcomes in middle childhood and adolescence: Conceptual issues and an empirical example. In *Neighborhood poverty: Context and consequences for children*, eds. Jeanne Brooks-Gunn, Greg J. Duncan, and J. Lawrence Aber. New York: Russell Sage Foundation.

Connell, James P., Bonnie L. Halpern-Felsher, Elizabeth Clifford, Warren Crichlow, and Peter Usinger. 1995. Hanging in there: Behavioral, psychological, and contextual factors affecting whether African American adolescents stay in high school. *Journal of Adolescent Research* 10: 41–63.

Connell, Robert W. 1995. *Masculinities*. Berkeley: University of California Press.

Cook, M. D., and W. M. Evans. 2000. Families or schools? Explaining the convergence in White and Black academic performance. *Journal of Labor Economics* 18(4): 729–55.

Cook, Philip J., and Jens Ludwig. 1997. Weighing the burden of 'acting white': Are there race differences in attitudes toward education? *Journal of Policy Analysis and Management* 16: 256–78.

———. 1998. The burden of acting white: Do black adolescents disparage academic achievement? In *The Black-white test score gap*, ed. Christopher Jencks and Meredith Phillips, 375–400. Washington, DC: Brookings.

Cookson, Peter, Jr., and Caroline Hodges Persell. 1985. *Preparing for power: America's elite boarding schools*. New York: Basic Books.

Corcoran, Mary, Roger Gordon, Deborah Laren, and Gary Solon. 1987. Intergenerational transmission of education, income and earnings. Unpublished paper. Political Science Department, University of Michigan, Ann Arbor.

Cose, Ellis, and Allison Samuels. 2003. The Black gender gap. *Newsweek*, March 3, p. 46.

Coulton, Claudia J., Shanta Pandey, and Julian Chow. 1990. Concentration of poverty and the changing ecology of low-income, urban neighborhoods: An analysis of the Cleveland area. *Social Work Research and Abstracts* 26: 5–16.

Cousins, L. H. 2006. Black students' individual and collective identity and 'acting black and white.' In *Collective identity and schooling*, ed. John U. Ogbu, Mahwah, NJ: Erlbaum.

Crane, Jonathan. 1991. The epidemic theory of ghettos and neighborhood effects on dropping out and teenage childbirth. *American Journal of Sociology* 96: 1226–59.

Crenshaw, Kimberlé W. 1992. Whose story is it anyway? Feminist and antiracist appropriations of Anita Hill. In *Race-ing justice, en-gendering power*, ed. Toni Morrison, pp. 402–436. New York: Pantheon Books.

———. 1997. Color-blind Dreams and Racial Nightmares: Reconfiguring Racism in the Post-Civil Rights Era. In *Birth of a Nation'hood*, ed. T. Morrison & C. B. Lacour, 97–168. New York: Pantheon Books.

Cross, T., and R. B. Slater. 2000. The alarming decline in the academic performance of African American men. *The Journal of Blacks in Higher Education* 27: 82–87.

Crowder, Kyle D. 1999. Residential segregation of West Indians in the New York/New Jersey metropolitan area: The roles of race and ethnicity. *International Migration Review* 33: 79–113.

Crowder, Kyle D., and Lucky M. Tedrow. 2001. West Indians and the residential landscape of New York. In *Islands in the city: West Indian migration to New York*, ed. Nancy Foner, 81–114. Berkeley: University of California Press.

Dachter-Loury, L. 1989. Family background and school achievement among low income blacks. *The Journal of Human Resources* 25(3): 528–44.

Darity, W. A. 2002. Intergroup disparity: Why culture is irrelevant. Unpublished manuscript, University of North Carolina, Chapel Hill.

Darling-Hammond, Linda. 2003. Colorblind education: Will it help us leave no child behind? Presentation at conference on Colorblind racism: The politics of controlling racial and ethnic data, Stanford University, Palo Alto, California.

Datcher, Linda. 1982. Effects of community and family background on achievement. *Review of Economics and Statistics* 64: 32–41.

Davidson, Ann Locke. 1996. *Making and molding identity in schools: Student narratives on race, gender, and academic engagement.* Albany: State University of New York Press.

Delpit, Lisa. 1995. *Other people's children: Cultural conflict in the classroom.* New York: New Press.

Deutsch, M. 1967. *The disadvantaged child: Selected papers of Martin Deutsch and associates.* New York: Basic Books.

Dickerson, D. 2004. *The end of blackness: Returning the souls of Black folk to their rightful owners.* New York: Pantheon Books.

DiMaggio, Paul. 1982. "Cultural Capital and School Success: The Impact of Status Culture Participation on the Grades of U.S. High School Students." *American Sociological Review* 47: 189–201.

Doane, Ashley W. 2003. Rethinking whiteness studies. In *White out: The continuing significance of racism*, ed. A. Doane and E. Bonilla-Silva, 3–20. New York: Routledge.

Dodoo, F. Nii-Amoo. 1991. Earning differences among Blacks in America. *Social Science Research* 20: 93–108.

———. 1997. Assimilation differences among Africans in America. *Social Forces* 76(2): 527–46.

Dornbusch, Sanford M., Phillip L. Ritter, and Laurence Steinberg. 1991. Community influences on the relation of family statuses to adolescent school performance: Differences between African Americans and non-Hispanic whites. *American Journal of Education* 99: 543–67.

Downey, D. B., and J. W. Ainsworth-Darnell. 2002. Reply: The search for oppositional culture among Black students. *American Sociological Review* 67: 156–64.

Drake, St. Clair, and Horace R. Cayton. 1962. *Black Metropolis: A Study of Negro Life in a Northern City.* New York: Harper & Row.

D'Souza, D. 1995. *The end of racism: Principles for a multiracial society.* New York: Free Press.

DuBois, W. E. B. 1999. *Black reconstruction in America 1860–1880.* New York: Free Press.

DuBois, W. E. B., and A. G. Dill. 1911. *The common school and the Negro American.* Atlanta: Atlanta University Press.

Duncan, Greg J. 1994. Families and neighbors as sources of disadvantage in the schooling decisions of White and Black adolescents. *American Journal of Education* 103: 20–53.

Duncan, Greg J., Jeanne Brooks-Gunn, and Pamela Kato Klebanov. 1994. Economic deprivation and early childhood development. *Child Development* 65: 296–318.

Duneier, Mitchell. 1992. *Slim's table: Race, respectability, and masculinity.* Chicago: University of Chicago Press.

Edsall, Thomas Byrne, and Mary D. Edsall. 1991. *Chain reaction: The impact of race, rights, and taxes on American politics.* New York: Norton.

Education Week. 2000. NAEP results indicate narrowing of race gap. September 6, p. 7.

Elder, Glen. 1985. Household, kinship, and the life course: Perspectives on Black families and children. In *Beginnings: The social and affective development of*

Black children, ed. Margaret Beale Spencer, G. K. Brookins, and W. R. Allen, 29–44. Mahwah, NJ: Erlbaum.

Elder, Glen H., Jr. 1998. The life course and human development. In *Handbook of child psychology*, Volume 1: *Theoretical models human development*, ed. Richard Lerner, 939–91. New York: Wiley.

Ellison, Ralph. 1973. An American dilemma: a review. In *The death of white sociology*, ed. Joyce A. Ladner, 81–95. New York: Vintage Books.

Ensminger, Margaret E., Rebecca P. Lamkin, and Nora Jacobson. 1996. School leaving: A longitudinal perspective including neighborhood effects. *Child Development* 67: 2400–2416.

Entwisle, Doris R., Karl L. Alexander, and Linda Steffel Olson. 1994. The gender gap in math: Its possible origins in neighborhood effects. *American Sociological Review* 59: 822–38.

Entwisle, Doris, and Leslie Hayduk. 1978. *Too great expectations: The academic outlook of young children*. Baltimore: Johns Hopkins University Press.

Epstein, Debbie, Jannette Elwood, Valerie Hey, and Janet Maw, eds. 1998. *Failing boys: Issues in gender & achievement*. Buckingham, UK: Open University Press.

Epstein, Jonathan. 1998. *Youth culture: Identity in a postmodern world*. Malden, MA: Blackwell.

Erickson, Frederick. 1987. Transformation and school success: The politics and culture of educational achievement. *Anthropology & Education Quarterly* 18(4): 335–56.

Essed, Philomena. 1991. *Understanding everyday racism: An interdisciplinary theory*. Newbury Park, CA: Sage.

———. 1997. Racial intimidation: Sociopolitical implications of the usage of racist slurs. In *The language and politics of exclusion*, ed. S. H. Riggins, 131–52. Thousand Oaks, CA: Sage.

Fainstein, N. 1986–1987. The underclass/mismatch hypothesis an as explanation for Black economic deprivation. *Politics and Society* 15: 403–15.

Farkas, George. 1996. *Human capital or cultural capital: Ethnicity and poverty groups in an urban school district*. New York: Aldine.

Farkas, George, Christy Lleras, and Steve Maczuga. 2002. Comment: Does oppositional culture exist in minority and poverty peer groups? *American Sociological Review* 67(1): 148–55.

Farley, Reynolds. 1988. After the starting line: Blacks and women in an uphill race. *Demography* 25: 477–95.

Farley, Reynolds, and Walter Allen. 1987. *The color line and the quality of life in America*. New York: Oxford University Press.

Favors, J. Martin. 1999. *Authentic Blackness: The folk in the new Negro renaissance*. Durham, NC: Duke University Press.

Feagin, Joe R. 2000. *Racist America: Roots, current realities, and future reparations*. New York: Routledge.

Feagin, Joe R., and Karyn D. McKinney. 2003. *The Many Costs of Racism*. Lanham, MD: Rowman and Littlefield.

Ferguson, Ann Arnett. 2000. *Bad boys: Public schools in the making of Black masculinity*. Ann Arbor: University of Michigan Press.

Ferguson, R. F. 1998. Comment on Cook and Ludwig. In *The Black-white test score gap*, ed. Christopher Jencks and Meredith Phillips, 394–97. Washington, DC: Brookings.

———. 2001. A diagnostic analysis of Black-white GPA disparities in Shaker Heights, Ohio. In *Brookings papers on education policy*, ed. Diane Ravitch, 347–414. Washington, DC: Brookings.

Fischer, C. S., M. Hout, M. S. Jankowski, S. R. Lucas, A. Swidler, and K. Voss. 1996. *Inequality by design: Cracking the bell curve myth*. Princeton, NJ: Princeton University Press.

Fisher, M. 1987. "Peers inhibit Black achievers, study of D.C. schools finds; Academic success derided as 'acting white.' *Washington Post*, March 14, final edition, A1.

Fivush, Robyn. 1991. The social construction of personal narratives. *Merrill-Palmer Quarterly* 37: 59–82.

———. 2001. Owning experience: Developing subjective perspective in autobiographical narratives. In *The self in time: Developmental perspectives*, ed. K. Lemmon and C. Moore, 35–52. Mahwah, NJ: Erlbaum.

Flynn, J. 1980. *Race, IQ, and Jensen*. London: Routledge and Kegan Paul.

Foley, Douglas E. 1991. Reconsidering anthropological explanations of ethnic school failure. *Anthropology and Education Quarterly* 22: 60–94.

Foner, Nancy. 1979. West Indians in New York City and London: A comparative analysis. *International Migration Review* 13: 284–313.

———. 1985. Race and color: Jamaican migrants in London and New York City. *International Migration Review* 19: 708–27.

———. 1987. The Jamaicans: Race and ethnicity among migrants in New York City. In *New Immigrants in New York*, ed. Nancy Foner, 195–217. New York: Columbia University Press.

———. 2001. West Indian migration to New York: An overview. In *Islands in the city: West Indian migration to New York*, ed. Nancy Foner, 1–22. Berkeley: University of California Press.

Ford, Donna Y. 1998. The underrepresentation of minority students in gifted education: Problems and promises in recruitment and retention. *The Journal of Special Education* 32(1): 4–14.

Ford, Donna Y., and J. John Harris. 1992. The American achievement ideology and achievement differentials among preadolescent gifted and nongifted African American males and females. *Journal of Negro Education* 61(1): 45–64.

———. 1996. Perceptions and attitudes of Black students toward school, achievement, and other educational variables. *Child Development* 67: 1141–52.

Ford, Donna Y., J. John Harris, and J. Schueger. 1993. Racial identity development among gifted Black students: counseling issues and concerns. *Journal of Counseling & Development* 71(4): 409–17.

Fordham, Signithia. 1988. Racelessness in Black students' school success: Pragmatic strategy or pyrrhic victory? *Harvard Educational Review* 58(1): 54–84.

———. 1991. Racelessness in private schools: Should we deconstruct the racial and cultural identity of African-American adolescents? *Teachers College Record* 92(3): 470–84.

———. 1996a. *Blacked out: Dilemmas of race, identity, and success at Capital High*. Chicago: University of Chicago Press.

216   *Bibliography*

------. 1996b. Racelessness as a factor in Black students' school success: Pragmatic strategy or pyrrhic victory? In *Facing racism in education*, 2nd edition, ed. T. Beauboeuf-Lafontant and D. S. Augustine, 209–244. Cambridge, MA: Harvard Education Review Reprint Series No. 28.

Fordham, Signithia, and John Ogbu. 1986. Black students and school success: Coping with the burden of acting white. *Urban Review* 18(3): 176–206.

Forman, Tyrone. 2004. "Color-blind Racism and Racial Indifference: The Role of Racial Apathy in Facilitating Enduring Inequalities." In *Changing Terrain of Race & Ethnicity*, ed. M. Krysan and A. E. Lewis, 43–66. New York: Russell Sage.

Foster, Michele. 1997. *Black teachers on teaching*. New York: New Press.

Frankenberg, Erica, Chungmei Lee, and Gary Orfield. 2003. *A multiracial society with segregated schools: Are we losing the dream?* Cambridge, MA: The Civil Rights Project, Harvard University.

Frankenberg, Ruth. 1993. *White women, race matters: The social construction of whiteness*. Minneapolis: University of Minnesota Press.

Franklin, Vincent. 1981. Continuity and discontinuity in black and immigrant minority education in urban America: An historical assessment. In *Educating an urban people*, ed. D. Ravitch, 44–66. New York: Teachers College Press.

Freeman, M. 1998. Mythical time, historical time, and the narrative fabric of the self. *Narrative Inquiry* 8: 37–50.

Fulwood, S., III. 2002. "Minority students equally motivated." *Plain Dealer*, November 21, final edition, metro, B1.

Gaines, J. 1996. "Two high-profile foes debate at BU forum on race, rationality." *The Boston Globe*, April 28, metro/region, p. 35.

Gans, Herbert. 1992. Second-generation decline: Scenarios for the economic and ethnic futures of the post-1965 American immigrants. *Ethnic and Racial Studies* 15(2): 173–92.

------. 1996. From "underclass" to "undercaste": Some observations about the future of the post-industrial economy and its major victims. In *Urban poverty and the underclass*, ed. Enzo Mingione, 173–92. Cambridge, MA: Blackwell Publishing.

Garner, Catherine L., and Stephen W. Raudenbush. 1991. Neighborhood effects on educational attainment: a multilevel analysis. *Sociology of Education* 64: 251–62.

Gee, James Paul. 2000–2001. Identity as an analytic lens for research in education. *Review of Research in Education* 25: 99–123.

George, Nelson. 1998. *Hip hop America*. New York: Viking Press.

Gibson, M., and John U. Ogbu. 1991. *Minority status and schooling: A comparative study of immigrant and involuntary minorities*. New York: Garland.

Gilliam, D. 1985. "You define yourself." *Washington Post*, March 28, final edition, metro, D3.

Glaser, Barney, and Anselm Strauss. 1967. *The discovery of grounded theory: Strategies for qualitative research*. New York: Aldine De Gruyter.

Goleman, D. 1988. "An emerging theory on Blacks' I.Q. scores." *New York Times*, April 10, late city, final edition, outlook, C1.

Goffman, Erving. 1959. *The presentation of self in everyday life*. New York: Doubleday.

Gordon, Edmund T. 1997. Cultural politics of Black masculinity. *Transforming Anthropology* 6(1&2): 36–53.

Gottlieb, D., and C. E. Ramsey. 1967. *Understanding children of poverty*. Chicago: Science Research Associates.

Gould, Mark. 1999. Race and theory: Culture, poverty, and adaptation to discrimination in Wilson and Ogbu. *Sociological Theory* 17(2): 171–200.

Grissmer, D., A. Flanagan, and S. Williamson. 1998. Why did the Black-white score gap narrow in the 1970s and 1980s? In *The Black-white test score gap*, ed. Christopher Jencks and Meredith Phillips, 182–226. Washington, DC: Brookings.

Hale, J. 1982. *Black children: Their roots, culture, and learning styles*. Baltimore: Johns Hopkins University Press.

Hallinan, M. T. 2001. Sociological perspectives on Black-white inequalities in American schooling. *Sociology of Education*, Extra Issue: 50–70.

Hallinan, M. T., and A. Sorensen. 1977. The dynamics of learning: A conceptual model. Discussion paper 444-77. Madison, WI: Institute for Research on Society.

Halpern-Felsher, Bonnie L., James P. Connell, Margaret Beale Spencer, J. Lawrence Aber, Greg J. Duncan, Elizabeth Clifford, Warren E. Crichlow, Peter A. Usinger, Steven P. Cole, LaRue Allen, and Edward Seidman. 1997. Neighborhood and family factors predicting educational risk and attainment in African American and white children and adolescents. In *Neighborhood poverty: Context and consequences for children*, ed. Jeanne Brooks-Gunn, Greg J. Duncan, and J. Lawrence Aber, 146-73. New York: Russell Sage Foundation.

Hannerz, Ulf. 1969. *Soulside: Inquiries into ghetto culture and community*. New York: Columbia University Press.

Harter, Susan. 1990. Self and identity development. In *At the threshold: The developing adolescent*, ed. S. S. Feldman and G. R. Elliott, 352–87. Cambridge, MA: Harvard University Press.

Healy, P. 2003. "Justice's 'deadline' confounds colleges." *Boston Globe*, June 29, third edition, education, A1.

Heath, Shirley Brice. 1983. *Ways with words: Language, life, and work in communities and classrooms*. New York: Cambridge University Press.

Hedges, L., and A. Nowell. 1998. Black-white test score convergence since 1965. In *The Black-white test score gap*, ed. Christopher Jencks and Meredith Phillips, 149–81. Washington, DC: Brookings.

Hemmings, Annette. 1996. Conflicting images? Being Black and a model high school student. *Anthropology & Education Quarterly* 27(1): 20–50.

———. 1998. Self-transformations of African American achievers. *Youth & Society* 29(3): 330–68.

———. 2000a. The "hidden" corridor curriculum. *High School Journal* 83(2): 1–10.

———. 2000b. Lona's links: Postoppositional identity work of urban youths. *Anthropology & Education Quarterly* 31(2): 152–72.

———. 2002. Youth culture of hostility: Discourses of money, respect, and difference. *International Journal of Qualitative Studies in Education* 15(3): 291–307.

———. 2004. *Coming of age in U.S. high schools: Economic, kinship, religious, and political crosscurrents*. Mahweh, NJ: Erlbaum.

Herrnstein, R., and C. Murray. 1994. *The bell curve: Intelligence and class structure in American life*. New York: Free Press.

Hewitt, John P. 1984. *Self and society: A symbolic interactionist social psychology*. Boston: Allyn and Bacon.

Hilliard, Asa G., III. 1995. Either a paradigm shift or no mental measurement. *Psych Discourse* 26(10): 6–20.

Hoberman, John. 1997. *Darwin's athletes: How sport has damaged Black America and preserved the myth of race.* New York: Houghton Mifflin Mariner Books.

Hochschild, Jennifer L. 1995. *Facing up to the American dream: Race, class, and the soul of the nation.* Princeton, NJ: Princeton University Press.

Hoffman, Diane M. 1998. Therapeutic moment? Identity, self, and culture in the anthropology of education. *Anthropology & Education Quarterly* 29(3): 324–46.

Holliday, B. 1985. Differential effects of children's self-perceptions and teachers' perceptions on Black children's academic achievement. *Journal of Negro Education* 54(1): 71–81.

hooks, bell. 1984. *From margin to center.* Boston: South End Press.

Hopkins, Ronnie. 1997. *Educating Black males: Critical lessons in schooling, community, and power.* Albany: State University of New York Press.

Horvat, E. M. 2001. Reassessing the 'burden of acting white': Black students, school success and the importance of school context and family habitus. Unpublished manuscript.

Horvat, E. M., and K. Lewis. 2003. Reassessing the "burden of 'acting white': The importance of peer groups in managing academic success. *Sociology of Education* 76(4): 265–80.

Horvat, E. M., Elliot Weininger, & Annette Lareau. 2003. From social ties to social capital: Class differences in the relation between school and parent networks. *American Educational Research Journal* 40(2): 319–51.

Hubbard, Lea, and Hugh Mehan. 1999. Race and reform: Educational 'niche picking' in a hostile environment. *Journal of Negro Education* 68(2): 213–26.

Hubbard, Lea, and Roslyn A. Mickelson. 2004. How racism ruins reform. University of San Diego. Unpublished manuscript under review.

Hughes, Mark Alan. 1989. Misspeaking truth to power: A geographical perspective on the 'underclass' fallacy. *Economic Geography* 65: 187–207.

Institute for Democracy, Education, and Access. 2004. Separate and unequal 50 years after Brown: California's racial 'opportunity gap.' UCLA, Graduate School of Education and Information Studies.

Jacobs, Jerry A. 1996. Gender inequality and higher education. *Annual Review of Sociology* 22: 153–85.

Jacoby, R., and N. Glauberman, eds. 1995. *The bell curve debate: history, documents, opinions.* New York: Times Books.

Jaggi, M. 2002. Review: Profile: Henry the first. *The Guardian,* July 6, p. 20.

Jargowsky, Paul A., and Mary Jo Bane. 1991. Ghetto poverty in the United States, 1970–1980. In *The urban underclass,* ed. Christopher Jencks and P. E. Peterson, 16–55. Washington, DC: Brookings.

Jencks, Christopher, and Susan E. Mayer. 1990. The social consequences of growing up in a poor neighborhood. In *Inner-city poverty in the United States,* ed. Laurence E. Lynn Jr. and Michael G. H. McGeary, 111–85. Washington, DC: National Academy Press.

Jencks, Christopher, and Meredith Phillips, eds. 1998a. The Black-white test score gap: An introduction. In *The Black-white test score gap,* ed. Christopher Jencks and Meredith Phillips, 1–51. Washington, DC: Brookings.

———, eds. 1998b. *The Black-white test score gap.* Washington, DC: Brookings.

Jensen, Arthur R. 1969. How much can we boost IQ and scholastic achievement? *Harvard Educational Review* 39(1): 1–123.

Kalmijn, Mattijs. 1996. The socioeconomic assimilation of Caribbean American Blacks. *Social Forces* 74: 911–30.

Kalmijn, Mattijs, and Gerbert Kraaykamp. 1996. Race, cultural capital, and schooling: An analysis of trends in the United States. *Sociology of Education* 69(1): 22–34.

Kao, Grace, and Marta Tienda. 1998. Educational aspirations of minority youth. *American Journal of Education* 106(3): 349–84.

Kao, Grace, Marta Tienda, and Barbara Schneider. 1995. Optimism and achievement: The educational performance of immigrant youth. *Social Science Quarterly* 76:1–19.

———. 1996. Racial and ethnic variation in academic performance. *Research in Sociology of Education and Socialization* 11: 263–97.

Kasarda, John D. 1988. Jobs, migration, and emerging urban mismatch. In *Urban change and poverty*, ed. Michael G. H. McGeary and Laurence E. Lynn, Jr., 148–98. Washington, DC: National Academy Press.

———. 1989. Urban industrial transition and the underclass. *Annals of the American Academy of Political and Social Sciences* 501: 26–47.

———. 1993. Inner-city concentrated poverty and neighborhood distress: 1970–1990. *Housing Policy Debate* 4: 253–302.

Kasinitz, Philip. 1987. The minority within: The new black immigrants. *New York Affairs* 10(1): 44–58.

———. 1992. *Caribbean New York: Black immigrants and the politics of race.* Ithaca, NY: Cornell University Press.

Kasinitz, Philip, Juan Battle, and Miyares Ines. 2001. Fade to Black? The children of West Indian immigrants in Southern Florida. In *Ethnicities: Children of immigrants in America*, ed. R. Rumbaut and A. Portes, 267–300. Berkeley: University of California Press.

Kazmin, B. R. 2003. "Mind-set is better than quotas." *The Columbus Dispatch*, January 20, home final edition, editorial & comment, 9A.

Kelley, Robin. 1994. *Race rebels: Culture, politics and the Black working class.* New York: Free Press.

Kelly, J. 2001. "Learn baby learn; Too many Black Americans choose self-sabatoge. Why?" *Pittsburgh Post-Gazette*, May 27, two-star edition, forum, E3.

King, Deborah K. 1996. Multiple jeopardy, multiple consciousness: The context of Black feminist ideology. In *Words of fire: An anthology of African-American feminist thought*, ed. B. Guy-Sheftall, pp. 294–317. New York: New Press.

Kinney, David A. 1993. From nerds to normals: The recovery of identity among adolescents from middle to high school. *Sociology of Education* 66(1): 21–40.

Kirschenman, Joleen, and Kathryn M. Neckerman. 1991. 'We'd love to hire them, but': The meaning of race for employers. In *The Urban underclass*, ed. Christopher Jencks and P. E. Peterson, 203–32. Washington, DC: Brookings.

Klebanov, Pamela K., Jeanne Brooks-Gunn, P. Lindsay Chase-Lansdale, and Rachel A. Gordon. 1997. Are neighborhood effects on young children mediated by features of the home environment? In *Neighborhood poverty: Context and consequences for children*, ed. Jeanne Brooks-Gunn, Greg J. Duncan, and J. Lawrence Aber, 119–45. New York: Russell Sage Foundation.

Kochman, Thomas. 1981. *Black and white: Styles in conflict.* Chicago: University of Chicago Press.

Kovach, J. A., and D. E. Gordon. 1997. Inclusive education: A modern day civil-rights struggle. *Educational Forum* 61: 247–57.

Kozol, Jonathan. 1991. *Savage inequalities.* New York: HarperPerennial.

———. 2005. *The shame of the nation: The restoration of apartheid schooling.* New York: Crown.

Krivo, Lauren J., Ruth D. Peterson, Helen Rizzo, and John R. Reynolds. 1998. Race, segregation, and the concentration of disadvantage: 1980–1990. *Social Problems* 45: 61–80.

Ladson-Billings, Gloria. 1994. *The dreamkeepers: Successful teachers of African American children.* San Francisco: Jossey-Bass.

Lamont, Michele, and Annette Lareau. 1988. "Cultural Capital: Allusions, Gaps and Glissandos in Recent Theoretical Developments." *Sociological Theory* 6: 153–68.

Lareau, Annette, and Erin McNamara Horvat. 1999. Moments of social inclusion and exclusion: Race, class and cultural capital in family-school relationships. *Sociology of Education* 72: 37–53.

Leacock, Eleanor. 1969. *Teaching and learning in city schools: A comparative study.* New York: Basic Books.

Lee, Carol. D., Margaret Beale Spencer, and Vinay Harpalani. 2003. Every shut eye ain't sleep: Studying how people live culturally. *Educational Researcher* 32: 6–13.

Lee, F. R. 2002. "Why are black students lagging?" *New York Times*, November 30, late edition, section B, p. 9, column 3.

Lee, Sara. 2004. Class matters: Racial and ethnic identities of working- and middle-class second generation Korean Americans in New York City. In *Becoming New Yorkers: Ethnographies of the new second generation*, ed P. Kasinitz, J. Mollenkopf, and M. Waters, 313–38. New York: Russell Sage Foundation.

Lesko, Nancy. 1990. Curriculum differentiation as social redemption: The case of school-aged mothers. In *Curriculum differentiation: Interpretive studies in U.S. secondary schools*, ed. Reba Page and Linda Valli, 113–36. Albany: State University of New York Press.

———. 2001. *Act your age. A cultural construction of adolescence.* New York: Routledge.

Lew, Jamie. 2004. The "other" story of model minorities: Korean American high school dropouts in an urban context. *Anthropology and Education Quarterly* 35(3): 297–311.

Lewin, Tamar. 1998. "How boys lost to girl power." *New York Times*, December 13, WK 3.

Lewin-Epstein, N. 1985. Neighborhoods, local labor markets, and employment opportunities for white and non-white youth. *Social Science Quarterly* 66: 163–71.

Lewis, Amanda. 2003a. *Race in the schoolyard: Negotiating the color line in classrooms and communities.* New Brunswick, NJ: Rutgers University Press.

———. 2003b. Some Are More Equal than Others: Lessons on Whiteness from School. In *White Out: The Continuing Significance of Racism*, ed. A. Doane and E. Bonilla-Silva, 159–72. New York: Routledge.

Lewis, Oscar. 1966. *La vida; a Puerto Rican family in the culture of poverty—San Juan and New York.* New York: Random House.

Liebow, Elliott. 1967. *Tally's corner: A study of Negro streetcorner men.* Boston: Little, Brown.

Lipsitz, George. 1998. *The possessive investment in whiteness: How white people profit from identity politics.* Philadelphia: Temple University Press.

Litwack, Leon. 1998. *Trouble in mind: Black southerners in the age of Jim Crow.* New York: Vintage Books.

Logan, John R., and Glenn Deane. 2003. *Black diversity in metropolitan America.* Report for the Lewis Mumford Center for Comparative Urban and Regional Research. Albany: State University of New York Press.

Lopez, Nancy. 2003. *Hopeful girls, troubled boys: Race and gender disparity in urban education.* New York: Routledge.

Louie, Vivian. 2004a. *Compelled to excel: Immigration, education, and opportunity among Chinese Americans.* Stanford, CA: Stanford University Press.

———. 2004b. "Being practical" or "doing what I want": The role of parents in the academic choices of Chinese Americans. In *Becoming New Yorkers: Ethnographies of the new second generation,* ed. P. Kasinitz, J. Mollenkopf, and M. Waters, 79–109. New York: Russell Sage Foundation.

Lovaglia, M., J. Lucas, J. Houser, S. Thye, and B. Markovsky. 1998. Status processes and mental ability test scores. *American Journal of Sociology* 104: 195–228.

Loveless, Tom. 1999. *The tracking wars.* Washington, DC: Brookings.

Lucas, Samuel. 1999. *Tracking inequality: Stratification and mobility in American high schools.* New York: Teachers College Press.

Lundy, Garvey. 2003. The myths of oppositional culture. *Journal of Black Studies* 33: 450–67.

Mac An Ghaill, Maírtín. 1994. *The making of men: Masculinities, sexualities and schooling.* Buckingham, UK: Open University Press.

Maccoby, Eleanor E., and Carol N. Jacklin. 1974. *Psychology of sex differences.* Stanford, CA: Stanford University Press.

MacLeod, Jay. 1995. *Ain't no makin it: Aspirations and attainment in a low-income neighborhood.* Boulder, CO: Westview.

Mahiri, Jabari. 1989. *Shooting for excellence: African American and youth culture in new century schools.* New York: Teachers College Press.

Majors, Richard, and Janet Mancini Billson. 1992. *Cool pose: The dilemmas of Black manhood in America.* New York: Lexington Books.

Marable, Manning. 1983. *The Underdevelopment of Black America.* Boston: South End Press.

———. 2002. *The great wells of democracy: The meaning of race in American life.* New York: Basic Civitas Books.

Marcus, George E., and Michael M. J. Fischer. 1986. *Anthropology as cultural critique: An experimental moment in the human sciences.* Chicago: University of Chicago Press.

Marks, J. L. 1985. *The enrollment of Black students in higher education: Can decline be prevented?* Atlanta: Southern Regional Education Board.

Massey, Douglas S., Camille Z. Charles, Garvey F. Lundy, and Mary J. Fischer. 2003. *The source of the river: The social origins of freshmen at America's selective colleges and universities.* Princeton, NJ: Princeton University Press.

Massey, Douglas S., and Nancy A. Denton. 1993. *American apartheid: Segregation and the making of the underclass.* Cambridge, MA: Harvard University Press.

Massey, Douglas S., and Mitchell L. Eggers. 1993. The spatial concentration of affluence and poverty during the 1970s. *Urban Affairs Quarterly* 29: 299–315.

Massey, Douglas S., and Eric Fong. 1990. Segregation and neighborhood quality: Blacks, Hispanics, and Asians in the San Francisco metropolitan area. *Social Forces* 69: 15–32.

Massey Douglas S., Andrew B. Gross, and Mitchell L. Eggers. 1991. Segregation, the concentration of poverty, and the life chances of individuals. *Social Science Research* 20: 397–420.

Matute-Bianchi, Maria E. 1986. Ethnic identities and patterns of school success and failure among Mexican-descent and Japanese-American students in a California high school. *American Journal of Education* 95(1): 233–55.

McCadden, Brian M. 1998. Why is Michael always getting timed out? Race, class, and the disciplining of other people's children. In *Classroom discipline in American schools: Problems and possibilities for democratic education*, ed. Ronald E. Butchart and Barbara McEwan, 109–34. Albany: State University of New York Press.

McCardle, Clare G., and Nancy F. Young. 1970. Classroom discussion of racial identity or how can we make it without 'acting white.' *American Journal of Orthopsychiatry* 41(1): 135–41.

McQuillan, Patrick J. 1998. *Educational opportunity in an urban American High School: A cultural analysis*. Albany: State University of New York Press.

McWhorter, John. 2000. *Losing the race: Self-sabotage in Black America*. New York: HarperCollins.

———. 2002. "Diversity's no longer the point, is it?" *Washington Post*, December 8, outlook, B04.

Mehan, H., L. Hubbard, and I. Villanueva. 1994. Forming academic identities: Accommodation without assimilation among involuntary minorities. *Anthropology & Education Quarterly* 25(2): 91–117.

Merton, Robert K. 1938. Social structure and anomie. *American Sociological Review* 3: 672–82.

Michaels, W. B. 1992. Race into culture: a critical genealogy of cultural identity. *Critical Inquiry* 18: 655–85.

Mickelson, Roslyn Arlin. 1989. Why does Jane read and write so well? The anomaly of women's achievement. *Sociology of Education* 62(1): 47–63.

———. 1990. The attitude-achievement paradox among Black adolescents. *Sociology of Education* 63(1): 44–61.

———. 2001. Subverting *Swann*: First- and second-generation segregation in the Charlotte-Mecklenburg schools. *American Educational Research Journal* 38: 215–52.

———. 2002. The contributions of abstract, concrete, and oppositional attitudes to understanding race and class differences in adolescents' achievement. Paper presented at the annual meeting of the American Sociological Association, Chicago.

———. 2003a. The academic consequences of desegregation and segregation: Evidence from the Charlotte-Mecklenburg schools. *North Carolina Law Review* 81(4): 120–65.

———. 2003b. When are racial disparities in education the result of racial discrimination? A social science perspective. *Teachers College Record* 105(6): 1052–86.

Mickelson, Roslyn Arlin, and C. A. Ray. 1994. Fear of falling from grace: The middle class, downward mobility, and school desegregation. *Research in Sociology of Education and Socialization* 10: 207–38.

Mickelson, Roslyn Arlin, and S. S. Smith. 1999. Race, tracking, and achievement among African-Americans in a desegregated school system: Evidence from the Charlotte-

Mecklenburg schools. Invited presentation, African Americans: Research and policy perspectives at the turn of the century, Stanford University, Palo Alto, California.

Milloy, C. 1988. "Partnerships pays off for students." *Washington Post*, May 15, final edition, metro, D3.

Mills, Charles. 1997. *The racial contract.* Ithaca, NY: Cornell University Press.

———. 2003. White supremacy as sociopolitical system: A philosophical perspective. In *White out: The continuing significance of racism*, ed. A. Doane and E. Bonilla-Silva, 35–48. New York: Routledge.

Mirande, Alfredo. 1997. *Hombres y machos: Masculinity and Latino culture.* Boulder, CO: Westview.

Model, Suzanne. 1991. Caribbean immigrants: A Black success story? *International Migration Review* 25: 248–76.

———. 1995. West Indian prosperity: Fact or fiction? *Social Problems* 42(4): 535–53.

Mollenkopf, J., P. Kasinitz, and M. Waters. 1995. The immigrant second generation in metropolitan New York. Unpublished manuscript (research proposal submitted to Russell Sage Foundation).

Mooar, Brian. 1997. "Urban League urges Black economic power; Issue deemed next frontier in civil rights." *Washington Post*, August 4, final edition, A12.

Moss, Philip, and Chris Tilly. 1996. 'Soft' skills and race: An investigation of Black men's employment problems. *Work and Occupations* 23: 252–76.

Moynihan, Daniel Patrick et al. 1965. *The Negro family: The case for national action.* Washington, DC: U.S. Department of Labor.

Munoz, Victoria I. 1995. *Where something catches: Work, love, and identity in youth.* Albany: State University of New York Press.

Myrdal, Gunnar. 1944. *An American dilemma: The Negro problem and modern democracy*, Volumes 1 and 2. New York: Harper and Row.

Nagel, Joane. 1994. Constructing ethnicity: Creating and recreating ethnic identity and culture. *Social Problems* 41: 152–76.

National Academy of Sciences. 2002. *Minority students in special and gifted education*, eds. M. Suzanne Donovan and Christopher T. Cross. Committee on Minority Representation in Special Education, Division of Behavioral and Social Sciences and Education, National Research Council. Washington, DC: National Academy Press.

National Center for Education Statistics (NCES). 2001. U.S. Department of Commerce, Bureau of the Census, Current Population Survey, October (various years): www.nces.ed.gov.

Neal-Barnett, Angela. 2001. Being Black: New thoughts on the old phenomenon of acting white. In *Forging links: African American children: Clinical developmental perspectives*, ed. A. Neal-Barnett, J. M. Contreras, and K. A. Kerns, 75–87. Westport, CT: Praeger.

Neckerman, Kathryn M., P. Carter, and J. Lee. 1999. Segmented assimilation and minority cultures of mobility. *Ethnic and Racial Studies* 22(6): 945–65.

Neckerman, Kathryn M., and Joleen Kirscherman. 1991. Hiring strategies, racial bias, and inner-city workers. *Social Problems* 38: 433–47.

Nelson, Katherine. 2003. Self and social functions: Individual autobiographical memory and collective narrative. *Memory* 11(2): 125–36.

Nettles, M. T. 1988. *Toward Black undergraduate student equality in American higher education.* New York: Greenwood Press.

Nettles, M. T., and L. W. Perna. 1997a. *The African American education data book,* Volume I: *Higher and adult education.* Fairfax, VA: Frederick D. Patterson Research Institute.

———. 1997b. *The African American education data book,* Volume II: *Preschool through high school education.* Fairfax, VA: Frederick D. Patterson Research Institute of the College Fund/UNCF.

New York Times. 1992. "Film; Just whose 'Malcolm' is it, anyway?" May 31, late edition, section 2, p. 13, column 1.

Nieto, Sonia. 2001. *Language, culture, and teaching: Critical perspectives for a new century.* Mahwah, NJ: Erlbaum.

Noguera, P. A. 2003. The trouble with black boys: The role and influence of environmental and cultural factors on academic performance of African American males. *Urban Education* 38(4): 431–59.

Nowell, Amy, and Larry V. Hedges. 1998. Trends in gender differences in academic achievement from 1960 to 1994: An analysis of differences in mean variance, and extreme scores. *Sex Roles* 39(1/2): 21–43.

Oakes, Jeannie. 1985. *Keeping track: How schools structure inequality.* New Haven, CT: Yale University Press.

———. 1990. *Multiplying inequalities: The effects of race, social class, and tracking on opportunities to learn mathematics and science.* Santa Monica, CA: RAND.

———. 1994. More than misapplied technology: A normative and political response to Hallinan on tracking. *Sociology of Education* 67: 84–88.

———. 1995. Two cities' tracking and within-school segregation. *Teachers College Record* 96(4): 681–90.

———. 2003. Presentation at conference on Colorblind racism: The politics of controlling racial and ethnic data, Stanford University, Palo Alto, California.

Oakes, Jeannie, K. Muir, and R. Joseph. 2000. Course taking and achievement in math and science: Inequalities that endure. Paper presented at National Institute for Science Education conference, Detroit.

O'Connor, Carla. 1997. Dispositions toward (collective) struggle and educational resilience in the inner city: A case analysis of six African-American high school students. *American Educational Research Journal* 34: 593–629.

———. 1999. Race, class, and gender in America: Narratives of opportunity among low-income African American youths. *Sociology of Education* 72: 137–57.

———. 2001. Making sense of the complexity of social identity in relation to achievement: A sociological challenge in the new millennium. *Sociology of Education,* Extra Issue: 159–68.

———. 2002. Black women beating the odds from one generation to the next: How the changing dynamics of constraint and opportunity affect the process of educational resilience. *American Educational Research Journal* 39(4): 855–903.

O'Connor, Carla, Amanda Lewis, and Jennifer Mueller. Forthcoming. Researching Black educational experiences and outcomes: Theoretical and practical considerations. In *Research methodology in African American communities,* ed. J. Jackson and C. Caldwell, Oakland, CA: Sage.

Ogbu, John U. 1974. *The next generation: An ethnography of education in an urban neighborhood.* New York: Academic Press.

———. 1978. *Minority education and caste.* New York: Academic Press.

———. 1981. Origins of human competence: A cultural ecological perspective. *Child Development* 52: 413–29.

Ogbu, John. 1983. Minority status and schooling in plural societies. *Comparative Education Review* 27(2): 168–90.

———. 1985. A cultural ecology of competence among inner-city Blacks. In *Beginnings: The social and affective development of Black children,* ed. Margaret Beale Spencer, G. Brookins, and W. Allen, 45–68. Hillsdale, NJ: Erlbaum.

———. 1987. Variability in minority school performance: A problem in search of an explanation. *Anthropology & Education Quarterly* 18: 312–34.

———. 1989. The individual in collective adaptation: A framework for focusing on academic under-performance and dropping out among involuntary minorities. In *Dropouts from school,* ed. L. Weis, 181–20. Albany: State University of New York Press.

———. 1990a. Minority education in a comparative perspective. *Journal of Negro Education* 59(1): 45–56.

———. 1990b. Minority status and literacy in comparative perspective. *Daedalus* 119(2): 141–68.

———. 1991a. Immigrant and involuntary minorities in comparative perspective. In *Minority status and schooling: A comparative study of immigrant and involuntary minorities,* ed. John Ogbu and M. Gibson, 3–33. New York: Garland.

———. 1991b. Low school performance as an adaptation: The case of Blacks in Stockton, California. In *Minority status and schooling: A comparative study of immigrant and involuntary minorities,* ed. John Ogbu and M. Gibson, 249–85. New York: Garland.

———. 1992. Adaptation to minority status and impact on school success. *Theory into Practice* 31(4): 287–95.

———. 1999. Beyond language: Ebonics, proper English, and identity in a Black-American speech community. *American Educational Research Journal* 36(2): 147–84.

———. 2003. *Black Americans students in an affluent suburb. A study of academic disengagement.* Mahwah, NJ: Erlbaum.

———. 2004. Collective identity and the burden of 'acting white' in Black history, community, and education. *The Urban Review* 36(1): 1–35.

Ogbu, John U., and Herbert D. Simons. 1998. Voluntary and involuntary minorities: A cultural-ecological theory of school performance with some implications for education. *Anthropology & Education Quarterly* 29(2): 155–88.

Oliver, Melvin, and Thomas Shapiro. 1995. *Black wealth, white wealth.* New York: Routledge.

Omi, Michael, and Howard Winant. 1994. *Racial formation in the United States: From the 1960s to the 1990s.* New York: Routledge.

Orfield, Gary, and Nora Gordon. 2001. *Schools more separate: Consequences of a decade of resegregation.* Cambridge, MA: The Civil Rights Project, Harvard University.

Orfield, Gary, and John T. Yun. 1999. *Resegregation in American schools.* Cambridge, MA: The Civil Rights Project, Harvard University.

Ortner, Sherry B. 1991. Reading America: Preliminary notes on class and culture. In *Recapturing anthropology: Working in the present,* ed. Richard G. Fox, 163–89. Santa Fe, NM: School of American Research Press.

Osborne, Jason W. 1997. Race and academic disidentification. *Educational Psychology* 89(4): 728–35.

Osterman, Paul. 1980. *Getting started*. Cambridge, MA: MIT Press.

Pappano, L. 2003. "The chalkboard/Laura Pappano; Fighting through theories: achievement gap feeds perceptions." *Boston Globe*, April 20, third edition, B9.

Parker, Sheila, Mimi Nichter, Mark Nichter, Nancy Vuckovic, Colette Sims, and Cheryl Ritenbaugh. 1995. Body image and weight concerns among African American and white adolescent females: Differences that make a difference. *Human Organization* 54(2): 103–14.

Parsons, Talcott. 1959. The school class as a social system. *Harvard Educational Review* 39: 297–318.

Pattillo-McCoy, Mary. 1999. *Black picket fences: Privilege and peril among the Black middle class*. Chicago: University of Chicago Press.

Patton, J. 1998. The disproportionate representation of African Americans in special education: Looking behind the curtain for understanding and solutions. *Journal of Special Education* 32(1): 25–31.

Patton, Michael Q. 1990. *Qualitative evaluation and research methods*. Newbury Park, CA: Sage.

Perry, Pamela. 2001. White means never having to say you're ethnic: White youth and the construction of 'cultureless' identities. *Contemporary Ethnography* 30: 56–91.

———. 2002. *Shades of white: White kids and racial identities in high school*. Durham, NC: Duke University Press.

Perry, Theresa, Claude Steele, and Asa G. Hilliard, III. 2003. *Young, gifted, and Black: Promoting high achievement among African-American students*. Boston: Beacon Press.

Petterson, Stephen M. 1997. Are young Black men really less willing to work? *American Sociological Review* 62: 605–13.

Philips, Susan U. 1972. Participant Structures and Communicative Competence: Warm Springs Children in Community and Classroom. In *Functions of Language in the Classroom*, ed. C. Cazden, V. John, and D. Hymes, 370–94. Prospect Heights, IL: Waveland Press.

Portes, Alejandro. 1995. Children of immigrants: Segmented assimilation and its determinants. In *The economic sociology of immigration: Essays on networks, ethnicity, and entrepreneurship*, ed. A. Portes. New York: Russell Sage Foundation.

Portes, Alejandro, and Dag MacLeod. 1996. Educational progress of children of immigrants: The role of class, ethnicity, and school context. *Sociology of Education* 69: 255–75.

Portes, Alejandro, and Ruben Rumbaut. 1996. *Immigrant America; A portrait*. Berkeley: University of California Press.

———. 2001. *Legacies: The story of the immigrant second generation*. Berkeley: University of California Press.

Portes, Alejandro, and Julia Sensenbrenner. 1993. Embeddedness and immigration: Notes on the social determinants of economic action. *American Journal of Sociology* 98(6): 1320–50.

Portes, Alejandro, and Min Zhou. 1993. The new second generation: Segmented assimilation and its variants. *Annals of the American Political and Social Sciences* 530: 74–96.

Pulido, Laura. 2000. "Rethinking Environmental Racism: White Privilege and Urban Development in Southern California." *Annals of the Association of American Geographers* 90(1): 12–40.

Qian, Zhenchao, and Sampson Lee Blair. 1999. Racial/ethnic differences in educational aspirations of high school seniors. *Sociological Perspectives* 42(4): 605–25.

Quadagno, Jill. 1994. *The color of welfare: How racism undermined the war on poverty.* New York: Oxford University Press.

Rainwater, Lee. 1966. *Behind ghetto walls: Black family life in a federal slum.* Chicago: Aldine.

Rasmussen, Birgit Brander, Irene J. Nexica, Eric Klinenberg, and Matt Wray. 2001. *The making and unmaking of whiteness.* Durham, NC: Duke University Press.

Raspberry, W. 1989. "Conspiracy against Blacks? Sure, Why not?" *Washington Post,* December 23, editorial, A19.

———. 2002. "Why Black kids lag." *Washington Post,* December 9, final edition, editorial, A23.

Ray, C. A., and R. A. Mickelson. 1990. Corporate leaders, resistant youth, and school reform in Sunbelt City: The political economy of education. *Social Problems* 37(2): 178–90.

———. 1993. Restructuring students for restructured work: The economy, school reform, and noncollege-bound youth. *Sociology of Education* 66(1): 1–23.

Renold, Emma. 2001. Learning the 'hard' way: boys, hegemonic masculinity and the negotiation of learner identities in the primary school. *British Journal of Sociology of Education* 22(3): 369–385.

Richey, W. 2003. "Affirmative action evolution." *Christian Science Monitor,* March 28, p. 1.

Ricketts, Erol R., and Isabel V. Sawhill. 1988. Defining and measuring the underclass. *Journal of Policy Analysis and Management* 7: 316–25.

Rioux, P. 1997. "District selects its gap chief." *Ann Arbor News,* October 16, A1, A10.

Rist, Ray. 1970. Student social class and teacher expectations: The self-fulfilling prophecy in ghetto education. *Harvard Educational Review* 40(3): 411–51.

Rogers, Reuel. 2001. Black like who? Afro-Caribbean immigrants, African Americans, and the politics of group identity. In *Islands in the city: West Indian migration to New York,* ed. Nancy Foner, 163–92. Berkeley: University of California Press.

Rollins, Judith. 1985. *Between women: Domestics and their employers.* Philadelphia: Temple University Press.

Roscigno, Vincent J., and James W. Ainsworth-Darnell. 1999. Race, cultural capital, and educational resources: Persistent inequalities and achievement returns. *Sociology of Education* 72: 158–78.

Rose, Tricia. 1994. *Black noise: Rap music and Black culture in contemporary America.* Hanover, NH: Wesleyan University Press.

Rowan, Carl. 1988. "Young, gifted, black—and inspired." *Washington Post,* May 18, final edition, A20.

Rumbaut, Ruben G. 1991. The agony of exile: A comparative study of Indochinese refugee adults and children. In *Refugee children: Theory, research and services,* ed. F. Ahearn, Jr., and J. Athey, pp. 53–59. Baltimore: Johns Hopkins University Press.

———. 1994. The crucible within: Ethnic identity, self-esteem, and segmented assimilation among children of immigrants. *International Migration Review* 28(4): 748–94.

Rumberger, Russell W., and Katherine A. Larson. 1998. Toward explaining ethnic differences in educational achievement among Mexican American language-minority
students. *Sociology of Education* 71(1): 69–92.

Sampson, Robert J., and W. Byron Groves. 1989. Community structure and crime:
testing social-disorganization theory. *American Journal of Sociology* 94:
774–802.

Santana, R. M. 2003a. "Shaker's academic gap gets close look; Authors conclusions on
black, white pupils bring intense debate." *Plain Dealer*, January 5, A1.

———. 2003b. "Black parents can make a difference, book says; Berkeley scholar
studied Shaker Hts. Schools." *Plain Dealer*, February 12, A1.

Segrue, Tom. 1996. *The Origins of the Urban Crisis*. Princeton, NJ: Princeton University Press.

Sellers, R. M., T. M. Chavous, and D. Y. Cooke. 1998. Racial ideology and racial cen-
trality as predictors of African American college students' academic performance.
Journal of Black Psychology 24(1): 8–27.

Sennett, Richard, and Jonathan Cobb. 1972. *The hidden injuries of class*. New York:
Vintage Books.

Sewell, T. 2004. "How blaming racism went out of fashion." *Times* (London), February 8, news review, p. 8.

Shade, B. 1982. Afro-American cognitive style: A variable in school success. *Review
of Educational Research* 52: 219–44.

Shapiro, Thomas. 2004. *The Hidden Cost of Being African American: How Wealth
Perpetuates Inequality*. New York: Oxford University Press.

Shaw, Clifford, and H. McKay. 1942. *Juvenile delinquency and urban areas*.
Chicago: University of Chicago Press.

Shaw, K. M., and H. B. London. 2001. Culture and ideology in keeping transfer commitment: Three community colleges. *Review of Higher Education* 25: 91–114.

Sheley, Joseph F., Zina T. McGee, and James W. Wright. 1995. Weapon related vic-
timization in selected inner-city high school samples. National Institute of Justice
Paper NCJ-151526. Washington, DC: U.S. Department of Justice.

Sheley, Joseph F., and James W. Wright. 1998. High school youths, weapons, and violence: A national survey. National Institute of Justice Paper NCJ-172857. Washington, DC: U.S. Department of Justice.

Simcha-Fagan, Ora, and Joseph E. Schwartz. 1986. Neighborhood and delinquency:
An assessment of contextual effects. *Criminology* 24: 667–99.

Skiba, R. 2001. When is disproportionality discrimination? The overrepresentation of
Black students in school suspension. In *Zero tolerance*, ed. W. Ayers, B. Dohrm,
and R. Ayers, 176–87. New York: New Press.

Slater, Robert Bruce. 1994. The growing gender gap in Black higher education. *Journal of Blacks in Higher Education* 3: 52–59.

Solomon, R. Patrick. 1992. *Black resistance in high school*. Albany: State University
of New York Press.

Solorzano, Daniel G. 1992. An exploratory analysis of the effects of race, class, and
gender on student and parent mobility aspirations. *Journal of Negro Education*
61(1): 30–44.

South, Scott J., and Erick P. Baumer. 2000. Deciphering community and race effects
on adolescent premarital childbearing. *Social Forces* 78(4): 1379–1408.

South, Scott J., Eric P. Baumer, and Amy Lutz. 2003. Interpreting community effects on youth educational attainment. *Youth & Society* 35: 3–36.

South, Scott J., and Kyle D. Crowder. 2000. The declining significance of neighborhoods? Marital transitions in community context. *Social Forces* 78: 1067–99.

Sowell, Thomas. 1978. Three Black histories. In *Essays and data on American ethnic groups*, ed. Thomas Sowell, 7–64. Washington, DC: The Urban Institute.

———. 1997a. "Lies harming black students," *Columbus Dispatch*, May 25, 3G.

———. 1997b. "Truth will set us free—but the lie won't allow it." *Chicago Sun-Times*, September 30, editorial, p. 25.

Spencer, Margaret Beale. 1983. Children's cultural values and parental child rearing strategies. *Developmental Review* 3: 351–70.

———. 1984. "Black children's race awareness, racial attitudes, and self-concept: A reinterpretation." *Journal of Child Psychology and Psychiatry* 25(3): 433–41.

———. 1990. Parental values transmission. In *Interdisciplinary perspectives on Black families*, ed. J. B. Stewart and H. Cheatham, 111–30. New Brunswick, NY: Transactions.

———. 1995. Old issues and new theorizing about African American youth: A phenomenological variant of ecological systems theory. In *Black youth: Perspectives on their status in the United States*, ed. R. L. Taylor, 37–70. Westport, CT: Praeger.

———. 1999. Social and cultural influences on school adjustment: The application of an identity-focused cultural ecological perspective. *Educational Psychologist* 34(1): 43–57.

———. 2004. Comments presented at conference on Beyond acting white: Reassessments and new directions in research on black students and school success. Philadelphia: Temple University.

Spencer, Margaret Beale, Steven P. Cole, Stephanie M. Jones, and Dena Phillips Swanson. 1997. Neighborhood and family influences on young urban adolescents' behavior problems: A multisample, multisite analysis. In *Neighborhood poverty: Context and consequences for children*, ed. Jeanne Brooks-Gunn, Greg J. Duncan, and J. Lawrence Aber, 200–218. New York: Russell Sage Foundation.

Spencer, Margaret Beale, Elizabeth Noll, Jill Stolzfus, and Vinay Harpalani. 2001. Identity and school adjustment: Revisiting the 'acting white' assumption. *Educational Psychologist* 36(1): 21–30.

Spencer, Margaret Beale, Dena Phillips Swanson, and M. Cunningham. 1991. Ethnicity, ethnic identity, and competence formation: Adolescent transition and cultural transformation. *Journal of Negro Education* 60(3): 366–87.

Spindler, George, and Louise Spindler. 1992. The enduring, situated, and endangered self in fieldwork: A personal account. In *The Psychoanalytical Study of Society*, ed. B. Boyer, 25–28. Hillsdale, NJ: Analytic Press.

———. 1993. The process of culture and person: Cultural therapy and culturally diverse schools. In *Renegotiating cultural diversity in American schools*, ed. Patricia Phelan and Ann Locke Davidson, 27–51. New York: Teachers College Press.

Stafford, C. 1987. "Fear of 'acting white' stifles Blacks; congressional panel searches for reasons for high drop out rate." *St. Petersburg Times*, November 11, 6A.

Stafford, Susan Buchanan. 1987. The Haitians: The cultural meaning of race and ethnicity. In *New immigrants in New York*, ed. Nancy Foner, 131–58. New York: Columbia University Press.

Staples, Robert. 1982. *Black masculinity: The Black male's role in American society.* San Francisco: Black Scholar Press.

Steele, Claude M. 1992. Race and the schooling of Black Americans. *Atlantic Monthly* (April): 68–78.

———. 1997. A threat in the air: How stereotypes shape intellectual identity and performance. *American Psychologist* 52: 613–29.

———. 1999. Thin ice: 'Stereotype threat' and Black college students. *Atlantic Monthly* (August): 44–54.

Steele, Claude M., and J. Aronson. 1995. Stereotype threat and the intellectual test performance of African Americans. *Journal of Personality and Social Psychology* 69: 797–811.

———. 1998. Stereotype threat and the test performance of academically successful African Americans. In *The Black-white test score gap*, ed. Christopher Jencks and Meredith Phillips, 401–30. Washington, DC: Brookings.

Steinberg, Laurence. 1987. Single parents, stepparents, and susceptibility of adolescents to antisocial peer-pressure. *Child Development* 58: 269–75.

———. 1989. Communities of families and education. In *Education and the American family: A research synthesis*, ed. W. Weston, 138–68. New York: New York University Press.

———. 1996. *Beyond the classroom: Why school reform has failed and what parents need to do.* New York: Simon and Schuster.

Steinberg, Laurence, Sanford M. Dornbusch, and Bradford B. Brown. 1992. Ethnic differences in adolescent achievement: An ecological perspective. *American Psychologist* 47(6): 723–29.

Stepick, Alex, Carol Dutton Stepick, and Emmanuel Eugene. 2001. Shifting identities and intergenerational conflict: Growing up Haitian in Miami. In *Ethnicities: Children of immigrants in America*, ed. R. Rumbaut and A. Portes, 229–66. Berkeley: University of California Press.

Stern, L. 1995. "Angry reception greets the messenger who weighs self-destructiveness against racism." *Ottawa Citizen*, November 26, C6.

Stevenson, H. C. 1994. Validation of the scale of racial socialization for African American adolescents: Steps toward multidimensionality. *Journal of Black Psychology* 20(4): 445–68.

Stevenson, Harold W., and Richard S. Newman. 1986. Long-term prediction of achievement and attitudes in mathematics and reading. *Child Development* 57: 646–59.

Stewart, Eric, Ronald Simons, and Rand Conger. 2002. Assessing neighborhood and social psychological influences on childhood violence in an African-American sample. *Criminology* 40: 301–30.

Stinchcombe, Arthur L. 1964. *Rebellion in a high school.* Chicago: Quadrangle Books.

Suarez-Orozco, Marcello, and Carola Suarez-Orozco. 1995. *Transformations: Migration, family life, and achievement motivation among Latino adolescents.* Stanford, CA: Stanford University Press.

Swann v. Charlotte-Mecklenburg Schools, 402 U.S. 1, 15. 1971.

Swanson, D., M. B. Spencer, and A. Peterson. 1998. Identity formation in adolescence. In *The adolescent years: Social influences and educational challenges, 97th yearbook for the national society for the study of education—Part 1*, ed. K. Borman and B. Schneider, 18–44. Chicago: University of Chicago Press.

Swidler, A. 1986. Culture in action: Symbols and strategies. *American Sociological Review* 51: 273–86.

Takaki, Ronald. 1993. *A Different Mirror: A History of Multicultural America*. Boston: Little, Brown.

Tampa Tribune. 2003. "Letters: Address the problem, not the system, do your part in education." *Tampa Tribune*, September 7, commentary, p. 3.

Tatum, Beverly Daniel. 1997. *Why are all the Black kids sitting together and other conversations about race*. New York: Basic Books.

Taylor, Jill McLean. 1996. Cultural stories: Latina and Portuguese daughters and mothers. In *Urban girls: Resisting stereotypes, creating identities*, ed. B. J. R. Leadbeater and N. Way, 117–31. New York: New York University Press.

Taylor, R. L. 1976. Psychosocial development among Black children and youth: A reexamination. *American Journal of Orthopsychiatry* 46: 4–19.

Tharp, R. G. 1989. Psychocultural variables and constants. *American Psychologist* 44(2): 349–59.

Thernstrom, Abigail, and Stephan Thernstrom. 2003. *No excuses: Closing the racial gap in learning*. New York: Simon & Schuster.

Trueba, Henry. 1988. Culturally-based explanations of minority students' academic achievement. *Anthropology & Education Quarterly* 19(3): 270–87.

Tuan, Mia. 1998. *Forever foreigners or honorary whites? The Asian ethnic experience today*. New Brunswick, NJ: Rutgers University Press.

Turley, Ruth N. L. 2003. When do neighborhoods matter? The role of race and neighborhood peers. *Social Science Research* 32: 61–79.

Turner, M., M. Fix, R. Struyk, et al. 1991. *Opportunities denied, opportunities diminished: Racial discrimination in hiring*. Washington, DC: Urban Institute.

Turner, Victor. 1969. *The ritual process: Structure and anti-structure*. Chicago: Aldine.

Tyson, K. 1998. Debunking a persistent myth: Academic achievement and the burden of "acting white" among Black students. Paper presented at the annual meeting of the American Sociological Association, San Francisco.

———. 2002. Weighing in: Elementary-age students and the debate on attitudes toward school among Black students. *Social Forces* 80: 1157–89.

———. 2003. Notes from the back of the room: Problems and paradoxes in the schooling of young Black students. *Sociology of Education* 76(4): 326–43.

Valdes, Guadalupe. 1997. Dual-language immersion programs: A cautionary note concerning the education of language-minority students. *Harvard Educational Review* 67: 391–423.

Valenzuela, Angela. 1999. *Subtractive schooling: Issues of caring in education of U.S.-Mexican youth*. Albany: State University of New York Press.

Van Gennep, Arnold. 1960. *The rites of passage*. London: Routledge.

Van Haitsma, Martha. 1989. A contextual definition of the underclass. *Focus: The Newsletter of the Institute for Research on Poverty* 12: 27–31.

Vickerman, Milton. 1999. *Crosscurrents: West Indian immigrants and race*. New York: Oxford University Press.

———. 2001. Tweaking a monolith: The West Indian immigrant encounter with 'Blackness.' In *Islands in the city: West Indian migration to New York*, ed. Nancy Foner, 237–56. Berkeley: University of California Press.

Wacquant, Loic J. D. 1996. Red belt, black belt: Racial division, class inequality and the state in the French urban periphery and the American ghetto. In *Urban poverty and the underclass*, ed. Enzo Mingione, 234–74. Malden, MA: Blackwell.

Wacquant, Loic J. D., and William Julius Wilson. 1989. The cost of racial and class exclusion in the inner city. *Annals of the American Academy of Political and Social Sciences* 501: 8–25.

Waldinger, Roger. 1996. The 'other side' of embeddedness: A case study of the interplay of economy and ethnicity. *Ethnic and Racial Studies* 18: 555–80.

Walters, Pamela Barnhouse. 2001. Educational access and the state: Historical continuities and discontinuities in racial inequality in American education. *Sociology of Education*, Special Issue: 35–49.

Wang, M., and E. Gordon. 1994. *Educational resilience in Inner City America: Challenges and prospects*. Hillsdale, NJ: Erlbaum.

Washington Post. 1994a. May 18, op-ed, A20.

———. 1994b. May 18, op-ed, A22.

Waters, Mary C. 1990. *Ethnic options: Choosing identities in America*. Berkeley: University of California Press.

———. 1996. The Intersection of gender, race, and ethnicity in identity development of Caribbean American teens. In *Urban adolescent girls: Resisting stereotypes*, ed. B. J. R. Leadbeater and N. Way, 65–81. New York: New York University Press.

———. 1999. *Black identities: West Indian immigrant dreams and American realities*. New York: Russell Sage Foundation.

———. 2001. Growing up West Indian and African American: Gender and class differences in the second generation. In *Islands in the city: West Indian migration to New York*, ed. Nancy Foner, 193–215. Berkeley: University of California Press.

Watkins, William. 2001. *The white architects of black education: Ideology and power in America 1865–1954*. New York: Teachers College Press.

Weinberg, M. 1977. *A chance to learn: The history of race and education in the United States*. New York: Cambridge University Press.

Weinstein, Rhona. 1981. Student perspectives on 'achievement' in varied classroom environments. Paper presented at the annual meeting of the American Educational Research Association, Los Angeles.

Weinstein, Rhona, Hermine Marshall, Karen Brattesani, and Lee Sharp. 1980. "Achieving in school: Children's views of causes and consequences: A preliminary report on methodology." Paper presented at the annual meeting of the American Psychological Association. Montreal, Canada.

Wellman, David T. 1993. *Portraits of white racism*. New York: Cambridge University Press.

Wells, Amy Stuart, and Robert L. Crain. 1997. *Stepping over the color line: African American students in white suburban schools*. New Haven, CT: Yale University Press.

Welner, K. G. 2001. *Legal rights, local wrongs. When community control collides with educational equity*. Albany: State University of New York Press.

Welner, K. G., and J. Oakes. 1996. (Li)ability grouping: The new susceptibility of school tracking systems to legal challenges. *Harvard Educational Review* 66: 451–70.

Welsh, P. 1988. "The Black talent trap: Top high-school students are caught between white racism and the jealousy of Blacks." *Washington Post*, May 1, C1.

Welsh, Wayne, Jack Greene, and Patricia Jenkins. 1999. School disorder: The influence of individual, institutional, and community factors. *Criminology* 37: 73–115.

Wheelock, A. 1992. *Crossing the tracks: How 'untracking' can save America's schools.* New York: New Press.

Willis, Paul. 1977. *Learning to labor: How working class kids get working class jobs.* New York: Columbia University Press.

Wilson, Carter. 1992. Restructuring and the growth of concentrated poverty in Detroit. *Urban Affairs Quarterly* 28: 187–205.

Wilson, William J. 1987. *The truly disadvantaged: The inner city, the underclass, and public policy.* Chicago: University of Chicago Press.

———. 1991. Studying inner-city social dislocations: The challenge of public agenda research. *American Sociological Review* 56: 1–14.

———. 1996. *When work disappears: The world of the new urban poor.* New York: Alfred A Knopf.

Winerip, Michael. 2003. "In the affluent suburbs, an invisible racial gap." *New York Times,* June 4, section B, p. 8.

Wittrock, Merlin C. 1986. "Students' thought processes." In *Handbook on research on teaching,* ed. Merlin C. Wittrock, 297–314. New York: Macmillan.

Woldemikael, Tekle. 1985. Black ethnics: A case study of Haitian immigrants. *New England Journal of Black Studies* 5: 15–30.

———. 1989. *Becoming Black American: Haitians and American institutions in Evanston, Illinois.* New York: AMS Press.

Woo, Deborah. 1992. The gap between striving and achieving: The case of Asian-American women. In *Race, class and gender: An anthology,* ed. M. L. Anderson and P. H. Collins, pp. 191–200. Belmont, CA: Wadsworth Publishing Company.

Woodson, Carter G. 1997. *The miseducation of the American Negro.* New York: AMS Press.

Yon, Daniel A. 2000. *Elusive culture: Schooling, race, and identity in global times.* Albany: State University of New York Press.

Yonazawa, Susan. 1997. Making decisions about students' lives: An interactive study of secondary school students' academic program selection. PhD diss., University of California, Los Angeles.

Young, C. 2003. "Upholding racial division." *Boston Globe,* June 30, op-ed, A13.

Zhou, Min. 1997. Growing up American: The challenge confronting immigrant children and children of immigrants. *Annual Review of Sociology* 23:63–95.

Zhou, Min, and Carl L. Bankston III. 1994. Social Capital and the Adaptation of the Second Generation: The Case of Vietnamese Youth in New Orleans. *International Migration Review* 28(4): 775–99.

———. 1998. *Growing up American: How Vietnamese children adapt to life in the United States.* New York: Russell Sage Foundation.

Index

ability. *See* achievement; intelligence

ability grouping. *See* tracking

ability shows, 71

acculturation, 135

achievement: acting white hypothesis and, 33–34, 37–40, 52, 61–62, 80–84, 85–87, 111–14, 116–17, 128, 131, 148–49; agency and, 50; American dream and, 5, 8–9; attitude and, 137–38; biology and, 9; collective socialization and, 166–68; costs of, 42–46; counselors and, 48; critical mass and, 49–50, 53; cultural ecological theory (CET) and, 133–37; culture and, 9–10; developmental stages and, 60, 65–67; discipline and, 126–27; education and, 5–6; ethnicity and, 133–52; evaluations and, 65–68, 85; family and, 127–28, 130; folk theory and, 8–9; friends and, 47–48; gender and, 17, 21, 111–14, 122–31, 179; genetics and, 9; heterogeneity and, 16–17, 20–22, 54–55, 107–9, 111–14, 131; identity and, 20–21, 107–9; immigrant minorities and, 133–52; institutional characteristics and, 171–72;

intelligence and, 66–68, 70; isolation and, 44–45, 82–84; language and, 101; limited occupational opportunity and, 170–71; meritocracy and, 5–6; neighborhoods and, 22, 162–73; opportunity for, 73–77; oppositional cultural frameworks (OCF) and, 27–30, 50–55; orientation to, 59, 61, 65–73, 84–87, 128–29, 140–52, 159–62, 166–68, 197–98; parents and, 48; race and, 2, 35–46; research on, 28, 152; school context and, 136; social capital and, 169–70; social control and, 168–69; social mobility and, 61, 65–66, 126–27; social networks and, 136, 149–51, 169–70; socioeconomic status and, 17; structure and, 49–55, 73–77, 84–87, 172–73; support systems and, 47–50, 53; teachers and, 48, 107; tracking and, 29–30, 47, 49–55, 73–77, 80–84. *See also* achievement gap; underachievement

achievement gap: acting white hypothesis and, 57; agency and, 1–2, 6–7, 29; closing of, 1, 27; college attendance and, 3; community and,

235

73–77; underachievement and, 2, 179. *See also* ethnicity
racelessness, 62, 189–90, 193–97
racialization, 183, 194
racism: achievement gap and, 86; acting white hypothesis and, 42; of counselors, 149–50; family and, 192–93; intelligence and, 39, 42, 45–46, 56n7, 60; opportunity and, 76–77; of students, 194–97; of teachers, 146–47, 149–50, 180–81, 188–97; tracking and, 76–77; underachievement and, 106. *See also* discrimination; segregation
Raspberry, William, 12, 13
Ravitch, Diane, 11
rebellion, 127
religion, 105–6, 109
representation, 42–44
reputation, 99–101, 108, 183
research: on achievement, 28, 152; on acting white hypothesis, 28; on adolescence, 86–87; on attitudes, 86–87, 152; on developmental stages, 86–87; diversity in teams for, 55n5; on heterogeneity, 15–17; on immigrant minorities, 152; on material conditions, 172–73; on neighborhoods, 172–73; on opportunity, 152; on oppositional cultural frameworks (OCF), 28; on race, 14–16, 20; on schools, 20, 23; on structure, 23, 86–87, 172–73
respectability, 98, 99–102, 108, 120
Ridgewood High School, 94–96, 102–3, 108–9
role models, 107, 165, 166–68, 170

school context, 136
schools: acting white hypothesis and, 17–18; agency and, 18–20; after Civil War, x; cultural ecological theory (CET) and, 17–18; culture of, 17–18; deterioration of, 96; developmental stages and, 19–20; discipline and, 17–18; founded by blacks, x; funding for, 96, 102, 202; language in,

182–83, 184–85, 186–88; neighborhoods and, 171–72; opportunity and, 73–77; organization of, 17–18, 29, 51–52; orientation to, 197–98; poverty and, 171–72; power in, 183–88, 190–91, 197–98; race and, 15–16, 17–18; racelessness in, 193–97; reputation of, 183; research on, 20, 23; segregation in, ix, 30–32, 51, 59, 202–3; social control in, 188–93; structure and, 8–10, 18–20, 22–23, 27, 29, 49–55, 57–58, 59–60, 73–77, 84–87, 103, 177–98; tracking and, 19–20; whiteness and, 177–98. *See also* education; school context
segregation, ix, 30–32, 51, 59, 62, 201–5. *See also* discrimination; isolation; racism
self-perception, 65–75, 85. *See also* identity
sexuality, 117–18
social capital, 169–70
social control, 120, 127–28, 168–69, 188–93
socialization, collective, 166–68
social mobility: achievement and, 61, 65–66, 126–27; cultural ecological theory (CET) and, 133–37; culture and, 133; education and, 61; ethnicity and, 133–37; identity and, 135–37; race and, 203; reputation and, 108; respectability and, 108; social networks and, 136; socioeconomic status and, 135–36, 203; structure and, 103; working hard and, 98
social networks, 136, 149–51, 169–70. *See also* community; friends; peer groups
society, 22–23, 203–5
socioeconomic status: achievement and, 17; achievement gap and, 3, 10, 17, 179; aspirations and, 127, 130; cultural capital and, 187; education and, 202, 203; material conditions compared, 174n3; neighborhoods

valley-girl culture, 118–19, 120, 121
victims, ix, 7, 12, 14, 197
violence, 100–101, 124–25, 169, 189

Waters, Mary, 118
wealth. *See* affluence
West City elementary school, 182–83, 188–93
West Indians, 133–52
whiteness, 104, 177–98
white supremacy, 178–79, 197–98, 204. *See also* power

Wilson, William J., 166–67, 170, 173
working class, 2, 3, 127. *See also* socioeconomic status
working hard: attitude toward, 87n9, 166–68, 170–71; immigrant minorities and, 140–41; social mobility and, 98; tracking and, 35–36; underachievement and, 70–71

Yonkers (New York), 114–15

Zhou, Min, 135

Contributors

James W. Ainsworth is associate professor of sociology at Georgia State University. His research interests include social stratification, race and ethnic relations, and sociology of education. His current research addresses how educational processes reproduce social inequality including the effect of involvement in high school vocational education on the school-to-work transition, and the attitude-achievement "paradox" among black students.

Walter Allen is professor of education and the Allan Murray Cartter Chair in Higher Education in the UCLA Graduate School of Education and Information Studies. He is also professor of sociology at UCLA and codirector of CHOICES, a longitudinal study of college access and attendance among African Americans and Latinos in California. His research and teaching focus on comparative race, ethnicity, and inequality; diversity in higher education; and family studies.

Sherri-Ann P. Butterfield is assistant professor of sociology at Rutgers University in Newark, New Jersey. Her research focuses on issues of race and ethnicity among contemporary immigrants; her main fields of interest are immigration, identity and culture, and urban education. Her work has specifically explored how race, ethnicity, class, and gender impact black immigrants within the diasporic West Indian community.

Prudence L. Carter is associate professor in the Department of Sociology at Harvard University. Her research interrogates prevalent cultural explanations of the mobility differences among various racial/ethnic groups. She is the author of *Keepin' It Real: School Success beyond Black and White*, which examines the intersecting identities of race/ethnicity, class, and gender and their influences on culture and achievement among black and Latino youths. Currently, she is pursuing a comparative study of race, culture, identity, and schools in South Africa and the United States.

Annette Hemmings is associate professor in the Educational Foundations Program at the University of Cincinnati. She is an educational anthropologist who has conducted extensive fieldwork in urban and suburban high schools on the identity work of African American students, teachers' work lives, classroom democratic dialogues and authority relations, and adolescent coming-of-age processes. Her work is informed by theories that explicate sociocultural differences and conflicts in formal educational contexts.

Erin McNamara Horvat is associate professor of urban education at Temple University in Philadelphia. Her research agenda has focused on issues of access and equity in education. Her main fields of interest are urban education, sociology of education, and higher education. Her work has explored empirically how race and class shape access throughout the educational pipeline.

Carol D. Lee is associate professor of education and social policy in the Learning Sciences Program at Northwestern University. Her research focuses on cultural supports for teaching and learning, specifically in the area of literacy. She has developed a framework called Cultural Modeling to guide the design and enactment of curriculum that is both culturally responsive and subject matter specific. She is active in urban school reform.

David Lemmel is director of youth development at the Big Picture Company. In that capacity, he facilitates the Bill & Melinda Gates Foundation's Alternative High School Initiative, a national collaboration of youth development organizations to create diploma-granting high schools for disconnected youth. His research focuses on small school reform as well as examines psychosocial factors related to race/ethnicity and their impact on educational opportunities and outcomes.

Amanda E. Lewis is associate professor in the Departments of Sociology and African American Studies. Her research focuses on how race shapes educational opportunities from kindergarten through graduate school and on how our ideas about race get negotiated in everyday life. Her recent book, *Race in the Schoolyard: Negotiating the Color-Line in Classrooms and Com-*

munities (Rutgers University Press, 2003) examines how race shapes school experiences and outcomes in elementary schools.

Roslyn Arlin Mickelson is professor of sociology and adjunct professor of public policy and women's studies at the University of North Carolina at Charlotte. Her research focuses on the political economy of schooling and school reform, particularly the relationships among race, ethnicity, gender, class, and educational processes and outcomes.

Carla O'Connor is associate professor of education at the University of Michigan at Ann Arbor. Her research examines the relationship between structure, culture, and human agency in explicating the educational experiences of black youth, particularly their experience with academic success. Currently, she is conducting a longitudinal study of how racial identity is implicated in black youths' transition to adulthood.

Karolyn Tyson is assistant professor of sociology at the University of North Carolina at Chapel Hill. Her research interests center on issues of educational equity and understanding how cultural, structural, and individual-level factors affect school achievement, particularly as they relate to African American students.

Anne E. Velasco currently serves as program manager for the Math/Science Equity Program, an NSF-funded project in Charlotte, North Carolina, which aims to increase the participation of African American students in upper-level high school courses. Her interest in equality in education began at New Kent High School, the focal point of the 1968 Supreme Court decision, *Green v. the [New Kent] County School Board*, where as a seventh grader she began to realize the benefits of a racially integrated education.

Greg Wiggan is assistant professor of sociology at Salem College in Winston-Salem, North Carolina. His research areas include racial and ethnic relations, globalization and inequality, sociology of education, and the Afro-Caribbean experience. Currently, he is exploring how race influences neighborhood and school processes.